PHILOSOPHY AS CULTURAL POLITICS

This volume presents a selection of the philosophical papers which Richard Rorty has written over the past decade, and complements three previous volumes of his papers: *Objectivity, Relativism, and Truth, Essays on Heidegger and Others*, and *Truth and Progress*. Topics discussed include the changing role of philosophy in Western culture over the course of recent centuries, the role of the imagination in intellectual and moral progress, the notion of "moral identity," the Wittgensteinian claim that the problems of philosophy are linguistic in nature, the irrelevance of cognitive science to philosophy, and the mistaken idea that philosophers should find the "place" of such things as consciousness and moral value in a world of physical particles. The papers form a rich and distinctive collection which will appeal to anyone with a serious interest in philosophy and its relation to culture.

PHILOSOPHY AS CULTURAL POLITICS

Philosophical Papers, Volume 4

RICHARD RORTY

CAMBRIDGE
UNIVERSITY PRESS

CAMBRIDGE UNIVERSITY PRESS
Cambridge, New York, Melbourne, Madrid, Cape Town,
Singapore, São Paulo, Delhi, Tokyo, Mexico City

Cambridge University Press
The Edinburgh Building, Cambridge CB2 8RU, UK

Published in the United States of America by
Cambridge University Press, New York

www.cambridge.org
Information on this title: www.cambridge.org/9780521698351

First published 2007
Third printing 2009

A catalogue record for this publication is available from the British Library

Library of Congress Cataloguing in Publication data

ISBN 978-0-521-87544-8 Hardback
ISBN 978-0-521-69835-1 Paperback

To Ruby Rorty, Flynn Rorty, and other grandchildren still to come

Contents

Preface

Most of the papers collected in this volume were written between 1996 and 2006. Like my previous writings, they are attempts to weave together Hegel's thesis that philosophy is its time held in thought with a non-representationalist account of language. That account, implicit in the later work of Wittgenstein, has been more carefully worked out in the writings of Wilfrid Sellars, Donald Davidson, and Robert Brandom. I argue that Hegelian historicism and a Wittgensteinian "social practice" approach to language complement and reinforce one another.

Dewey agreed with Hegel that philosophers were never going to be able to see things under the aspect of eternity; they should instead try to contribute to humanity's ongoing conversation about what to do with itself. The progress of this conversation has engendered new social practices, and changes in the vocabularies deployed in moral and political deliberation. To suggest further novelties is to intervene in cultural politics. Dewey hoped that philosophy professors would see such intervention as their principal assignment.

In Dewey's work, historicism appears as a corollary of the pragmatist maxim that what makes no difference to practice should make no difference to philosophy. "Philosophy," Dewey wrote, "is not in any sense whatever a form of knowledge." It is, instead, "a social hope reduced to a working program of action, a prophecy of the future."[1] From Dewey's point of view, the history of philosophy is best seen as a series of efforts to modify people's sense of who they are, what matters to them, what is most important.

Interventions in cultural politics have sometimes taken the form of proposals for new roles that men and women might play: the ascetic, the prophet, the dispassionate seeker after truth, the good citizen, the aesthete,

[1] John Dewey, "Philosophy and Democracy," in *The Middle Works*, ed. Jo Ann Boydston (Carbondale: Southern Illinois University Press, 1982), vol. XI, 43.

the revolutionary. Sometimes they have been sketches of an ideal community – the perfected Greek polis, the Christian Church, the republic of letters, the cooperative commonwealth. Sometimes they have been suggestions about how to reconcile seemingly incompatible outlooks – to resolve the conflict between Greek rationalism and Christian faith, or between natural science and the common moral consciousness. These are just a few of the ways in which philosophers, poets, and other intellectuals have made a difference to the way human beings live.

In many of these papers, I urge that we look at relatively specialized and technical debates between contemporary philosophers in the light of our hopes for cultural change. Philosophers should choose sides in those debates with an eye to the possibility of changing the course of the conversation. They should ask themselves whether taking one side rather than another will make any difference to social hopes, programs of action, prophecies of a better future. If it will not, it may not be worth doing. If it will, they should spell out what that difference amounts to.

The professionalization of philosophy, its transformation into an academic discipline, was a necessary evil. But it has encouraged attempts to make philosophy into an autonomous quasi-science. These attempts should be resisted. The more philosophy interacts with other human activities – not just natural science, but art, literature, religion and politics as well – the more relevant to cultural politics it becomes, and thus the more useful. The more it strives for autonomy, the less attention it deserves.

Readers of my previous books will find little new in this volume. It contains no novel ideas or arguments. But I hope that these further efforts to tie James' and Dewey's ideas up with Hegel's and Wittgenstein's may lead a few readers to think of pragmatism in a more favorable light. In an exuberant moment, James compared pragmatism's potential for producing radical cultural change to that of the Protestant Reformation.[2] I would like to persuade my readers that the analogy is not as absurd as it might seem.

---

[2] Letter to Henry James, Jr. of May 4, 1907, in *The Correspondence of William James*, vol. XI, ed. Ignas K. Skrupskelis and Elizabeth M. Berkeley (Charlottesville: University Press of Virginia, 2003).

Acknowledgments

"Cultural politics and the question of the existence of God" was published in *Radical Interpretation in Religion*, ed. Nancy Frankenberry (Cambridge University Press, 2002).

"Pragmatism as romantic polytheism" was published in *The Revival of Pragmatism: New Essays on Social Thought, Law and Culture*, ed. Morris Dickstein (Duke University Press, 1998).

"Justice as a larger loyalty" was written for the Seventh East–West Philosophy Conference and was first published in *Justice and Democracy: Cross-Cultural Perspectives*, ed. Ron Bontekoe and Marietta Stepaniants (University of Hawaii Press, 1997).

"Honest mistakes" was written for a conference on "The Cold War" organized in 2003 by Louis Menand for the English Institute. Under the title "Whittaker Chambers and Alger Hiss: Two Men of Honor," the paper is forthcoming in the *Proceedings of the English Institute*.

"Grandeur, profundity, and finitude" is a revised version of the first of two Smythies Lectures given at Balliol College, Oxford, in 2004. An earlier version was read at a UNESCO conference in Benin and published as "Universalist Grandeur, Romantic Depth, Pragmatist Cunning" in *Diogenes*, no. 202.

"Philosophy as a transitional genre" is a shortened and revised version of an essay published under the same title in *Pragmatism, Critique, Judgment: Essays for Richard J. Bernstein*, ed. Seyla Benhabib and Nancy Fraser (MIT Press, 2004).

"Pragmatism and romanticism" was the third of three Page-Barbour Lectures given at the University of Virginia in 2005. It has not been published previously.

"Analytic and conversational philosophy" is a revised version of a paper published, under the same title, in *A House Divided: Comparing Analytic and Continental Philosophy*, ed. Carlos Prado (Humanties Press, 2003).

"A pragmatist view of contemporary analytic philosophy" was published, under the same title, in *The Pragmatic Turn in Philosophy: Contemporary Engagements between Analytic and Continental Thought*, ed. William Egginton and Mike Sandbothe (State University of New York Press, 2004).

"Naturalism and quietism" has not been published previously.

"Wittgenstein and the linguistic turn" was written in response to an invitation from the Kirchberg Wittgenstein Symposium. It has not been published previously.

"Holism and historicism" is a revised and shortened version of the second of two Smythies Lectures at Oxford; an earlier version was published in *Kant im Streit der Fakultaeten*, ed. Volker Gerhardt (De Gruyter, 2005).

"Kant vs. Dewey: the current situation of moral philosophy" was published under the title "Trapped between Kant and Dewey: The Current Situation of Moral Philosophy," in *New Essays on the History of Autonomy: A Collection Honoring J. B. Schneewind*, ed. Natalie Brender and Larry Krasnoff (Cambridge University Press, 2004).

I am very grateful to the institutions mentioned above for their invitations to give lectures or to contribute to symposia. These invitations led me to write on various topics I should otherwise not have discussed. I also appreciate the willingness of the publishers I have listed to let me include previously published papers in this volume.

I also want to thank Gideon Lewis-Kraus, my former research assistant at Stanford, for indispensable assistance in preparing this volume for publication. He gave me excellent advice about which papers to include, which to omit, and which to revise. He also did most of the work of seeing it through the press.

Religion and Morality from a Pragmatist Point of View

Cultural politics and the question of the existence of God

CULTURAL POLITICS

The term "cultural politics" covers, among other things, arguments about what words to use. When we say that Frenchmen should stop referring to Germans as "Boches," or that white people should stop referring to black people as "niggers," we are practicing cultural politics. For our sociopolitical goals – increasing the degree of tolerance that certain groups of people have for one another – will be promoted by abandoning these linguistic practices.

Cultural politics is not confined to debates about hate speech. It includes projects for getting rid of whole topics of discourse. It is often said, for example, that we should stop using the concepts of "race" and "caste," stop dividing the human community up by genealogical descent. The idea is to lessen the chances that the question "who are his or her ancestors?" will be asked. Many people urge that words like "noble blood," "mixed blood," "outcaste," "intermarriage," "untouchable," and the like should be dropped from the language. For, they argue, this would be a better world if the suitability of people as spouses or employees or public officials were judged entirely on the basis of their behavior, rather than partially by reference to their ancestry.

This line of thinking is sometimes countered by saying "but there really *are* inherited differences – ancestry *does* matter." The rejoinder is: there certainly are inheritable physical characteristics, but these do not, in themselves, correlate with any characteristics that could provide a good reason for breaking up a planned marriage, or voting for or against a candidate. We may need the notion of genetic transmission for medical purposes, but not for any other purposes. So instead of talking about different races, let us just talk about different genes.

In the case of "race," as in that of "noble blood," the question "is there such a thing?" and the question "should we talk about such a thing?" seem pretty well interchangeable. That is why we tend to classify discussion of whether to stop talking about different races as "political" rather than "scientific" or "philosophical." But there are other cases in which it seems odd to identify questions about what exists with questions about what it is desirable to discuss.

The question of whether to talk about neutrons, for example, seems a strictly scientific question. That is why people who regret that physicists ever investigated radioactivity, or speculated about the possibility of splitting the atom, are accused of confusing science with politics. It seems natural to separate the political question of whether it was a good thing for humanity that scientists began to think about the possibility of atomic fission from scientific questions about the existence and properties of elementary particles.

I have sketched this contrast between the case of races and that of neutrons because it raises the question I want to discuss: how do we tell when, if ever, an issue about what exists should be discussed without reference to our sociopolitical goals? How should we split up culture into areas to which cultural politics is relevant and areas which should be kept free of it? When is it appropriate to say "we had *better* talk about them, because they *exist*" and when is that remark not to the point?

These questions are important for debates about what roles religion should play in contemporary society. Many people think that we should just stop talking about God. They think this for much the same reasons that they believe talk of race and caste to be a bad thing. Lucretius' *Tantum religio potuit suadere malorum* has been quoted for two millennia in order to remind us that religious conviction can easily be used to excuse cruelty. Marx's claim that religion is the opiate of the people sums up the suspicion, widespread since the Enlightenment, that ecclesiastical institutions are among the principal obstacles to the formation of a global cooperative commonwealth. Many people agree with Marx that we should try to create a world in which human beings devote all their energies to increasing human happiness in this world, rather than taking time off to think about the possibility of life after death.

To say that talk about God should be dropped because it impedes the search for human happiness is to take a pragmatic attitude toward religion that many religious believers find offensive and that some theologians think beside the point. The point, they would insist, is that God *exists*, or perhaps that human beings really *do* have immortal souls. Granted that the existence of God or of an immortal soul is controversial, that controversy should be explicitly about what exists, not about whether religious belief conduces to human happiness. First things first: ontology precedes cultural politics.

WILLIAM JAMES' VIEW OF RELIGION

I want to argue that cultural politics should replace ontology, and also that whether it should or not is *itself* a matter of cultural politics. Before turning to the defense of these theses, however, I want to underline the importance of such issues for philosophers who, like myself, are sympathetic to William James' pragmatism. James agreed with John Stuart Mill that the right thing to do, and a fortiori the right belief to acquire, is always the one that will do most for human happiness. So he advocated a utilitarian ethics of belief. James often comes close to saying that *all* questions, including questions about what exists, boil down to questions about what will help create a better world.

James' willingness to say this sort of thing has made him subject to accusations of intellectual perversity. For his view seems to suggest that, when notions like "race-mixing" and "atomic fission" are brought into the conversation, it is apposite to exclaim: "Let's not talk about that sort of thing! It's too dangerous! Let's not go there!" James seems to countenance doing what Peirce forbade: blocking the road of inquiry, refusing to find out what the world is really like because doing so might have harmful effects on human beings.

To give a concrete example, many people have argued that psychologists should not try to find out whether inheritable physical features are correlated with intelligence, simply because of the social harm that a positive answer to this question might produce. James' view of truth seems to suggest that these people are making a good point. People who are suspicious of pragmatism, on the other hand, argue that preventing scientists from doing experiments to find out whether intelligence is genetically transmissible, or to find out whether a neutron bomb is feasible, is to sin against truth. On their view, we should separate practical questions about whether eugenics or racial discrimination should be practiced, from the straightforwardly empirical question about whether Europeans are, on average, stupider than Asiatics – just as we divide the question of whether we *can* build a neutron bomb from the question of whether we *should*.

James was criticized not only for blocking the road of inquiry, and thus for being too restrictive, but also for being too permissive. That criticism was most frequently directed at "The Will to Believe," an essay which he said should have been titled "The Right to Believe." There he argued that one had a right to believe in the existence of God if that belief contributed to one's happiness, for no reason other than that very contribution.

I think that the best way for those of us who find James' pragmatism sympathetic to restate his position is to say that questions about what is too permissive and what is too restrictive are themselves questions of cultural politics. For example, the question of whether religious believers should be asked for evidence of the truth of their belief, and condemned as uneducated or irrational if they are unable to produce sufficient evidence, is a question about what sort of role we want religion to play in our society. It is on all fours with the question raised by the Inquisition: should scientists be allowed cavalierly to disregard scripture when they formulate hypotheses about the motions of heavenly bodies?

The question of whether we should, for the sake of preserving ancient traditions, allow parents to perpetuate a caste system by dictating choices of marriage partners to their children, is the same sort of question. Such questions arise whenever new social practices are beginning to compete with old ones – when, for example, the New Science of seventeenth-century Europe began to compete with the Christian churches for control of the universities, or when a traditional African culture is exposed to European ways.

The question of whether scientists should have been allowed to find out whether the atom could be split, or should be allowed to investigate the correlation of intelligence with skin color, is not a question that can be answered simply by saying "do not block the road of inquiry!" or "seek the truth, though the heavens fall!" Neither is the question of whether France and Germany are right to criminalize Holocaust-denial. There is much to be said on both sides. The argument for letting scientists investigate whatever they please is that the more ability to predict we can get, the better off we shall be in the long run. The argument for blocking them off from certain topics is that the short-run dangers are so great as to outweigh the chances of long-term benefit. There are no grand philosophical principles that can help us solve such problems of risk-management.

To say that James is basically right in his approach to truth and reality is to say that arguments about relative dangers and benefits are the only ones that matter. That is why the statement "we should be talking about it because it's real" is as useless as "we should believe it because it's true." Attributions of reality or truth are, on the view I share with James, compliments we pay to entities or beliefs that have won their spurs, paid their way, proved themselves useful, and therefore been incorporated into accepted social practices. When these practices are being contested, it is of no use to say that reality or truth is on the side of one of the contestants. For such claims will always be mere table-thumping, not serious contributions to cultural politics.

Another way to put James' point is to say that truth and reality exist for the sake of social practices, rather than vice versa. Like the Sabbath, they are made for man. This is a dark saying, but I think that it can be defended by appealing to the work of a contemporary neo-Hegelian, Robert Brandom, whose writings provide the best weapons for defending my version of James' pragmatism. Brandom is not a utilitarian, and his work follows out the line of thought that leads from Kant to Hegel, rather than the one that leads from Mill to James. But his construal of assertions as the assumption of responsibilities to other members of society, rather than to "the world" or "the truth," brings him into alignment with James.

BRANDOM ON THE PRIORITY OF THE SOCIAL

The germ of Brandom's later work can be found in an early article he published on Heidegger. There he treats Heidegger as putting forward a doctrine he calls "the ontological priority of the social." The doctrine of the priority of the social is perhaps not happily thought of as an "ontological" one, but Brandom is using it as a way of explicating the consequences of Heidegger's quasi-pragmatist attempt to make the *Zuhanden* prior to the *Vorhanden*. The priority in question consists in the fact that "all matters of authority or privilege, in particular *epistemic* authority, are matters of social practice, and not objective matters of fact."[1]

Brandom enlarges on this claim by remarking that society divides culture up into three areas. In the first of these the individual's authority is supreme (as when she makes sincere first-person reports of feelings or thoughts). In the second, the non-human world is supreme (as when the litmus paper, or the DNA-analysis apparatus, is allowed to determine whether the accused will be freed or punished, or whether a given scientific theory will be accepted or rejected). But there is a third area in which society does not delegate, but retains the right to decide for itself. This last is the arena of cultural politics. Brandom analogizes this situation to the constitutional arrangements of the USA, according to which, as he says, "the judiciary is given the authority and responsibility to interpret the proper region of authority and responsibility of each branch [that is to say,

---

[1] Robert Brandom, "Heidegger's Categories in *Being and Time*," *The Monist* 66 (1983), 389–90.

of the executive, the legislative, and the judiciary branches of government], itself included."[2]

The question at issue between James and his opponents boiled down to this: is there an authority beyond that of society which society should acknowledge – an authority such as God, or Truth, or Reality? Brandom's account of assertions as assumptions of social responsibilities leaves no room for such an authority, and so he sides with James. Both philosophers can appeal to Occam's Razor. The authority traditionally attributed to the non-human can be explained sociologically, and such a sociological account has no need to invoke the rather mysterious beings that theological or philo-sophical treatments of authority require. (Such entities include "the divine will," "the intrinsic nature of reality, as it is in itself, apart from human needs and interests," and "the immediately given character of experience.")

Suppose that one accepts the thesis of the ontological primacy of the social. Then one will think that the question of the existence of God is a question of the advantages and disadvantages of using God-talk over against alternative ways of talking. As with "race," so with "God." Instead of taking about races we can, for many purposes, talk about genes. Instead of talking about God the Creator we can (as physicists do) talk about the Big Bang. For other purposes, such as providing foundations for morality, we can talk (as Habermas does) about consensus under ideal communica-tive conditions rather than about the divine will. When discussing the future of humanity, we can talk (as Marx did) about a secularist social utopia instead of about the Last Judgment. And so on.

Suppose, however, one does not accept the priority of the social, pre-cisely *because* one is a religious believer, and holds that God has authority over human society, as well as over everything else. From Brandom's point of view, this is like holding that human society is subject to the authority of "reality" or of "experience" or of "truth." All attempts to name an author-ity which is superior to that of society are disguised moves in the game of cultural politics. That is what they *must* be, because it is the only game in town. (But in saying that it is the only such game, Brandom is not claim-ing to have made an empirical discovery, much less to have revealed a "con-ceptual necessity." He is, I would claim, articulating a cultural–political stance by pointing to the social advantages of his account of authority.)

Brandom's view can be made more plausible by considering what people actually have in mind when they say that God has authority over human society. They do not say this unless they think they know what God wants human beings to do – unless they can cite sacred scriptures, or the words of a guru, or the teachings of an ecclesiastical tradition, or something of the sort, in support of their own position. But, from the point of view of both atheists and people whose scripture or guru or tradition is different, what is purportedly said in the name of God is actually said in the name of some interest group – some sect or church, for example. Two competing religious groups (say the Hindus and the Muslims, or the Mormons and the Catholics) will typically say that the other willfully and blasphemously refuses to submit to God's authority.

The battles between two such groups are analogous to arguments between opposing counsel, presenting appellate briefs to a court. Both sets of lawyers will claim to have the authority of "the law" on their side. Alternatively, it can be analogized to the battle between two scientific theories, both of which claim to be true to the "nature of reality." Brandom's point is that the appeal to God, like the appeal to "the law," is always super-fluous, since, as long as there is disagreement about what the purported authority says, the idea of "authority" is out of place.[3] Only when the com-munity decides to adopt one faith rather than another, or the court decides in favor of one side rather than another, or the scientific community in favor of one theory rather than another, does the idea of "authority" become applicable. The so-called "authority" of anything other than the community (or some person or thing or expert culture authorized by the community to make decisions in its name) can only be more table-thumping.

THE APPEAL TO EXPERIENCE, RELIGIOUS AND OTHERWISE

The counterintuitive character of Brandom's claims is due in part to the popularity of empiricism. For empiricists tell us that we can break out from under the authority of the local community by making unmediated contact with reality. This view has encouraged the idea that Europe finally got in touch with reality when scientists like Galileo had the courage to believe the evidence of their senses rather than bowing to the authority of Aristotle and the Catholic Church.

Brandom agrees with his teacher Wilfrid Sellars that the idea of getting in direct touch with reality through the senses is a confusion between relations of justification, which hold between propositions, and causal rela-tions, which hold between events. We should not treat the causal ability of

---

[3] This is a point which has been made repeatedly, and very persuasively, by Stanley Fish. See his book *Professional Correctness: Literary Studies and Political Change* (New York: Clarendon Press, 1995).

certain events to produce non-inferential beliefs in suitably programmed organisms as a justification for their holding those beliefs.

Brandom agrees with Sellars that "all awareness is a linguistic affair." On this view, creatures not programmed to use language, such as dogs and human infants, react to stimuli but are no more aware of the characteristics of things than thermostats are aware of heat and cold. There can be no such thing as by-passing the linguistic practices of the community by using one's senses to find out how things really are, for two reasons. First: all non-inferential perceptual reports ("this is red," "this is disgusting," "this is holy") are made in the language of one or another community, a language adapted to that community's needs. Second: the community grants authority to such reports not because it believes in a special relation between reality and human sense-organs, but because it has empirical evidence that such reports are reliable (in the sense that they will be confirmed by the application of independent criteria).

This means that when somebody reports experiencing an object about which the community has no reason to think her a reliable reporter, her appeal to experience will fall flat. If I say that round squares are, contrary to popular opinion, possible, because I have in fact recently encountered several such squares, nobody takes me seriously. The same goes if I come out of the forest claiming to have spotted a unicorn. If I say that I experienced God, this may or may not be taken seriously, depending on what uses of the term "God" are current in my community. If I explain to a Christian audience that personal observation has shown me that God is, contrary to popular opinion, female, that audience will probably just laugh. But if I say that I have seen the Risen Christ in the disk of the sun on Easter morning, it is possible that I shall be viewed with respect and envy.

In short, God-reports have to live up to previous expectations, just as do reports of physical objects. They cannot, all by themselves, be used to repudiate those expectations. They are useful for this purpose only when they form part of a full-fledged, concerted, cultural–political initiative. This is what happens when a new religion or church replaces an old one. It was not the disciples' reports of an empty tomb, all by themselves, that made Europe believe that God was incarnate in Christ. But, in the context of St. Paul's overall public relations strategy, those reports had their effect. Analogously, it was not Galileo's report of spots moving across the face of the planet Jupiter, possibly caused by the transits of moons, that overthrew the authority of the Aristotelian–Ptolemaic cosmology. But, in the context of the initiative being mounted by his fellow Copernican cultural politicians, that report had considerable importance.

I can sum up what I have been saying about appeals to experience as follows: experience gives us no way to drive a wedge between the cultural–political question of what we should talk about and the question of what really exists. For what counts as an accurate report of experience is a matter of what a community will let you get away with. Empiricism's appeal to experience is as inefficacious as appeals to the Word of God unless backed up with a predisposition on the part of a community to take such appeals seriously. So experience cannot, by itself, adjudicate disputes between warring cultural politicians.

THE EXISTENCE OF GOD AND THE EXISTENCE OF CONSCIOUSNESS

I can make my point about the irrelevance of religious experience to God's existence a bit more vivid by comparing the God of orthodox Western monotheism with consciousness as it is understood by Cartesian dualists. In the unphilosophical sense of the term "conscious," the existence of consciousness is indisputable. People in a coma lack consciousness. People are conscious as long as they are walking and talking. But there is a special philosophical sense of the term "consciousness" in which the very existence of consciousness is in dispute.

In this sense of "consciousness," the word refers to something the absence of which is compatible with walking and talking. It is what zombies lack that the rest of us possess. Zombies behave just like normal people, but have no inner life. The light bulb in their brains, so to speak, never goes on. They do not feel anything, although they can answer questions about how they feel in the conventional ways, ways which have the place they do in the language game by virtue of, for example, correlations between their utterances of "it hurts" and their having recently touched hot stoves, been pricked by pins, and the like. Talking to a zombie is just like talking to anybody else, since the zombie's lack of an inner life never manifests itself by any outward and visible sign. That is why, unless neurology someday discovers the secret of non-zombiehood, we shall never know whether our nearest and dearest share our feelings, or are what James called "automatic sweethearts."

Philosophers have spent decades arguing about whether this sense of "consciousness" and this sense of "zombie" make sense. The question at issue is: can a descriptive term have a sense if its application is regulated by no public criteria? Wittgenstein thought that the answer to this question was "no." That negative answer is the upshot of arguments like this one:

Suppose everyone had a box with something in it: we call it a "beetle." No one can look into anyone else's box, and everyone says he knows what a beetle is only by looking at *his* beetle. – Here it would be possible for everyone to have something different in his box. One might even imagine such a thing constantly changing. – But suppose the word "beetle" had a use in these people's language? – If so, it would not be used as the name of a thing. The thing in the box has no place in the language-game at all; not even as a *something*: for the box might even be empty. – No, one can "divide through" by the thing in the box; it cancels out, whatever it is.[4]

The analogues of these private beetles are what philosophers who believe in the possibility of zombies call "raw feels" or "qualia" – the sort of thing that shows "what it is *like*. . . [e.g. to be in pain, to see something red]." We all know what it is like be in pain, these philosophers believe, but (despite their sincere avowals that they do) zombies do not. Wittgenstein would say that the word "pain" has a sense only as long as philosophers do *not* treat it as the name of something whose presence or absence swings free of all differences in environment or behavior. On his view, the philosophers who believe in "qualia" and who deploy expressions like "what it is like to be in pain" are proposing, and commending, a new language game. In this specifically philosophical game, we use expressions whose *only* function is to help us disjoin pain from pain-behavior. We use them to separate off the outer behavior and its neurological correlates from something that is a state neither of the body nor of the nervous system. Wittgenstein, when he is being properly cautious, thinks that anything has a sense if you give it one by playing an appropriate language game with it. But he can see no point in playing the "qualia" game. So he thinks that we are entitled to "divide through" by the qualia just as we do by the beetles – to treat them, as Wittgenstein says in another passage, as "a wheel that turns though nothing else moves with it" and which is therefore "not part of the mechanism."[5]

Philosophers of mind like Daniel Dennett and Sellars agree with Wittgenstein about this. But they are criticized by philosophers more sympathetic to Descartes, such as David Chalmers and Thomas Nagel. The latter say that the existence of raw feels, of the experience of "what it is like . . ." is incontestable. They reject Sellars' and Brandom's doctrine that all awareness is a linguistic affair. There is, they say, more awareness than we can put into words – language can point to things that it cannot describe. To think otherwise, they say, is to be a verificationist, and verificationists display what Nagel regards as an undesirable lack of "the ambition for

---

[4] Ludwig Wittgenstein, *Philosophical Investigations*, Part I, section 293 (Oxford: Blackwell, 1953).
[5] Ibid., section 271.

transcendence." Nagel writes as follows: "Only a dogmatic verificationist would deny the possibility of forming objective concepts that reach beyond our current capacity to apply them. The aim of reaching *a conception of the world which does not put us at the center in any way* [emphasis added] requires the formation of such concepts."[6]

Brandom's doctrine of the ontological priority of the social would, of course, only be adopted by someone who has little interest in "reaching a conception of the world which does not put us at the center." Brandom, Sellars, and Wittgenstein simply lack the "ambition of transcendence" that Nagel, resembling in this respect the orthodox theologians of Western monotheism, thinks it desirable to have. Those theologians, in their anxiety to make God truly transcendent, separated him from the things of this world by describing him as without parts or passions, non-spatiotemporal, and therefore incomparable to his creatures. They went on to insist that the fact of God's incomparability is nonetheless compatible with his making himself known to us in experience. Nagel and those who wish to preserve the special philosophical notion of consciousness (i.e. the thing that zombies lack) are trying to give sense to a descriptive term by a series of negations. But they insist that the fact that consciousness is like nothing else in the universe is compatible with our being directly and incorrigibly aware that we have it, for we know that *we* are not zombies.

Both those who want to use "God" in the way that orthodox theology does and those who want to use "consciousness" as Chalmers and Nagel do claim that their opponents, the people who do not want to play any such language game, are denying the obvious. Many orthodox theologians have claimed that denial of the existence of God simply flies in the face of the common experience of mankind. Nagel thinks that philosophical views such as Dennett's "stem from an insufficiently robust sense of reality and of its independence of any particular form of human understanding." Many religious believers think that it requires considerable perversity to even imagine being an atheist. Nagel, I imagine, thinks that it requires similar perversity to weaken one's sense of reality to the point at which one takes seriously the doctrine of the ontological priority of the social.

The moral I want to draw from the analogy between God and consciousness is that the existence of either is not a matter which appeals to experience could ever resolve, any more than one can appeal to experience to determine whether or not marriage across caste or racial lines is or is not intrinsically disgusting. Cultural politics can create a society that will find

[6] Thomas Nagel, *The View from Nowhere* (New York: Oxford University Press, 1986), 24.

the latter repulsive, and cultural politics of a different sort can create one
that finds such marriages unobjectionable. There is no way to show that
belief in God or in qualia is more or less "natural" than disbelief, any more
than there is a way to figure out whether a sense of caste membership or
race membership is more or less "natural" than utter indifference to human
blood-lines. What one side of the argument calls "natural," the other is
likely to call "primitive," or perhaps "contrived."

Similarly, cultural politics of the sort conducted in Europe since the
Enlightenment can alternately diminish or increase the obviousness of
God's existence, as well as the frequency of reports to have experienced God's
presence. Cultural politics of the sort conducted within philosophy departments can diminish or increase the numbers of philosophy students who
find the existence of qualia obvious, and find it equally obvious that some
humanoids might be zombies. There are Dennett-leaning departments and
Chalmers-leaning departments. The disagreement between them is no
more susceptible to neutral adjudication than is the disagreement between
atheists and theists.[7]

To say that cultural politics has the last word on these matters is to say,
once again, that the questions "should we be talking about God?" "should
we be speculating about zombies?" "should we talk about what race people
belong to?" are not posterior to the questions "does God exist?" "could
some of the humanoids in this room be zombies?" "are there such things as
distinct races within the human species?" They are the *same* questions, for
any consideration relevant to the cultural–political question is equally relevant to the ontological question, and conversely. But, from the point of
view of philosophers like Nagel, who warn against the lures of verificationism, to think them the same questions is itself a confusion.

OBJECTS AS MADE FOR MAN

The view that I have been ascribing to Brandom may make it seem as
if acknowledging the ontological priority of the social entails allowing

---

[7] In this *The Conscious Mind: In Search of a Fundamental Theory* (Oxford: Oxford University Press,
1996), Chalmers discusses the analogy between consciousness (in the sense of what zombies lack)
and God at 186–9 and again at 249. At 187 he says that the difference is that we can explain God-
talk sociologically: God was postulated as an explanation of various phenomena. Consciousness,
however, is an explanandum. So the only way to account for talk about it is by saying that its existence is obvious to all (except, mysteriously, a few oddballs like Dennett). I would argue that "consciousness" is an artifact of Cartesian philosophy in the same way that God is an artifact of early
cosmology. (That was one of the claims made in my book *Philosophy and the Mirror of Nature*,
Princeton, NJ: Princeton University Press, 1979). On the view I share with Sellars and Brandom,
there are no such things as "natural" explananda.

existence to be ascribed to anything society finds it convenient to talk about. This may seem ridiculously counterintuitive. Even though society might set its face against caste-talk or against God-talk, it can hardly set its face against talk of stars and animals, pains and pleasures, truths and falsehoods – all the uncontroversial matters that people have talked about always and every-where. There are, critics of the ontological priority of the social will say, limits to society's ability to talk things into or out of existence.

Brandom, James, and Sellars would agree, but they would insist that it is important to specify just which considerations set these limits. There are three sorts of limits: (1) *transcendental* limits set by the need to talk *about* something – to refer to objects, things we can represent well or badly, rather than just making noises which, though they may change behavior, lack intentionality; (2) *practical* limits, set by the transcultural need all human beings have to distinguish between, for example, poisonous and nourish-ing substances, up and down, humans and beasts, true and false, male and female, pain and pleasure, right and left; (3) *cultural* limits set by our pre-vious social decisions – by a particular society's actually existing norms.

Brandom argues for the existence of the first sort of limit by claiming that no society can make much use of language unless it can wield the notion of a certain locution being about a certain object. To be an object, Brandom argues, is to be something that one can be wrong about. Indeed, it is to be something that everybody might always get wrong in certain respects (though not, obviously, in *all* respects).[8] The notion of "object" is thus derivative from that of social practice, as is that of "truth about an object." This is the point of saying, as I did earlier, that truth and reality exist for the sake of social practices. We talk about them because our social practices are improved by doing so.

In contrast, for most of the philosophers who hold to what Brandom calls "representationalism" (as distinguished from his own "inferentialism"), the concept of "object" is primitive and inexplicable. Representationalists think that you must grasp this concept in order to have any idea of what language, or mind, or rationality might be. For all of these notions must be understood in terms of the notion of accurate representation of objects. In contrast, Brandom's argument is that the true primitives are those that make possible the application of social norms – notions like "having done A, or said P, you cannot get away with doing B, or saying Q." The latter notions are the ones that enable us to articulate what he calls "proprieties of inference."

---

[8] Donald Davidson has famously argued that most of our beliefs must be true, for if most of our beliefs about beavers (for example)were wrong we should not be talking about beavers at all.

Doing things Brandom's way amounts to dropping the old skeptical question "how can the human mind manage to get accurate representations of reality?" in favor of such questions as "why does the human community need the notion of accurate representation of objects?" "why should the question of getting in touch with reality ever have arisen?" "how did we ever come to see an abyss between subject and object of the sort which the sceptic describes?" "how did we ever get ourselves into a position in which skeptical doubts like Descartes' seemed plausible?"

The change Brandom is urging parallels the change from a theistic to a humanistic world-view. In recent centuries, instead of asking whether God exists, people have started asking whether it is a good idea for us to continue talking about Him, and which human purposes might be served by doing so – asking, in short, what use the concept of God might be to human beings. Brandom is suggesting that philosophers, instead of asking whether we really are in touch with objects "outside the mind" – objects that are as they are regardless of what we think about them – should ask what human purposes are served by conceiving of such objects. We should reflect on whether talking about them was a good idea.

In the course of his book he argues that it was not only a good idea but a pragmatically indispensable one. For if we had never talked of such objects, we should never have had much to say. Our language would not have developed beyond an exchange of causally efficacious grunts. Talk about objects independent of the mind was valuable because it helped the anthropoids become human, not because humans awakened to their obligation to represent such objects accurately – their obligation to "the Truth."

The "loss of the world" which idealism seemed helpless to avoid is thus not a problem for Brandom's inferentialism, since "objectivity is a structural aspect of the social–perspectival form of conceptual contents. The permanent distinction between how things are and how they are taken to be by some interlocutor is built into the social – inferential articulation of concepts."[9] Yet Brandom is not exactly a "realist," for that distinction is permanent only as long as we humans behave as we do – namely sapiently. This is why he can say that "the facts about having physical properties" supervene upon "the facts about seeming to have such properties."[10] In the causal order which can be accurately represented once humans have initiated the practice of distinguishing causes from effects, the world comes before the practices. Yet space, time, substance, and causality are what they

⁹ Robert Brandom, *Making it Explicit* (Cambridge, MA: Harvard University Press, 1994), 597.
¹⁰ Ibid., 292.

are because human beings need to talk in certain ways to get certain things done. In the place of Kant's inexplicable transcendental constitution of the mind, Brandom substitutes practices which helped a certain biological species flourish. So the question about the existence of God is: "can we get as good an argument for the utility of God-talk as we can for the utility of talk about time, space, substance, and causality?"

For Brandom, the answer to this question is "no." For a priori philosophical inquiry into what exists is exhausted once such questions as "why do we need to talk about reidentifiable spatiotemporal particulars?" have been answered. Giving a transcendental argument for the existence of objects, and of these particular sorts of objects, exhausts the capacity of philosophy to tell you what there just *has* to be (if we are to make inferences at all). There is no further discipline called "ontology" which can tell you what singular terms we need to have in the language – whether or not we need "God" for example.

Brandom often points to analogies between his inferentialism and Spinoza's. But there are, of course, obvious disanalogies. Brandom and Spinoza are both holists, but Brandom's whole, like Hegel's, is the ongoing conversation of mankind, a conversation always subject to the contingencies that afflict finite existence. Spinoza's whole is an atemporal being that can be the object of what he called *scientia intuitiva*, the sort of direct acquaintance that makes further conversation, further inquiry, and further use of language, superfluous. This difference between Brandom and Spinoza encapsulates the difference between philosophers who see no end to the process of inquiry, and no court of appeal other than our descendants, and those who think that cultural politics cannot be the last word – that there must be what Plato hoped for, a way to rise above the contingent vagaries of conversation to a vision which transcends politics.

BRANDOM ON THE NATURE OF EXISTENCE

Brandom's explicit discussion of existence is confined to a rather brief excursus.[11] He starts out by agreeing with Kant that existence is not a predicate, but his way of making this point is very different from Kant's. Kant distinguished between "logical" notions such as "thing" and "is identical with," which apply to both the phenomenal and the noumenal, and categories of the understanding such as "substance" and "cause" which apply only to the former. Brandom thinks that Kant (and later Frege) erred by thinking of

---

[11] Ibid., 440ff.

"thing" and "object" as what he calls "genuine sortals," and by treating identity as a property that can be attributed to things without specification of the sorts to which they belong. These errors make plausible the bad idea that things come in two flavors – existent and non-existent – and thereby suggest that one might be able to explain what all the existent ones have in common. They also encourage the view that the sentence "everything is identical with itself" is more than what Wittgenstein said it was – a splendid example of a completely useless proposition.[12]

To get rid of these bad beliefs, Brandom thinks, we have to take "thing" as always short for "thing of the following kind . . ." and "identical with" as always short for "identical with in the following respect . . ." He thinks that Frege should have seen quantifiers as coming with sortal restrictions. "For," as he says, "quantifiers quantify, they specify, at least in general terms, *how many*, and how many there are depends (as Frege's remarks about playing cards indicate), on *what* one is counting – on the sortal used to identify and individuate them."[13]

Kant's discussion of existence takes for granted that it comes in two sorts – the generic sort had both by pencils and God and the more specific, phenomenal, sort had only by the pencils and their fellow-inhabitants of space and time. Brandom responds that it comes in many sorts, as many as there are sets of what he calls canonical designators. For him, an existential commitment – a belief that something of a certain description exists – is "a particular quantificational commitment in which the vindicating commitments that determine its content are restricted to canonical designators."[14]

The best way to understand what Brandom means by "canonical designators" is to consider the paradigm case thereof – "egocentric spatio-temporal coordinate descriptions."[15] These designators are the descriptions of spatiotemporal locations on a grid whose zero point is the place where the speaker is now. To say that a physical object exists is to say that the object in question occupies one of those points – that it occupies an address specified with reference to the coordinates of that grid.

Analogously, to say that an object has existence not physically but "in the Sherlock Holmes stories" is to choose as a set of canonical designators all and only descriptions of persons and things mentioned in those stories, or entailed by what is said in those stories. When we say that Dr. Watson's wife exists but Holmes' does not, we mean that appeal to that list of

[12] Wittgenstein, *Philosophical Investigations*, Part I, section 216.
[13] Brandom, *Making it Explicit*, 439. Frege remarks that it matters whether it is packs, or cards, or honors that are being counted.   [14] Ibid., 443.   [15] Ibid., 445.

designators will settle the question. Again, to say that there exists a prime between 21 and 25 but no prime between 48 and 50 is to take the numerals as canonical designators. Any such list of designators acquaints us with an exhaustive (finite or infinite) set of things, things that an entity must be identical with if it is to exist, in the relevant sense of "exist."

The only sort of existence that Kant thought we could discuss intelligibly was physical existence. In this logical space the canonical designators are, indeed, the same ones Kant picks – the niches on the spatiotemporal grid. In Kant's system, God inhabits logical space but not empirical, physical, space. So, Kant thought, the question of the existence of God is beyond our knowledge, for knowledge of existence is coextensive with knowledge of physical existence. (But, Kant goes on to say, this question can somehow be dealt with by "pure practical reason.")

For Brandom, however, the matter is more complicated. We have lots of logical spaces at our disposal (and doubtless more to come) and we can discuss existence within any of them. We have as many such spaces as we have infinite sequences, or finite lists, of canonical designators. We can, for example, treat the sacred scriptures of a given religious tradition as we treat the Holmes stories – as providing canonical designators that permit us to confirm or disconfirm the existence of objects, albeit not physical objects. Kant was right to think that there is no reason why existence has to be physical (for neither that of prime numbers nor that of the Baker Street Irregulars is), but he was wrong in thinking that knowledge of existence is limited to knowledge of physical existence.

This is because the question of whether or not to talk about the existence of immaterial and infinite beings is not one for transcendental philosophy but rather one to be turned over to cultural politics. A representationalist like Nagel or Kant can picture us as surrounded by possibly unknowable facts – objects for which we shall never have words entering into relations we may never understand. But, for an inferentialist, what counts as an object is determined by what a culture has definite descriptions of, and argument about what exists is determined by what canonical designators are in place. Yet any culture may be surpassed by another, since the human imagination may dream up many more definite descriptions and equally many lists of canonical designators. There are no "natural," transcultural, limits to this process of self-transcendence, nor does it have any predetermined goal.

When a culture wants to erect a logical space that includes, say, the gods and goddesses of the Olympian pantheon, nothing stands in its way, any more than anything stood in Conan Doyle's way when he created the list of Holmesian canonical designators. But to ask, after such a culture has become entrenched, "are there *really* gods and goddesses?" is like asking "are there *really* numbers?" or "are there *really* physical objects?" The person asking such a question has to have a good reason for raising it. "Intellectual curiosity" is not such a reason. If one is going to challenge an ongoing cultural practice, one must both explain what practice might be put in its place, and how this substitute will tie in with surrounding practices. That is why to turn a question over to cultural politics is not to turn it over to "unreason." Arguments within cultural politics are usually just as rational, though typically not as conclusive, as those within natural science. To give good reasons for raising skeptical questions about a set of entities, one will have to at least sketch reasons for thinking that the culture would be in better shape if the sort of thing in question were no longer discussed.

TWO BAD DISTINCTIONS: LITERAL–SYMBOLIC AND SENSE–NONSENSE

Brandom's point can be clarified by comparing it with the quasi-Heideggerian claim, made by Tillich and other Christian theologians, that, since God is Being-as-such, and not a being among other beings, the attempt to characterize him – or, in Brandomian language, the attempt to identify him with the help of an already available list of canonical designators – is hopeless. Tillich concluded that "does God exist?" is a bad question – as bad as "is there *really* something it is like to be conscious?" or "are numbers *really* real? Do the numerals *really* refer to entities?"

There is no problem about giving either "what it is like to be conscious" or "God, a being without parts or passions" a place in a language game. We know how the trick is done, and we have had lots of experience watching both games being played. But in neither case is there any point in raising questions about existence, because there is no neutral logical space within which discussion can proceed between people inclined to deny and people inclined to affirm existence of the relevant entity. Metaphysical questions like "does God exist?" and "is the spatiotemporal world real?" are undiscussable because there is no list of "neutral" canonical designators by reference to which they might be answered.

That is why "existent thing," a universal as opposed to a local sortal, is only a pseudo-sortal. The very idea of a universal sortal is incoherent, for to be a sortal is to come with a set of canonical designators in tow. If discussion of God's existence or the reality of the world of common sense were to be discussable (in a way that does *not* boil down to cultural politics), we should have to have somehow transcended both God and the world so as to see them against a "neutral" background.

The fact that "does God exist?" is a bad question suggests that a better question would be: "do we want to weave one or more of the various religious traditions (with their accompanying pantheons) together with our deliberation over moral dilemmas, our deepest hopes, and our need to be rescued from despair?" Alternatively: "does one or more of these religious traditions provide language we wish to use when putting together our self-image, determining what is most important to us?" If none of them do, we shall treat all such traditions, and their pantheons, as offering mere "mythologies." Nevertheless, within each such mythology, as within the Holmes stories, there will be truth and falsity – *literal* truth and falsity – about existence claims. It will be true, for example, that there exists a child of Zeus and Semele but false that there is a child of Uranus and Aphrodite, true that there is a Third Person of the Godhead but false that there is a Thirteenth.

Our decision about whether to treat the religious tradition in which we were brought up as offering literal truths or as telling stories for which we no longer have any use will depend on many things – for example, whether we continue to think that prayer and worship will make a difference to what happens to us. But there are no criteria for when it is rational and when irrational to switch from adhesion to a tradition to a skeptical "mere myth" view of it. Decisions about what language games to play, what to talk about and what not to talk about, and for what purposes, are not made on the basis of agreed-upon criteria. Cultural politics is the least norm-governed human activity. It is the site of generational revolt, and thus the growing point of culture – the place where traditions and norms are all up for grabs at once. (Compare, as Brandom suggests, the decisions of the US Supreme Court in such cases as *Plessy* and *Brown*.)

Paul Tillich remarked that, in a post-Enlightenment Western culture, the vision of a social democratic utopia has begun to play the role of God. This vision has become the symbol of ultimate concern for many intellectuals whose ancestors' symbol was Jesus Christ. Tillich offered various arguments to the effect that that vision was an inadequate symbol, but his arguments are all of the non-criteria-governed sort that I have been putting under the heading "cultural politics." Like most recommendations of religious belief in the West since the Enlightenment, they were arguments that we shall eventually be driven to despair without specifically *religious* symbols of ultimate concern – the sort that Paine and Shelley thought we could perfectly well do without. Such arguments claim, for example, that a person whose sense of what is ultimately important is framed in purely secular terms will be less successful in achieving what Tillich called "the courage to be" than those who use Christian terms.

Tillich's term "finding an adequate symbol of ultimate concern" is, however, not an improvement on such old-fashioned phrases as "finding meaning in life," "formulating a satisfactory self-image," or "discovering what the Good is." Indeed, it is slightly worse than those, because it relies upon a distinction between the symbolic and the literal that is a relic of representationalist philosophy. Tillich thought that scientific and common-sense beliefs could have literal truth, but religious truths could have only "symbolic" truth. He thought this because he believed that the former could be considered accurate representations of reality, whereas the notion of "accuracy" was inappropriate to the latter. A Brandomian inferentialist, however, has no use for the literal-vs.-symbolic distinction. The only relevant distinction she can countenance is one between logical spaces constructed for certain purposes (e.g. those of physical science, of mathematics, or of chess) and other logical spaces constructed for other purposes (e.g. those provided by the Platonic dialogues, the Jataka, the Holmes stories, the New Testament, etc.).

Debate about the utility of such logical spaces and about the desirability or undesirability of uniting them with, or disjoining them from, one another is the substance of cultural politics. From the point of view common to Brandom and Hegel, there is nothing special about natural science (or, better, to the discourse constituted by the union of the logical space of everyday transcultural common sense with that of modern natural science) which entitles it to the term "literal truth." That term harks back to the bad Kantian idea that discourse about physical objects is the paradigm case of making truth claims, and that all other areas of discourse must be thought of as "non-cognitive." If we drop this idea, we shall have no use for what Nancy Frankenberry has called "the theology of symbolic forms" – no use for the attempt (which goes back at least to Schleiermacher) to make room for God by saying that there is something like "symbolic truth" or "imaginative truth" or "emotional truth" or "metaphorical truth" as well as "literal" truth.

Dropping these notions will lead us to drop the idea that God requires to be talked about in a special way because he is a special kind of being. For Brandom, there is no such thing as a certain kind of object demanding to be spoken of in a certain kind of language. To say that God requires to be talked about in a certain way is no more illuminating than to say that transfinite cardinal numbers, or neutrinos, demand to be talked about in a certain way. Since we would not know what any of these entities were if we did not know that they were the entities talked about in these ways, the idea that they "demand" this treatment is unhelpful. It is as if we praised a poet's choice of metaphor for fitting our otherwise indescribable experience perfectly. Such praise rings hollow, simply because we cannot identify the experience without the help of the metaphor. It as if, to paraphase Wittgenstein, we were to exclaim with delight over the fact that a plane figure fits perfectly into its surroundings.

Like Wittgenstein, Brandom thinks that anything has a sense if you give it a sense. More consistently than Wittgenstein, he can follow up on this by saying that whatever philosophy is, it is not the detection of nonsense (*pace* Kant, the *Tractatus*, Carnap, and some misbegotten passages in *Philosophical Investigations*). The language game played by theologians with the transcendental terms, or with Heideggerese, and the one played by philosophers of mind who talk about the independence of qualia from behavior and environment, is as coherent as that played with numbers or physical objects. *But the coherence of talk about X does not guarantee the discussability of the existence of X.* Talk about numbers is ideally coherent, but this coherence does not help us discuss the question of whether the numerals are names of real things. Nor does the coherence of Christian theology help us discuss the existence of God. This is not because of an ontological fact about numbers or God, but because of sociological facts about the unavailability of norms to regulate discussion.

Brandom's favorite philosopher is Hegel, and in this area the most salient difference between Kant and Hegel is that Hegel does not think philosophy can rise above the social practices of its time and judge their desirability by reference to something that is not itself an alternative social practice (past or future, real or imagined). For Hegel as for Brandom, there are no norms which are not the norms of some social practice. So, when asked "are these desirable norms?" or "is this a good social practice?" all either can do is ask "by reference to what encompassing social practice are we supposed to judge desirability?" or, more usefully, "by comparison to the norms of what proposed alternative social practice?"

Early in the Introduction to *The Phenomenology of Spirit*, there is a passage that anticipates what James said in "The Will to Believe" about W. K. Clifford, a philosopher who held that we have no right to believe in the existence of God, given the lack of relevant evidence. Clifford, James said, was too willing to sacrifice truth in order to be certain that he would never fall into error. Hegel criticized the Cliffords of his own day as follows:

if the fear of falling into error sets up a mistrust of Science, which in the absence of such scruples gets on with the work itself, and actually cognizes something, it is hard to see why we should not turn round and mistrust this very mistrust. This fear takes something – a great deal in fact – for granted as truth, supporting its scruples and inferences on what is itself in need of prior scrutiny to see if it is true. To be specific, it takes for granted certain ideas about cognition as an instrument and as a medium, and assumes that there is a difference between ourselves and this cognition. Above all, it presupposes that the Absolute stands on one side and cognition on the other, independent and separated from it, and yet is something real; or in other words, it presupposes that cognition which, since it is excluded from the Absolute, is surely outside of the truth as well, is nevertheless true, an assumption whereby what calls itself fear of error reveals itself rather as fear of the truth.[16]

In place of the words "Science" and "cognition" in Hegel's text, Brandom would put "conversation." If one makes this substitution, one will construe Hegel as saying that we should not think that there is a difference between ourselves and the discursive practices in which we are engaged, and that we should not think that those practices are a means to some end, nor that they are a medium of representation used to get something right. A fortiori, we should not think that there is a goal of inquiry which is what it is apart from those practices, and foreknowledge of which can help us decide which practices to have.

We should rather, as Hegel says elsewhere, be content to think of philosophy as its time (that is to say, our present discursive practices) held in thought (that is to say, contrasted with alternative past or proposed practices). We should stop trying to put our discursive practices within a larger context, one which forms the background of all possible social practices and which contains a list of "neutral" canonical designators that delimit the range of the existent once and for all. If there were such a context, it would of course be the proper object of study of an expert culture charged with determining the future direction of the Conversation of Humankind. But there is no such context. "Ontology" is not the name of an expert culture, and we should stop imagining that such an expert culture would be desirable. Only when we do so will we put what Heidegger called "onto-theology" behind us.

PRIVATE AND PUBLIC RELIGION

I have been arguing that we should substitute the question of the cultural desirability of God-talk for the ontological question about the existence of

---

[16] G. W. F. Hegel, *Phenomenology of Spirit*, trans. A. V. Miller (Oxford: Clarendon Press, 1977), paragraph 74.

God. But I have said little about what discussion of the former question looks like.

As I see it, the question of whether to keep on talking about God, whether to keep that logical space open, needs to be divided into two sub-questions. The first is a question about an individual's right to be religious, even though unable to justify her religious beliefs to others. It might be formulated in the first person as "have I the right to my religious devotions even though there is no social practice that legitimizes inferences from or to the sentences that I employ in this devotional practice – a lack which makes it impossible for many, and perhaps all, of my fellow-humans to make sense of this practice?"

Aside from a few science-worshipping philosophers who retain Clifford's antagonism to religious belief, most intellectuals of the present day would answer this question affirmatively, just as James did. The increasing privatization of religion during the last 200 years has created a climate of opinion in which people have the same right to idiosyncratic forms of religious devotion as they do to write poems or paint pictures that nobody else can make any sense out of. It is a feature of a democratic and pluralist society that our religion is our own business – something we need not even discuss with others, much less try to justify to them, unless we feel like doing so. Such a society tries to leave as much free space as possible for individuals to develop their own sense of who they are and what their lives are for, asking only that they obey Mill's precept and extend to others the tolerance they themselves enjoy. Individuals are free to make up their own semi-private language games (as Henry James, Sr. and William Blake did, for example), as long as they do not insist that everybody else plays them as well.

But such societies have, of course, been troubled by other questions: "what about organized religion?" "what about the churches?" Even if one follows James' advice and ignores Clifford-like strictures against the "irrationality" of religious belief, one might still think that both Lucretius and Marx had a point. So it is possible to agree that society should grant private individuals the right to formulate private systems of belief while remaining militantly anti-clerical. James and Mill agree that there is nothing wrong with churches unless their activities do social harm. But when it comes to deciding whether actually existing churches in fact do such harm, things get complicated. The sociopolitical history of the West in the last 200 years is spotted with controversies such as those over Jefferson's Virginia Statute of Religious Freedom, the laicization of education in France, the *Kulturkampf* in Germany, and the controversy in Turkey about female students wearing veils on campus.

Issues like these require different resolutions in different countries and different centuries. It would be absurd to suggest that there are universally valid norms that might be invoked to settle them. But I would urge that debate over such concrete political questions is more useful for human happiness than debate over the existence of God. They are the questions which remain once we realize that appeals to religious experience are of no use for settling what traditions should be maintained and which replaced, and after we have come to think natural theology pointless.

We shall not appeal to religious experiences in order to decide what social practices to abandon or adopt if we follow Wittgenstein, Sellars, and Brandom in thinking that there is no intermediary called "what the experience was really *of*"in between the altered state of the nervous system associated with the onset of the claimed experience and the resulting discursive commitments undertaken by a member of a language-using community. We shall dismiss natural theology if we see the undiscussability of God's existence not as a testimony to his superior status but as a consequence of the attempt to give him that status – a side-effect of making him so incomparably special as to be a being whose existence cannot be discussed by reference to any antecedent list of canonical designators. If we grant the Sellarsian doctrine that all awareness is a linguistic affair and the Brandomian doctrine that "existent object" is not a genuine sortal, we shall cut ourselves off from many of the traditional varieties of God-talk.

Inferentialist philosophy of language and mind helps us understand why neither appeals to "experience" nor appeals to "reason" have been of much help to us when we are choosing between alternative social practices. To move into the intellectual world to which Brandom's inferentialism facilitates access would be to treat questions of which language games to play as questions of how members of democratic societies may best adjust the balance between their responsibilities to themselves and their responsibilities to their fellow-citizens.[17]

[17] I am grateful to Jeffrey Stout for detailed and very helpful comments on an earlier draft of this chapter.

2

Pragmatism as romantic polytheism

In 1911 a book appeared in Paris with the title *Un romantisme utilitaire: étude sur le mouvement pragmatiste*. This was the first of three volumes on the subject by René Berthelot. Berthelot had been struck by the resemblances between the views of William James, John Dewey, Nietzsche, Bergson, Poincaré, and certain Catholic Modernists. He was the first to treat them as belonging to the same intellectual movement. A convinced Cartesian, Berthelot disliked and distrusted all these thinkers, but he wrote about them with acuity and verve. He traced the romantic roots of pragmatism back behind Emerson to Schelling and Hoelderlin, and the utilitarian roots to the influence of Darwin and Spencer.[1] But he thought that the difference between these two modes of thought was too great to permit synthesis. "In all its different forms," Berthelot said, "pragmatism reveals itself to be a romantic utilitarianism: that is its most obviously original feature and also its most private vice and its hidden weakness."[2]

Berthelot was probably the first to call Nietzsche "a German pragmatist," and the first to emphasize the resemblance between Nietzsche's perspectivism and the pragmatist theory of truth. This resemblance – frequently noted since, notably in a seminal chapter of Arthur Danto's book on Nietzsche – is most evident in *The Gay Science*. There Nietzsche says "We do not even have any organ at all for *knowing*, for 'truth'; we 'know' . . . just as much as may be *useful* in the interest of the human herd."[3] This

---

[1] René Berthelot, *Un romantisme utilitaire: étude sur le mouvement pragmatiste*, vol. I (Paris: F. Alcan, 1911), 62–3. Berthelot also looked back behind Darwin and Spencer to Hume, whom he regarded as "la transition entre la psychologie utilitaire et intellectualiste d'Helvétius et la psychologie vitaliste de l'instinct que nous rencontrons chez les Ecossais." He views Lamarck as "la transition entre cette conception vitaliste de la biologie et ce qu'on peut appeler l'utilitarisme mécanique de Darwin" (vol. I, 85).   [2] Ibid., vol. I, 128.
[3] Friedrich Nietzsche, *The Gay Science*, section 354: "Wir haben eben gar kein Organ fuer das *Erkennen*, fuer die 'Wahrheit'; wir 'wissen' . . . gerade so viel, als im Interesse der Menschen-Herde, der Gattung, *nuetzlich* sein mag."

Darwinian view lies behind James' claim that "thinking is for the sake of behavior" and his identification of truth as "the good in the way of belief."

That identification amounts to accepting Nietzsche's claim that human beings should be viewed, for epistemological purposes, as what Nietzsche called "clever animals." Beliefs are to be judged solely by their utility in fulfilling these animals' varied needs. James and Nietzsche did for the word "true" what John Stuart Mill had done for the word "right." Just as Mill says that there is no ethical motive apart from the desire for the happiness of human beings, so James and Nietzsche say that there is no will to truth distinct from the will to happiness. All three philosophers think that the terms "true" and "right" gain their meaning from their use in evaluating the relative success of efforts to achieve happiness.

Nietzsche, to be sure, had no use for Mill, but this was a result of arrogant ignorance, which resulted in a failure to grasp the difference between Mill and Bentham. James, on the other hand, dedicated his first philosophical treatise to Mill's memory, and tried to cultivate not only the debunking, Benthamite strain in Mill's thought but also the romantic, Coleridgean strain. The latter led Mill to choose an epigraph from Wilhelm von Humboldt for *On Liberty*: "The grand, leading principle, towards which every argument unfolded in these pages directly converges, is the absolute and essential importance of human development in its richest diversity." As a romantic utilitarian, Mill wanted to avoid Benthamite reductionism, and to defend a secular culture against the familiar charge of blindness to higher things.

This led him, as M. H. Abrams has pointed out, to share Arnold's view that literature could take the place of dogma. Abrams quotes Alexander Bain as saying of Mill that "he seemed to look upon Poetry as a Religion, or rather as Religion and Philosophy in One." Abrams also quotes a letter of Mill's which says that "the new utilitarianism" – his own as opposed to Bentham's – holds "Poetry not only on a par with, but the necessary condition of, any true and comprehensive Philosophy." Abrams argues that Mill and Arnold, despite their differences, drew the same moral from the English Romantics: that poetry could and should take on "the tremendous responsibility of the functions once performed by the exploded dogmas of religion and religious philosophy."[4] The exploded dogmas included the claim that, whereas there can be many great poems, there can be only one true religion, because only one true God. Poetry cannot be a substitute for

---

[4] M. H. Abrams, *The Mirror and the Lamp* (New York: Oxford University Press, 1953), quotes on 334–5, 333 (quoting a letter to Bulwer-Lytton), and 335 respectively.

a monotheistic religion, but it can serve the purposes of a secular version of polytheism.

The substitution of poetry for religion as a source of ideals, a movement that began with the Romantics, seems to me usefully described as a return to polytheism. For if, with the utilitarians, you reject the idea that a non-human authority can rank human needs, and thus dictate moral choices to human beings, you will favor what Arnold called "Hellenism" over what he called "Hebraism." You will reject the idea, characteristic of the evangelical Christians whom Arnold thought of as "Hebraist," that it suffices to love God and keep his commandments. You will substitute what Arnold called the idea of "a human nature perfect on all its sides."[5] Different poets will perfect different sides of human nature, by projecting different ideals. A romantic utilitarian will probably drop the idea of diverse immortal persons, such as the Olympian deities, but she will retain the idea that there are diverse, conflicting, but equally valuable forms of human life.

A polytheism of this sort is recommended in a famous passage near the end of *The Varieties of Religious Experience* at which James says:

If an Emerson were forced to be a Wesley, or a Moody forced to be a Whitman, the total human consciousness of the divine would suffer. The divine can mean no single quality, it must mean a group of qualities, by being champions of which in alternation, different men may all find worthy missions. Each attitude being a syllable in human nature's total message, it takes the whole of us to spell the meaning out completely.[6]

James' loose use of the term "the divine" makes it pretty much equivalent to "the ideal." In this passage he is doing for theology what Mill had done for politics when he cited von Humboldt's claim that "human development in its richest diversity" is the aim of social institutions.

There is a passage in Nietzsche in praise of polytheism that complements the one I have just quoted from James. In section 143 of *The Gay Science* he argues that morality – in the wide sense of the need for acceptance of binding laws and customs – entails "hostility against the impulse to have an ideal of one's own." But, he says, the pre-Socratic Greeks provided an outlet for individuality by permitting human beings "to behold, in some distant overworld, a *plurality of norms*: one god was not considered a denial of another god, nor blasphemy against him." In this way, Nietzsche says, "the luxury of individuals was first permitted; it was here that one first

5 Matthew Arnold, *Culture and Anarchy*, ed. Samuel Lipman (New Haven, CT: Yale University Press, 1994), 37.
6 William James, *Varieties of Religious Experience* (Cambridge, MA: Harvard University Press, 1985), 384.

honored the rights of individuals." For in pre-Socratic polytheism "the free-spiriting and many-spiriting of man attained its first preliminary form – the strength to create for ourselves our own new eyes."[7]

Here is a definition of "polytheism" that covers both Nietzsche and James. You are a polytheist if you think that there is no actual or possible object of knowledge that would permit you to commensurate and rank all human needs. Isaiah Berlin's well-known doctrine of incommensurable human values is, in my sense, a polytheistic manifesto. To be a polytheist in this sense you do not have to believe that there are non-human persons with power to intervene in human affairs. All you need do is abandon the idea that we should try to find a way of making everything hang together, which will tell all human beings what to do with their lives, and tell all of them the same thing.

Polytheism, in the sense I have defined it, is pretty much coextensive with romantic utilitarianism. For once one sees no way of ranking human needs other than playing them off against one another, human happiness becomes all that matters. Mill's *On Liberty* provides all the ethical instruction you need – all the philosophical advice you are ever going to get about your responsibilities to other human beings. For human perfection becomes a private concern, and our responsibility to others becomes a matter of permitting them as much space to pursue these private concerns – to worship their own gods, so to speak – as is compatible with granting an equal amount of space to all. The tradition of religious toleration is extended to moral toleration.

This privatization of perfection permits James and Nietzsche to agree with Mill and Arnold that poetry should take over the role that religion has played in the formation of individual human lives. They also agree that nobody should take over the function of the clergy. For poets are to a secularized polytheism what the priests of a universal church are to monotheism. Once you become polytheistic, you will turn away not only from priests but from such priest-substitutes as metaphysicians and physicists – from anyone who purports to tell you how things *really* are, anyone who invokes the distinction between the true world and the apparent world that Nietzsche ridiculed in *Twilight of the Idols*. Both monotheism and the kind of metaphysics or science that purports to tell you what the world is *really*

7 "Aber ueber sich and ausser sich, in einer fernen Ueberwelt, durfte man eine *Mehrzahl von Normen* sehen; der eine Gott war nicht die Leugnung oder Laesterung des anderen Gottes . . . Hier erlaubte man sich zuerst Individuen, hier ehrte man zuerst das Recht von Individuen . . . In Polytheismus lag die Freigeisterei und Vielgeisterei des Menschen vorgebildet; die Kraft, sich neue und eigne Augen zu schaffen" (Nietzsche, *The Gay Science*, section 143).

like are replaced with democratic politics. A free consensus about how much space for private perfection we can allow each other takes the place of the quest for "objective" values, the quest for a ranking of human needs that does not depend upon such consensus.

So far I have been playing along with Berthelot's emphasis on the similarities between Nietzsche and the American pragmatists. Now I want to turn to the two most obvious differences between them: their attitude toward democracy and their attitude toward religion. Nietzsche thought democracy was "Christianity for the people" – Christianity deprived of the nobility of spirit of which Christ himself, and perhaps a few of the more strenuous saints, had been capable. Dewey thought of democracy as Christianity cleansed of the hieratic, exclusionist elements. Nietzsche thought those who believed in a traditional monotheistic God were foolish weaklings. Dewey thought of them as so spellbound by the work of one poet as to be unable to appreciate the work of other poets. Dewey thought that the sort of "aggressive atheism" on which Nietzsche prided himself is unnecessarily intolerant. It has, he said, "something in common with traditional supernaturalism."[8]

I want first to argue that Nietzsche's contempt for democracy was an adventitious extra, inessential to his overall philosophical outlook. Then I shall get down to my main task in this chapter – defending Dewey's tolerance for religious belief against those who think that pragmatism and religion do not mix.

Nietzsche was a utilitarian only in the sense that he saw no goals for human beings to pursue other than human happiness. He had no interest in the greatest happiness of the greatest number, but only in that of a few exceptional human beings – those with the capacity to be *greatly* happy. Democracy seemed to him a way of trivializing human existence. By contrast, James and Dewey took for granted, as Mill had, the ideal of universal human fraternity. Echoing Mill, James wrote, "Take any demand, however slight, which any creature, however weak, may make. Ought it not, for its own sole sake, to be desired?"[9]

Romantic utilitarianism, pragmatism, and polytheism are compatible with both wholehearted enthusiasm and wholehearted contempt for democracy. The frequent complaint that a philosopher who holds the

[8] John Dewey, "A Common Faith," in *Later Works of John Dewey*, ed. Jo Ann Boydston (Carbondale: Southern Illinois University Press, 1986), vol. IX, 36.
[9] William James, *The Will to Believe* (Cambridge, MA: Harvard University Press, 1979), 149.

pragmatic theory of truth cannot give you a reason not to be a fascist is perfectly justified. But neither can that person give you a reason to be a fascist. For once you become a polytheist in the sense I just defined, you have to give up on the idea that philosophy can help you choose among the various deities and the various forms of life offered. The choice between enthusiasm and contempt for democracy becomes more like a choice between Walt Whitman and Robinson Jeffers than between competing sets of philosophical arguments.

Those who find the pragmatist identification of truth with what is good to believe morally offensive often say that Nietzsche, rather than James and Dewey, drew the proper inference from the abandonment of the idea of an object of knowledge that tells one how to rank human needs. Those who think of pragmatism as a species of irrationalism, and of irrationalism as selling the pass to fascism, say that James and Dewey were blind to the anti-democratic consequences of their own ideas, and naive to think that one can be both a good pragmatist and a good democrat.

Such critics make the same mistake that Nietzsche made. They think that the idea of fraternity is inextricable from Platonism. Platonism, in this sense, is the idea that the will to truth is distinct from the will to happiness – or, to be a bit more precise, the claim that human beings are divided between a quest for a lower, animal form of happiness and a higher, God-like form of happiness. Nietzsche mistakenly thought that once (with Darwin's help) you had given up this idea, and had gotten used to the idea that you are just a clever animal, you could have no reason to wish for the happiness of all human beings. He was so impressed by the fact that Christianity would have seemed ludicrous to the Homeric heroes that he was unable, except at occasional fleeting moments, to think of Christianity as the work of strong poets. So Nietzsche assumed that once poetry had replaced religion as the source of ideals, there would be no place for either Christianity or democracy.

Nietzsche would have done better to ask himself whether the Christian emphasis on human fraternity – the idea that for Christians there is neither Jew nor Greek, and the related idea that love is the only law – might have been only accidentally, for contingent historical reasons, associated with Platonism. This ideal might have gotten along nicely without the logocentrism of the Gospel of John, and without Augustine's unfortunate suggestion that Plato had prefigured Christian truth. In a different, but possible, world, some early Christian might have anticipated James' remark about Emerson and Wesley by writing "If Caesar were forced to be Christ, the total human consciousness of the divine would suffer."

A Christianity that was merely ethical – the sort Jefferson and other Enlightenment thinkers commended and was later propounded by theologians of the social gospel – might have sloughed off exclusionism by viewing Jesus as one incarnation of the divine among others. The celebration of an ethics of love would then have taken its place within the relatively tolerant polytheism of the Roman Empire, having disjoined the ideal of human brotherhood from the claim to represent the will of an omnipotent and monopolistic Heavenly Father (not to mention the idea that there is no salvation outside the Christian Church).

Had they preached such a merely moral and social gospel, the Christians would never have bothered to develop a natural theology. So thirteenth-century Christians would not have worried about whether the Scriptures could be reconciled with Aristotle. Seventeenth-century believers would not have worried about whether they could be reconciled with Newton, nor those in the nineteenth century about whether they could be reconciled with Darwin. These hypothetical Christians would have treated Scripture as useful for purposes for which Aristotle, Newton, and Darwin were useless, and as useless for purposes of prediction and control of the environment. As things stood, however, the Christian churches remained obsessed by the Platonic idea that both Truth and God are One. So it was natural, when physical science began to make some progress, that its practitioners should take over this rhetoric, and thereby stir up a war between science and theology, between Scientific Truth and Religious Faith.

I have imagined such a non-Platonic and non-exclusivist form of Christianity in order to emphasize that no chain of inference links the ideal of human fraternity to the ideal of escaping from a world of appearance inhabited by animals to a real world in which humans will become as gods. Nietzsche and contemporary critics who see Nietzsche and Dewey as holding similarly dangerous "irrationalist" doctrines have been tricked by Plato into believing that, unless there is such a real world, Thrasymachus, Callicles, and Hitler are unanswerable. But they are unanswerable only in the sense that, *pace* Habermas, there are no premises to which they must assent simply by virtue of being rational, language-using animals. A fortiori, there are no such premises that would lead them to agree that they should treat all other human beings as brothers and sisters. Christianity as a strong poem, one poem among many, can be as socially useful as Christianity backed up by the Platonist claim that God and Truth are interchangeable terms.

Although I do not think that there is an inferential path that leads from the anti-representationalist view of truth and knowledge common to

Nietzsche, James, and Dewey either to democracy or anti-democracy, I do think there is a plausible inference from democratic convictions to such a view. Your devotion to democracy is unlikely to be wholehearted if you believe, as monotheists typically do, that we can have knowledge of an "objective" ranking of human needs that can overrule the result of democratic consensus. But if your devotion is wholehearted, then you will welcome the utilitarian and pragmatist claim that we have no will to truth distinct from the will to happiness.

So much for the disagreement between Nietzsche and his American colleagues about the value of democracy. I turn now to the other big difference between Nietzsche on the one hand and James and Dewey on the other. Nietzsche thinks religious belief is intellectually disreputable; James and Dewey do not.

In order to defend James and Dewey's tolerance for theism against Nietzsche, I shall sketch a pragmatist philosophy of religion in five brief theses. Then I shall try to relate these theses to what James and Dewey actually said about belief in God.

First, it is an advantage of the anti-representationalist view of belief that James took over from Bain and Peirce – the view that beliefs are habits of action – that it frees us from the responsibility to unify all our beliefs into a single worldview. If our beliefs are all parts of a single attempt to represent a single world, then they must all hang together fairly tightly. But if they are habits of action, then, because the purposes served by action may blamelessly vary, so may the habits we develop to serve those purposes.

Second, Nietzsche's attempt to "see science through the optic of art, and art through that of life," like Arnold's and Mill's substitution of poetry for religion, is an attempt to make more room for individuality than can be provided either by orthodox monotheism, or by the Enlightenment's attempt to put science in the place of religion as a source of Truth. So the attempt, by Tillich and others, to treat religious faith as "symbolic," and thereby to treat religion as poetic and poetry as religious, and neither as competing with science, is on the right track. But to make it convincing we need to drop the idea that some parts of culture fulfill our need to know the truth and others fulfill lesser aims. The pragmatists' romantic utilitarianism does drop this idea: if there is no will to truth apart from the will to happiness, there is no way to contrast the cognitive with the non-cognitive, the serious with the non-serious.

Third, pragmatism does permit us to make another distinction, one that takes over some of the work previously done by the old distinction between the cognitive and the non-cognitive. The new distinction is between projects of social cooperation and projects of individual self-development. Intersubjective agreement is required for the former projects, but not for the latter. Natural science is a paradigmatic project of social cooperation: the project of improving man's estate by taking account of every possible observation and experimental result in order to facilitate the making of predictions that will come true. Law is another such paradigm. Romantic art, by contrast, is a paradigmatic project of individual self-development. Religion, if it can be disconnected from both science and morals – from the attempt to predict the consequences of our actions and the attempt to rank human needs – may be another such paradigm.

Fourth, the idea that we should love Truth is largely responsible for the idea that religious belief is "intellectually irresponsible." But there is no such thing as the love of Truth. What has been called by that name is a mixture of the love of reaching intersubjective agreement, the love of gaining mastery over a recalcitrant set of data, the love of winning arguments, and the love of synthesizing little theories into big theories. It is never an objection to a religious belief that there is no evidence for it. The only possible objection to it can be that it intrudes an individual project into a social and cooperative project, and thereby offends against the teachings of *On Liberty*. Such intrusion is a betrayal of one's responsibilities to cooperate with other human beings, not of one's responsibility to Truth or to Reason.

Fifth, the attempt to love Truth, and to think of it as One, and as capable of commensurating and ranking human needs, is a secular version of the traditional religious hope that allegiance to something big, powerful, and non-human will persuade that powerful being to take your side in your struggle with other people. Nietzsche despised any such hope as a sign of weakness. Pragmatists who are also democrats have a different objection to such hope for allegiance with power. They see it as a betrayal of the ideal of human fraternity that democracy inherits from the Judeo-Christian religious tradition. That ideal finds its best expression in the doctrine, common to Mill and James, that every human need should be satisfied unless doing so causes too many other human needs to go unsatisfied. The pragmatist objection to religious fundamentalists is not that fundamentalists are *intellectually* irresponsible in disregarding the results of natural science. Rather it is that they are *morally* irresponsible in attempting to circumvent the process of achieving democratic consensus about how to maximize happiness. They sin not by ignoring Mill's inductive methods, but by ignoring his reflections on liberty.

I turn now to the question of how the view of religious belief epitomized in my five theses accords with the views of James and Dewey. It would not, I think, have been congenial to James. But I think it might have suited Dewey. So I shall argue that it is Dewey's rather unambitious and half-hearted *A Common Faith*, rather than James' brave and exuberant "Conclusion" to *Varieties of Religious Experience*, that coheres best with the romantic utilitarianism which both accepted.

James says, in that chapter of *Varieties*, that "the pivot round which the religious life revolves . . . is the interest of the individual in his private personal destiny." By "repudiating the personal point of view," however, science gives us a picture of nature that "has no distinguishable ultimate tendency with which it is possible to feel a sympathy." The "driftings of the cosmic atoms" are "a kind of aimless weather, doing and undoing, achieving no proper history, and leaving no result."[10] On the view I have just outlined, he should have followed this up by saying "But we are free to describe the universe in many different ways. Describing it as the drifting of cosmic atoms is useful for the social project of working together to control our environment and improve man's estate. But that description leaves us entirely free to say, for example, that the Heavens proclaim the glory of God."

Sometimes James seems to take this line, as when, with obvious approval, he quotes James Henry Leuba as saying:

God is not known, he is not understood, he is used – sometimes as meat-purveyor, sometimes as moral support, sometimes as friend, sometime as an object of love. If he proves himself useful, the religious consciousness can ask no more than that. Does God really exist? How does he exist? What is he? are so many irrelevant questions. Not God, but life, more life, a larger, richer, more satisfying life, is, in the last analysis, the end of religion.

Unfortunately, however, almost immediately after quoting Leuba James says "we must next pass beyond the point of view of merely subjective utility and make inquiry into the intellectual content itself." He then goes on to argue that the material he has gathered together in *Varieties* provides empirical evidence for the hypothesis that "the conscious person is continuous with a wider self through which saving experiences come." He calls this "a positive content of religious experience which, it seems to me, is literally and objectively true as far as it goes."[11]

On the view I have been suggesting, this claim to literal and objective truth is unpragmatic, hollow, and superfluous. James should have rested

---

[10] James, *Varieties of Religious Experience*, pp. 387–8.   [11] Ibid., 399 and 405, respectively.

content with the argument of "The Will to Believe." As I read that essay, it says that we have a right to believe what we like when we are, so to speak, on our own time.[12] But we abandon this right when we are engaged in, for example, a scientific or a political project. For when so engaged it is necessary to reconcile our beliefs, our habits of action, with those of others. On our own time, by contrast, our habits of action are nobody's business but our own. A romantic polytheist will rejoice in what Nietzsche called the "free-spiritedness and many-spiritedness" of individuals, and see the only constraint on this freedom and this diversity as the need not to injure others.

James wobbled on the question of whether what he called "the religious hypothesis" was something to be adopted on "passional" or on "intellectual" grounds. This hypothesis says that "the best things are the more eternal things, the overlapping things, the things in the universe that throw the last stone, so to speak, and say the final word."[13] In "The Will to Believe" this is put forward as a hypothesis to which considerations of evidence are irrelevant, and must therefore be turned over to our emotions. But in the "Conclusion" to *Varieties of Religious Experience*, the hypothesis that "God's existence is the guarantee of an ideal order that shall be permanently preserved" is one for which he has accumulated evidence. There he also says that the least common denominator of religious beliefs is that "The solution [to the problem presented by a 'sense that there is something wrong about us as we naturally stand'] is that we are saved from the wrongness by making proper connection with the higher powers." Again, he says that "the conscious person is continuous with a wider self from which saving experiences come."[14]

James should not have made a distinction between issues to be decided by intellect and issues to be decided by emotion. If he had not, he might have wobbled less. What he should have done instead was to distinguish issues that you must resolve cooperatively with others and issues that you are entitled to resolve on your own. The first set of issues is about conciliating your habits of action with those of other human beings. The second set is about getting your own habits of action to cohere with each other sufficiently so that you acquire a stable, coherent self-image. But such a self-image does not require monotheism, or the belief that Truth is One. It is compatible with the idea that you have many different needs, and that the

---

[12] See my "Religious Faith, Intellectual Responsibility, and Romance," in *The Cambridge Companion to William James*, ed. Ruth Anna Putnam (Cambridge: Cambridge University Press, 1997).
[13] James, *The Will to Believe*, 29.
[14] James, *Varieties of Religious Experience*, 407, 400, 405 respectively.

beliefs that help you fill one set of needs are irrelevant to, and need not be made to cohere with, those that help you to fill another set.

Dewey avoided James' mistakes in this area. One reason he did so is that he was much less prone to a sense of guilt than was James. After he realized that his mother had made him unnecessarily miserable by burdening him with a belief in original sin, Dewey simply stopped thinking that, in James' words, "there is something wrong about us as we naturally stand." He no longer believed that we could be "saved from the wrongness by making proper connection with the higher powers." He thought that all that was wrong with us was that the Christian ideal of fraternity had not yet been achieved – society had not yet become pervasively democratic. That was not a problem to be solved by making proper connection with higher powers, but a problem of men to be solved by men.

Dewey's steadfast refusal to have any truck with the notion of original sin, and his suspicion of anything that smacked of such a notion, is bound up with his lifelong distaste for the idea of authority – the idea that anything could have authority over the members of a democratic community save the free, collective decisions of that community. This anti-authoritarian motif is perhaps clearest in his "Christianity and Democracy" – an early essay to which Alan Ryan has recently called our attention, saying that it is "a dazzling and dazzlingly brave piece of work."[15] Indeed it is. It must have seemed strange to the University of Michigan's Christian Students Association to be told, in 1892, that "God is essentially and only the self-revealing" and that "the revelation is complete only as men come to realize him."

Dewey spelled out what he meant by going on to say, "Had Jesus Christ made an absolute, detailed and explicit statement upon all the facts of life, that statement would not have had meaning – it would not have been revelation – until men began to realize in their own action the truth that he declared – until they themselves began to *live* it."[16] This amounts to saying that even if a non-human authority tells you something, the only way to figure out whether what you have been told is true is to see whether it gets you the sort of life you want. The only way is to apply the utilitarian test for whether the suggestion made proves to be "good in the way of belief." Granted that hearing what such a being has to say may change your wants, you nevertheless test those new wants and that purported truth in the same way: by living them, trying them out in everyday life, seeing whether they make you and yours happier.

[15] Alan Ryan, *John Dewey and the High Tide of American Liberalism* (New York: Norton, 1995), 102.
[16] John Dewey, *Early Works of John Dewey* (Carbondale: Southern Illinois University Press, 1969), vol. III, 6–7.

Suppose that a source you believe to be non-human tells you that all men are brothers, that the attempt to make yourself and those you cherish happier should be expanded into an attempt to make all human beings happy. For Dewey, the source of this suggestion is irrelevant. You might have heard it from a god or a guru, but you might just as well have found it carved out by the waves on a sandy beach. It has no validity unless it is treated as a hypothesis, tried out, and found successful. The good thing about Christianity, Dewey is saying, is that it has been found to work.

More specifically, what has been found to work is the idea of fraternity and equality as a basis for social organization. This worked not just as a Thrasymachian device for avoiding pain – what Rawls calls a "mere modus vivendi" – but as a source of the kind of spiritual transfiguration that Platonism and the Christian churches have told us would have to wait upon a future intersection of time with eternity. It makes possible precisely the sort of nobility of spirit that Nietzsche mistakenly thought could be had only by the exceptional few – those who were capable of being greatly happy.

"Democracy," Dewey says, "is neither a form of government nor a social expediency, but a metaphysic of the relation of man and his experience in nature."[17] The point of calling it a metaphysic is not, of course, that it is an accurate account of the fundamental relation of reality, but that if one shares Whitman's sense of glorious democratic vistas stretching on indefinitely into the future one has everything which Platonists hoped to get out of such an account. For Whitman offers what Tillich called "a symbol of ultimate concern," of something that can be loved with all one's heart and soul and mind.

Plato's mistake, in Dewey's view, was having identified the ultimate object of *eros* with something unique, atemporal, and non-human rather than with an indefinitely expansible pantheon of transitory temporal accomplishments, both natural and cultural. This mistake lent aid and comfort to monotheism. Dewey might well have agreed with Nietzsche that "Monotheism, this rigid consequence of the doctrine of one normal human type – the faith in one normal god beside whom there are only pseudo-gods – was perhaps the greatest danger that has yet confronted humanity."[18]

[17] John Dewey, "Maeterlinck's Philosophy of Life," in *The Middle Works of John Dewey*, ed. Jo Ann Boydston (Carbondale: Southern Illinois University Press, 1978), vol. VI. Dewey says that Emerson, Whitman, and Maeterlinck are the only three to have grasped this fact about democracy.

[18] Nietzsche, *The Gay Science*, section 143: "Der Monotheismus . . . diese starre Konsequenz der Lehre von einem Normalmenschen – also der Glaube an einen Normalgott, neben dem es nur noch falsche Luegengoetter gibt – war vielleicht die groesste Gefahr der bisherigen Menscheit."

When Christianity is treated as a merely social gospel, it acquires the advantage which Nietzsche attributes to polytheism: it makes the most important human achievement "creating for ourselves our own new eyes," and thereby "honors the rights of individuals." As Dewey put it, "Government, business, art, religion, all social institutions have . . . a purpose[:] . . . to set free the capacities of human individuals . . . [T]he test of their value is the extent to which they educate every individual into the full stature of his possibility."[19] In a democratic society, everybody gets to worship his or her personal symbol of ultimate concern, unless worship of that symbol interferes with the pursuit of happiness by his or her fellow-citizens. Accepting that utilitarian constraint, the one Mill formulated in *On Liberty*, is the only obligation imposed by democratic citizenship, the only exception to democracy's commitment to honor the rights of individuals.

This means that nobody is under any constraint to seek Truth, nor to care, whether the earth revolves around the sun or conversely. Scientific theories become, as do theological and philosophical ones, optional tools for the facilitation of individual or social projects. Scientists thereby lose the position they inherited from the monotheistic priesthood, as the people who pay proper tribute to the authority of something "not ourselves."

"Not ourselves" is a term that tolls like a bell throughout the text of Arnold's *Literature and Dogma*, and this may be one of the reasons Dewey had a particular dislike for Arnold.[20] Once he got out from under his mother's Calvinism, Dewey distrusted nothing more than the suggestion that there was a non-human authority to which human beings owed respect. He praised democracy as the *only* form of "moral and social faith" that does *not* "rest upon the idea that experience must be subjected at some point or other to some form of external control: to some 'authority' alleged to exist outside the process of experience."[21]

This passage in an essay of 1939 echoes one written forty-seven years earlier. In "Christianity and Democracy" Dewey had said that "The one claim that Christianity makes is that God is truth; that as truth He is love and reveals Himself fully to man, keeping back nothing of Himself; that man is so one with the truth thus revealed that it is not so much revealed *to* him

---

[19] Dewey, *Reconstruction in Philosophy*, in *Middle Works*, vol. XII, 186.

[20] See Dewey, *A Common Faith*, in *Later Works*, vol. IX, 36, and also Dewey's early essay "Poetry and Philosophy." In the latter Dewey says that "the source of regret which inspires Arnold's lines is his consciousness of a twofold isolation of man – his isolation from nature, his isolation from his fellow-man" (Dewey, *Early Works*, vol. III, 115).

[21] John Dewey "Creative Democracy – The Task Before Us" (1939). The passage cited is in *Later Works*, vol. XIV, 229. Dewey says that he is here "stating briefly the democratic faith in the formal terms of a philosophic position."

as *in* him; he is its incarnation."[22] For Dewey God is in no way Kierkegaard's Wholly Other. Nor is he One. Rather, he is all the varied sublimities human beings come to see through the eyes that they themselves create.

If atheism were identical with anti-monotheism, then Dewey would have been as aggressive an atheist as has ever lived. The idea that God might have kept something back, that there might be something not ourselves that it was our duty to discover, was as distasteful to him as was the idea that God could tell us which of our needs took priority over others. He reserved his awe for the universe as a whole, "the community of causes and consequences in which we, together with those not born, are enmeshed." "The continuing life of this comprehensive community of beings," he said, "includes all the significant achievement of men in science and art and all the kindly offices of intercourse and communication."

Notice, in the passages I have just quoted, the phrase "together with those not born" and also the adjective "continuing." Dewey's distaste for the eternity and stability on which monotheism prides itself is so great that he can never refer to the universe as a whole without reminding us that the universe is still evolving – still experimenting, still fashioning new eyes with which to see itself.

Wordsworth's version of pantheism meant a great deal to Dewey, but Whitman's insistence on futurity meant more. Wordsworth's pantheism saves us from what Arnold called "Hebraism" by making it impossible to treat, as Dewey put it, "the drama of sin and redemption enacted within the isolated and lonely soul of man as the one thing of ultimate import- ance." But Whitman does something more. He tells us that non-human nature culminates in a community of free men, in their collaboration in building a society in which, as Dewey said, "poetry and religious feeling will be the unforced flowers of life."[23]

Dewey's principal symbol of what he called "the union of the ideal and the actual" was the United States of America treated as Whitman treated it: as a symbol of openness to the possibility of as yet undreamt of, ever more diverse, forms of human happiness. Much of what Dewey wrote consists of endless reiteration of Whitman's caution that "America . . . counts, as I reckon, for her justification and success, (for who, as yet, dare claim success?) almost entirely on the future . . . For our New World I consider far less important for what it has done, or what it is, than for results to come."[24]

[22] Dewey, *Early Works*, vol. IV, 5.
[23] Dewey, *Reconstruction in Philosophy*, in *Middle Works*, vol. XII, 201.
[24] Walt Whitman, *Democratic Vistas*, in *Complete Poetry and Selected Prose* (New York: Library of America, 1982), 929.

3

Justice as a larger loyalty

All of us would expect help if, pursued by the police, we asked our family to hide us. Most of us would extend such help even when we know our child or our parent to be guilty of a sordid crime. Many of us would be willing to perjure ourselves in order to supply such a child or parent with a false alibi. But if an innocent person is wrongly convicted as a result of our perjury, most of us will be torn by a conflict between loyalty and justice.

Such a conflict will be felt, however, only to the extent to which we can identify with the innocent person whom we have harmed. If the person is a neighbor, the conflict will probably be intense. If a stranger, especially one of a different race, class, or nation, it may be considerably weaker. There has to be *some* sense in which he or she is "one of us," before we start to be tormented by the question of whether or not we did the right thing when we committed perjury. So it may be equally appropriate to describe us as torn between conflicting loyalties – loyalty to our family and to a group large enough to include the victim of our perjury – rather than between loyalty and justice.

Our loyalty to such larger groups will, however, weaken, or even vanish altogether, when things get really tough. Then people whom we once thought of as like ourselves will be excluded. Sharing food with impoverished people down the street is natural and right in normal times, but perhaps not in a famine, when doing so amounts to disloyalty to one's family. The tougher things get, the more ties of loyalty to those near at hand tighten, and the more those to everyone else slacken.

Consider another example of expanding and contracting loyalties: our attitude toward other species. Most of us today are at least half-convinced that the vegetarians have a point, and that animals do have some sort of rights. But suppose that the cows, or the kangaroos, turn out to be carriers of a newly mutated virus, which, though harmless to them, is invariably fatal to humans. I suspect that we would then shrug off accusations of "speciesism" and participate in the necessary massacre. The idea of justice

42

between species will suddenly become irrelevant, because things have gotten very tough indeed, and our loyalty to our own species must come first. Loyalty to a larger community – that of all living creatures on our home planet – would, under such circumstances, quickly fade away.

As a final example, consider the tough situation created by the accelerating export of jobs from the First World to the Third. There is likely to be a continuing decline in the average real income of most American families. Much of this decline can plausibly be attributed to the fact that you can hire a factory worker in Thailand for a tenth of what you would have to pay a worker in Ohio. It has become the conventional wisdom of the rich that American and European labor is overpriced on the world market. When American business people are told that they are being disloyal to the United States by leaving whole cities in our Rust Belt without work or hope, they sometimes reply that they place justice over loyalty.[1] They argue that the needs of humanity as a whole take moral precedence over those of their fellow-citizens and override national loyalties. Justice requires that they act as citizens of the world.

Consider now the plausible hypothesis that democratic institutions and freedoms are viable only when supported by an economic affluence that is achievable regionally but impossible globally. If this hypothesis is correct, democracy and freedom in the First World will not be able to survive a thoroughgoing globalization of the labor market. So the rich democracies face a choice between perpetuating their own democratic institutions and traditions and dealing justly with the Third World. Doing justice to the Third World would require exporting capital and jobs until everything is leveled out – until an honest day's work, in a ditch or at a computer, earns no higher a wage in Cincinnati or Paris than in a small town in Botswana. But then, it can plausibly be argued, there will be no money to support free public libraries, competing newspapers and networks, widely available liberal arts education, and all the other institutions that are necessary to produce enlightened public opinion, and thus to keep governments more or less democratic.

What, on this hypothesis, is the right thing for the rich democracies to do? Be loyal to themselves and each other? Keep free societies going for a third of mankind at the expense of the remaining two-thirds? Or sacrifice the blessings of political liberty for the sake of egalitarian economic justice?

[1] Donald Fites, the CEO of the Caterpillar tractor company, explained his company's policy of relocation abroad by saying that "as a human being, I think what is going on is positive. I don't think it is realistic for 250 million Americans to control so much of the world's GNP." Quoted in Edward Luttwak, *The Endangered American Dream* (New York: Simon and Schuster, 1993), 184.

These questions parallel those confronted by the parents of a large family after a nuclear holocaust. Do they share the food supply they have stored in the basement with their neighbors, even though the stores will then only last a day or two? Or do they fend those neighbors off with guns? Both moral dilemmas bring up the same question: Should we contract the circle for the sake of loyalty, or expand it for the sake of justice?

I have no idea of the right answer to these questions, neither about the right thing for these parents to do, nor about the right thing for the First World to do. I have posed them simply to bring a more abstract, and merely philosophical, question into focus. That question is: should we describe such moral dilemmas as conflicts between loyalty and justice, or rather, as I have suggested, between loyalties to smaller groups and loyalties to larger groups?

This amounts to asking: would it be a good idea to treat "justice" as the name for loyalty to a certain very large group, the name for our largest current loyalty, rather than the name of something distinct from loyalty? Could we replace the notion of "justice" with that of loyalty to that group – for example, one's fellow-citizens, or the human species, or all living things? Would anything be lost by this replacement?

Moral philosophers who remain loyal to Kant are likely to think that a *lot* would be lost. Kantians typically insist that justice springs from reason, and loyalty from sentiment. Only reason, they say, can impose universal and unconditional moral obligations, and our obligation to be just is of this sort. It is on another level from the sort of affectional relations that create loyalty. Juergen Habermas is the most prominent contemporary philosopher to insist on this Kantian way of looking at things: the thinker least willing to blur either the line between reason and sentiment, or the line between universal validity and historical consensus. But contemporary philosophers who depart from Kant, either in the direction of Hume (like Annette Baier) or in the direction of Hegel (like Charles Taylor) or in that of Aristotle (like Alasdair MacIntyre), are not so sure.

Michael Walzer is at the other extreme from Habermas. He is wary of terms like "reason" and "universal moral obligation." The heart of his *Thick and Thin* is the claim that we should reject the intuition that Kant took as central: the intuition that "men and women everywhere begin with some common idea or principle or set of ideas and principles, which they then work up in many different ways." Walzer thinks that this picture of morality "starting thin" and "thickening with age" should be inverted. He says that: "Morality is thick from the beginning, culturally integrated, fully resonant, and it reveals itself thinly only on special occasions, when moral language is turned to special purposes."[2] Walzer's inversion suggests, though it does not entail, the neo-Humean picture of morality sketched by Annette Baier in her book *Moral Prejudices*. On Baier's account, morality starts out not as an obligation but as a relation of reciprocal trust among a closely knit group, such as a family or clan. To behave morally is to do what comes naturally in your dealings with your parents and children or your fellow-clanmembers. It amounts to respecting the trust they place in you. Obligation, as opposed to trust, enters the picture only when your loyalty to a smaller group conflicts with your loyalty to a larger group.[3]

When, for example, the families confederate into tribes, or the tribes into nations, you may feel obliged to do what does not come naturally: to leave your parents in the lurch by going off to fight in the wars, or to rule against your own village in your capacity as a federal administrator or judge. What Kant would describe as the resulting conflict between moral obligation and sentiment, or between reason and sentiment, is, on a non-Kantian account of the matter, a conflict between one set of loyalties and another set of loyalties. The idea of a *universal* moral obligation to respect human dignity gets replaced by the idea of loyalty to a very large group – the human species. The idea that moral obligation extends beyond that species to an even larger group becomes the idea of loyalty to all those who, like yourself, can experience pain – even the cows and the kangaroos – or perhaps even to all living things, even the trees.

This non-Kantian view of morality can be rephrased as the claim that one's moral identity is determined by the group or groups with which one identifies – the group or groups to which one cannot be disloyal and still like oneself. Moral dilemmas are not, in this view, the result of a conflict between reason and sentiment but between alternative selves, alternative self-descriptions, alternative ways of giving a meaning to one's life. Non-Kantians do not think that we have a central, true self by virtue of our membership in the human species – a self that responds to the call of reason. They can, instead, agree with Daniel Dennett that a self is a center of narrative gravity. In non-traditional societies, most people have several such narratives at their disposal, and thus several different moral identities. It is this plurality of identities that accounts for the number and variety of moral dilemmas, moral philosophers, and psychological novels in such societies.

[2] Michael Walzer, *Thick and Thin: Moral Argument at Home and Abroad* (Notre Dame: Notre Dame University Press, 1994), 4.

[3] Baier's picture is quite close to that sketched by Wilfrid Sellars and Robert Brandom in their quasi-Hegelian accounts of moral progress as the expansion of the circle of beings who count as "us."

Walzer's contrast between thick and thin morality is, among other things, a contrast between the detailed and concrete stories you can tell about yourself as a member of a smaller group and the relatively abstract and sketchy story you can tell about yourself as a citizen of the world. You know more about your family than about your village, more about your village than about your nation, more about your nation than about humanity as a whole, more about being human than about simply being a living creature. You are in a better position to decide what differences between individuals are morally relevant when dealing with those whom you can describe thickly, and in a worse position when dealing with those whom you can only describe thinly. This is why, as groups get larger, law has to replace custom, and abstract principles have to replace *phronēsis*. So Kantians are wrong to see *phronēsis* as a thickening up of thin abstract principles. Plato and Kant were misled by the fact that abstract principles are designed to trump parochial loyalties into thinking that the principles are somehow prior to the loyalties – that the thin is somehow prior to the thick.

Walzer's thick–thin distinction can be aligned with Rawls' contrast between a shared *concept* of justice and various conflicting *conceptions* of justice. Rawls sets out that contrast as follows:

the concept of justice, applied to an institution, means, say, that the institution makes no arbitrary distinctions between persons in assigning basic rights and duties, and that its rules establish a proper balance between competing claims . . . [A] conception includes, besides this, principles and criteria for deciding which distinctions are arbitrary and when a balance between competing claims is proper. People can agree on the meaning of justice and still be at odds, since they affirm different principles and standards for deciding these matters.[4]

Phrased in Rawls' terms, Walzer's point is that thick "fully resonant" *conceptions* of justice, complete with distinctions between the people who matter most and the people who matter less, come first. The thin concept, and its maxim "do not make arbitrary distinctions between moral subjects," is articulated only on special occasions. On those occasions, the thin concept can often be turned against any of the thick conceptions from which it emerged, in the form of critical questions about whether it may not be merely arbitrary to think that certain people matter more than others.

Neither Rawls nor Walzer think, however, that unpacking the thin concept of justice will, by itself, resolve such critical questions by supplying a criterion of arbitrariness. They do not think that we can do what Kant hoped to do – derive solutions to moral dilemmas from the analysis of

---

[4] John Rawls, *Political Liberalism* (New York: Columbia University Press, 1993), 14n.

moral concepts. To put the point in the terminology I am suggesting: we cannot resolve conflicting loyalties by turning away from them all toward something categorically distinct from loyalty – the universal moral obligation to act justly. So we have to drop the Kantian idea that the moral law starts off pure but is always in danger of being contaminated by irrational feelings that introduce arbitrary discriminations among persons. We have to substitute the Hegelian-Marxist idea that the so-called moral law is, at best, a handy abbreviation for a concrete web of social practices. This means dropping Habermas' claim that his "discourse ethics" articulates a transcendental presupposition of the use of language, and accepting his critics' claim that it articulates only the customs of contemporary liberal societies.[5]

Now I want to raise the question of whether to describe the various moral dilemmas with which I began as conflicts between loyalty and justice, or rather as conflicting loyalties to particular groups, in a more concrete form. Consider the question of whether the demands for reform made on the rest of the world by Western liberal societies are made in the name of something not merely Western – something like morality, or humanity, or rationality – or are simply expressions of loyalty to local, Western, conceptions of justice. Habermas would say that they are the former. I would say that they are the latter, but are none the worse for that. I think it is better not to say that the liberal West is better informed about rationality and justice, and instead to say that, in making demands on non-liberal societies, it is simply being true to itself.

In a paper called "The Law of Peoples," Rawls discusses the question of whether the conception of justice he has developed in his books is something peculiarly Western and liberal or rather something universal. He would like to be able to claim universality. He says that it is important to avoid "historicism," and believes that he can do this if he can show that the conception of justice suited to a liberal society can be extended beyond such societies through formulating what he calls "the law of peoples."[6] He

---

[5] This sort of debate runs through a lot of contemporary philosophy. Compare, for example, Walzer's contrast between starting thin and starting thick with that between the Platonic-Chomskian notion that we start with meanings and descend to use, and the Wittgensteinian-Davidsonian notion that we start with use and then skim off meaning as needed for lexicographical or philosophical purposes.

[6] John Rawls, "The Law of Peoples," in Stephen Shute and Susan Hurley, eds., *On Human Rights: The Oxford Amnesty Lectures, 1993*, (New York: Basic Books, 1993), 44. I am not sure why Rawls thinks historicism is undesirable, and there are passages, both early and recent, in which he seems to throw in his lot with the historicists. (See the passage quoted in note 9 below from his recent "Reply to Habermas.") Some years ago I argued for the plausibility of an historicist interpretation of the metaphilosophy of Rawls' *A Theory of Justice* (Cambridge, MA: Harvard University Press, 1971) in my "The Priority of Democracy to Philosophy," reprinted in my *Objectivity, Relativism and Truth* (Cambridge: Cambridge University Press, 1991).

outlines, in that paper, an extension of the constructivist procedure proposed in his *A Theory of Justice* – an extension which, by continuing to separate the right from the good, lets us encompass liberal and non-liberal societies under the same law.

As Rawls develops this constructivist proposal, however, it emerges that this law applies only to *reasonable* peoples, in a quite specific sense of the term "reasonable." The conditions that non-liberal societies must honor in order to be "accepted by liberal societies as members in good standing of a society of peoples" include the following: "its system of law must be guided by a common good conception of justice . . . that takes impartially into account what it sees not unreasonably as the fundamental interests of all members of society."[7]

Rawls takes the fulfillment of that condition to rule out violation of basic human rights. These rights include "at least certain minimum rights to means of subsistence and security (the right to life), to liberty (freedom from slavery, serfdom, and forced occupations) and (personal) property, as well as to formal equality as expressed by the rules of natural justice (for example, that similar cases be treated similarly)."[8] When Rawls spells out what he means by saying that the admissible non-liberal societies must not have unreasonable philosophical or religious doctrines, he glosses "unreasonable" by saying that these societies must "admit a measure of liberty of conscience and freedom of thought, even if these freedoms are not in general equal for all members of society." Rawls' notion of what is reasonable, in short, confines membership of the society of peoples to societies whose institutions encompass most of the hard-won achievements of the West in the two centuries since the Enlightenment.

It seems to me that Rawls cannot both reject historicism and invoke this notion of reasonableness. For the effect of that invocation is to build most of the West's recent decisions about which distinctions between persons are arbitrary into the conception of justice that is implicit in the law of peoples. The differences between different *conceptions* of justice, remember, are differences between what features of people are seen as relevant to the adjudication of their competing claims. There is obviously enough wriggle room in phrases like "similar cases should be treated similarly" to allow for arguments that believers and infidels; men and women, blacks and whites, gays and straights should be treated as relevantly *dis*similar. So there is room to argue that discrimination on the basis of such differences is *not* arbitrary.

---

[7] Rawls "The Law of Peoples," 81, 61.   [8] Ibid., 62.

If we are going to exclude from the society of peoples societies in which infidel homosexuals are not permitted to engage in certain occupations, those societies can, quite reasonably say that we are, in excluding them, appealing not to something universal, but to very recent developments in Europe and America.

I agree with Habermas when he says, "What Rawls in fact prejudges with the concept of an 'overlapping consensus' is the distinction between modern and premodern forms of consciousness, between 'reasonable' and 'dogmatic' world interpretations." But I disagree with Habermas, as I think Walzer also would, when he goes on to say that Rawls

can defend the primacy of the right over the good with the concept of an overlapping consensus only if it is true that postmetaphysical worldviews that have become reflexive under modern conditions are epistemically superior to dogmatically fixed, fundamentalistic worldviews – indeed, only if such a distinction can be made with absolute clarity.

Habermas' point is that Rawls needs an argument from transculturally valid premises for the superiority of the liberal West. Without such an argument, he says, "the disqualification of 'unreasonable' doctrines that cannot be brought into harmony with the proposed 'political' concept of justice is inadmissible."[9]

Such passages make clear why Habermas and Walzer are at opposite poles. Walzer is taking for granted that there can be no such thing as a non-question-begging demonstration of the epistemic superiority of the Western idea of reasonableness. There is, for Walzer, no tribunal of transcultural reason before which to try the question of superiority. Walzer is presupposing what Habermas calls "a strong contextualism for which there is no single 'rationality.'" On this conception, Habermas continues, "individual 'rationalities' are correlated with different cultures, worldviews, traditions, or forms of life. Each of them is viewed as internally interwoven with a particular understanding of the world."[10]

---

[9] All quotations in this paragraph are from Juergen Habermas, *Justification and Application: Remarks on Discourse Ethics* (Cambridge, MA: MIT Press, 1993), 95. Habermas is here commenting on Rawls' use of "reasonable" in writings earlier than "The Law of Peoples," since the latter appeared subsequent to Habermas' book.

When I wrote the present chapter, the exchange between Rawls and Habermas published in *The Journal of Philosophy* (vol. 92, no. 3, March 1995) had not yet appeared. This exchange rarely touches on the question of historicism versus universalism. But one passage in which this question emerges explicitly is to be found on 179 of Rawls' "Reply to Habermas": "Justice as fairness is substantive ... in the sense that it springs from and belongs to the tradition of liberal thought and the larger community of political culture of democratic societies. It fails then to be properly formal and truly universal, and thus to be part of the quasi-transcendental presuppositions (as Habermas sometimes says) established by the theory of communicative action."   [10] Ibid.

I think that Rawls' constructivist approach to the law of peoples can work if he adopts what Habermas calls a "strong contextualism." Doing so would mean giving up the attempt to escape historicism, as well as the attempt to supply a universalistic argument for the West's most recent views about which differences between persons are arbitrary. The strength of Walzer's *Thick and Thin* seems to me to be its explicitness about the need to do this. The weakness of Rawls' account of what he is doing lies in an ambiguity between two senses of universalism. When Rawls says that "a constructivist liberal doctrine is universal in its reach, once it is extended to . . . a law of peoples,"[11] he is not saying that it is universal in its validity. Universal reach is a notion that sits well with constructivism, but universal validity is not. It is the latter that Habermas requires. That is why Habermas thinks that we need really heavy philosophical weaponry, modeled on Kant's – why he insists that only transcendental presupposi-tions of any possible communicative practice will do the job.[12] To be faith-ful to his own constructivism, I think, Rawls has to agree with Walzer that this job does not need to be done.

Rawls and Habermas often invoke, and Walzer almost never invokes, the notion of "reason." In Habermas, this notion is always bound up with that of context-free validity. In Rawls, things are more complicated. Rawls dis-tinguishes the reasonable from the rational, using the latter to mean simply the sort of means–end rationality that is employed in engineering, or in working out a Hobbesian *modus vivendi*. But he often invokes a third notion, that of "practical reason," as when he says that the authority of a constructivist liberal doctrine "rests on the principles and conceptions of practical reason."[13] Rawls' use of this Kantian term may make it sound as if he agreed with Kant and Habermas that there is a universally distributed human faculty called practical reason (existing prior to, and working quite independently of, the recent history of the West), a faculty that tells us what counts as an arbitrary distinction between persons and what does not. Such a faculty would do the job Habermas thinks needs doing; detecting trans-cultural moral validity.

But this cannot, I think, be what Rawls intends. For he also says that his own constructivism differs from all philosophical views that appeal to a source of authority, and in which "the universality of the doctrine is the

---

[11] Rawls, "The Law of Peoples," 46.

[12] My own view is that we do not need, either in epistemology or in moral philosophy, the notion of universal validity. I argue for this in "Universality and Truth," included in Robert Brandom (ed.), *Rorty and his Critics* (Oxford Blackwell, 2000). Habermas and Apel find my view paradoxical and likely to produce performative self-contradiction.   [13] Rawls "The Law of Peoples," 46.

direct consequence of its source of authority." As examples of sources of authority, he cites "(human) reason, or an independent realm of moral values, or some other proposed basis of universal validity."[14] So I think we have to construe his phrase "the principles and conceptions of practical reason" as referring to *whatever* principles and conceptions are in fact arrived at in the course of creating a community.

Rawls emphasizes that creating a community is not the same thing as working out a *modus vivendi* – a task which requires only means–end rationality, not practical reason. A principle or conception belongs to practical reason, in Rawls' sense, if it emerged in the course of people starting thick and getting thin, thereby developing an overlapping consensus and setting up a more inclusive moral community. It would not so belong if it had emerged under the threat of force. Practical reason for Rawls is, so to speak, a matter of procedure rather than of substance – of how we agree on what to do rather than of what we agree on.

This definition of practical reason suggests that there may be only a verbal difference between Rawls' and Habermas' positions. For Habermas' own attempt to substitute "communicative reason" for "subject-centered reason" is itself a move toward substituting "how" for "what." Subject-centered reason is a source of truth, truth somehow coeval with the human mind. Communicative reason is not a source of anything, but simply the activity of justifying claims by offering arguments rather than threats. Like Rawls, Habermas focuses on the difference between persuasion and force, rather than, as Plato and Kant did, on the difference between two parts of the human person – the good rational part and the dubious passionate or sensual part. Both would like to de-emphasize the notion of the *authority* of reason – the idea of reason as a faculty which issues decrees – and substitute the notion of rationality as what is present whenever people communicate, whenever they try to justify their claims to one another, rather than threatening each other.

The similarities between Rawls and Habermas seem even greater in the light of Rawls' endorsement of Thomas Scanlon's answer to the "fundamental question why anyone should care about morality at all," namely that "we have a basic desire to be able to justify our actions to others on grounds that they could not reasonably reject – reasonably, that is, given the desire to find principles that others similarly motivated could not reasonably reject."[15] This suggests that the two philosophers might agree on

---

14 Both quotations are from ibid., 45.
15 I quote here from Rawls' summary of Scanlon's view in *Political Liberalism*, 49n.

the following claim: the only notion of rationality we need, at least in moral and social philosophy, is that of a situation in which people do not say "your own current interests dictate that you agree to our proposal," but rather "your own central beliefs, the ones which are central to your own moral identity, suggest that you should agree to our proposal."

This notion of rationality can be delimited using Walzer's terminology by saying that rationality is found wherever people envisage the possibility of getting from different thicks to the same thin. To appeal to interests rather than beliefs is to urge a *modus vivendi*. Such an appeal is exemplified by the speech of the Athenian ambassadors to the unfortunate Melians, as reported by Thucydides. But to appeal to your enduring beliefs as well as to your current interests is to suggest that what gives you your *present* moral identity – your thick and resonant complex of beliefs – may make it possible for you to develop a new, supplementary, moral identity.[16] It is to suggest that what makes you loyal to a smaller group may give you reason to cooperate in constructing a larger group, a group to which you may in time become equally loyal or perhaps even more loyal. The difference between the absence and the presence of rationality, on this account, is the difference between a threat and an offer – the offer of a new moral identity and thus a new and larger loyalty, a loyalty to a group formed by an unforced agreement between smaller groups.

In the hope of minimizing the contrast between Habermas and Rawls still further, and of rapprochement between both and Walzer, I want to suggest a way of thinking of rationality that might help to resolve the problem I posed earlier: the problem of whether justice and loyalty are different sorts of things, or whether the demands of justice are simply the demands of a larger loyalty. I said that question seemed to boil down to the question of whether justice and loyalty had different sources – reason and sentiment, respectively. If the latter distinction disappears, the former one will not seem particularly useful. But if by rationality we mean simply the sort of activity that Walzer thinks of as a thinning-out process – the sort that, with luck, achieves the formulation and utilization of an overlapping consensus – then the idea that justice has a different source than loyalty no longer seems plausible.[17]

---

[16] Walzer thinks it is a good idea for people to have lots of different moral identities. "[T]hick, divided selves are the characteristic products of, and in turn require, a thick, differentiated, and pluralistic society" (*Thick and Thin*, 101).

[17] Note that in Rawls' semitechnical sense an overlapping consensus is not the result of discovering that various comprehensive views already share common doctrines, but rather something that might never have emerged had the proponents of these views not started trying to cooperate.

For, on this account of rationality, being rational and acquiring a larger loyalty are two descriptions of the same activity. This is because *any* unforced agreement between individuals and groups about what to do creates a form of community, and will, with luck, be the initial stage in expanding the circles of those whom each party to the agreement had previously taken to be "people like ourselves." The opposition between rational argument and fellow-feeling thus begins to dissolve. For fellow-feeling may, and often does, arise from the realization that the people whom one thought one might have to go to war with, use force on, are, in Rawls' sense, "reasonable." They are, it turns out, enough like us to see the point of compromising differences in order to live in peace, and of abiding by the agreement that has been hammered out. They are, to some degree at least, trustworthy.

From this point of view, Habermas' distinction between a strategic use of language and a genuinely communicative use of language begins to look like a difference between positions on a spectrum – a spectrum of degrees of trust. Baier's suggestion that we take trust rather than obligation to be our fundamental moral concept would thus produce a blurring of the line between rhetorical manipulation and genuine validity-seeking argument – a line that I think Habermas draws too sharply. If we cease to think of reason as a source of authority, and think of it simply as the process of reaching agreement by persuasion, then the standard Platonic and Kantian dichotomy of reason and feeling begins to fade away. That dichotomy can be replaced by a continuum of degrees of overlap of beliefs and desires.[18] When people whose beliefs and desires do not overlap very much disagree, they tend to think of each other as crazy or, more politely, as irrational. When there is considerable overlap, on the other hand, they may agree to differ and regard each other as the sort of people one can live with – and eventually, perhaps, the sort one can be friends with, intermarry with, and so on.[19]

To advise people to be rational is, on the view I am offering, simply to suggest that somewhere among their shared beliefs and desires there may

---

[18] Davidson has, I think, demonstrated that any two beings that use language to communicate with one another necessarily share an enormous number of beliefs and desires. He has thereby shown the incoherence of the idea that people can live in separate worlds created by differences in culture or status or fortune. There is always an immense overlap – an immense reserve army of common beliefs and desires to be drawn on at need. But this immense overlap does not, of course, prevent accusations of craziness or diabolical wickedness. For only a tiny amount of non-overlap about certain particularly touchy subjects (the border between two territories, the name of the One True God) may lead to such accusations, and eventually to violence.

[19] I owe this line of thought about how to reconcile Habermas and Baier to Mary Rorty.

be enough resources to permit agreement on how to coexist without violence. To conclude that someone is irredeemably *ir*rational is not to realize that she is not making proper use of her God-given faculties. It is rather to realize that she does not seem to share enough relevant beliefs and desires with us to make possible fruitful conversation about the issue in dispute. So, we reluctantly conclude, we have to give up on the attempt to get her to enlarge her moral identity, and settle for working out a *modus vivendi* – one which may involve the threat, or even the use, of force.

A stronger, more Kantian, notion of rationality would be invoked if one said that being rational guarantees a peaceful resolution of conflicts – that if people are willing to reason together long enough, what Habermas calls "the force of the better argument" will lead them to concur.[20] This stronger notion strikes me as pretty useless. I see no point in saying that it is more rational to prefer one's neighbors to one's family in the event of a nuclear holocaust, or more rational to prefer leveling off incomes around the world to preserving the institutions of liberal Western societies. To use the word "rational" to commend one's chosen solution to such dilemmas, or to use the term "yielding to the force of the better argument" to characterize one's way of making up one's mind, is to pay oneself an empty compliment.

More generally, the idea of "the better argument" makes sense only if one can identify a natural, transcultural relation of relevance, which connects propositions with one another so as to form something like Descartes' "natural order of reasons." Without such a natural order, one can only evaluate arguments by their efficacy in producing agreement among particular persons or groups. But the required notion of natural, intrinsic relevance – relevance dictated not by the needs of any given community but by human reason as such – seems no more plausible or useful than that of a God whose Will can be appealed to in order to resolve conflicts between communities. It is, I think, merely a secularized version of that earlier notion.

Non-Western societies in the past were rightly skeptical of Western conquerors who explained that they were invading in obedience to divine commands. More recently, they have been skeptical of Westerners who suggest that they should adopt Western ways in order to become more rational. (This suggestion has been abbreviated by Ian Hacking as "Me rational, you Jane.") On the account of rationality I am recommending, both forms of skepticism are equally justified. But this is not to deny that these societies *should* adopt recent Western ways by, for example, abandoning slavery,

---

[20] This notion of "the better argument" is central to Habermas' and Apel's understanding of rationality. I criticize it in the article cited above in note 12.

practicing religious toleration, educating women, permitting mixed marriages, tolerating homosexuality and conscientious objection to war, and so on. As a loyal Westerner, I think they should indeed do all these things. I agree with Rawls about what it takes to count as reasonable, and about what kind of societies we Westerners should accept as members of a global moral community.

But I think that the rhetoric we Westerners use in trying to get everyone to be more like us would be improved if we were more frankly ethnocentric, and less professedly universalist. It would be better to say: here is what we in the West look like as a result of ceasing to hold slaves, beginning to educate women, separating church and state, and so on. Here is what happened after we started treating certain distinctions between people as arbitrary rather than fraught with moral significance. If you would try treating them that way, you might like the results. Saying that sort of thing seems preferable to saying: look at how much better we are at knowing what differences between persons are arbitrary and which not – how much more *rational* we are.

If we Westerners could get rid of the notion of universal moral obligations created by membership in the species, and substitute the idea of building a community of trust between ourselves and others, we might be in a better position to persuade non-Westerners of the advantages of joining in that community. We might be better able to construct the sort of global moral community that Rawls describes in "The Law of Peoples." In making this suggestion, I am urging, as I have on earlier occasions, that we need to peel apart Enlightenment liberalism from Enlightenment rationalism.

I think that discarding the residual rationalism that we inherit from the Enlightenment is advisable for many reasons. Some of these are theoretical and of interest only to philosophy professors, such as the apparent incompatibility of the correspondence theory of truth with a naturalistic account of the origin of human minds.[21] Others are more practical. One practical reason is that getting rid of rationalistic rhetoric would permit the West to approach the non-West in the role of someone with an instructive story to tell, rather than in the role of someone purporting to be making better use of a universal human capacity.

---

[21] For a claim that such a theory of truth is essential to "the Western Rationalist Tradition," see John Searle, "Rationality and Realism: What Difference Does It Make?" *Daedalus* 122, no. 4 (Fall 1992), 55–84. See also my reply to Searle in "John Searle on Realism and Relativism," included in my *Truth and Progress* (Cambridge: Cambridge University Press, 1998). I argue there that Dewey and Davidson have shown us how to keep the benefits of Western rationalism without the philosophical hangups caused by attempts to explicate this notion.

4

Honest mistakes

People do not call themselves, without irony, cold war liberals. The term was designed to be pejorative. Like "parlor pink" and "Gucci Marxist," it is intended to describe a particular kind of hypocrite – in this case, a person who supported the cold war and nevertheless continued to call herself a "liberal," a description to which she must have known perfectly well she was no longer entitled. To describe someone as a cold war liberal is to suggest that he or she sold out. Why, after all, would they have supported a reactionary enterprise if not to further, or safeguard, their careers?

The most conspicuous and influential cold war liberals were ex-Stalinists, or ex-Trotskyists, or ex-fellow-travelers who had experienced the bitter factionalism that pervaded leftist politics in the 1930s. That factionalism was caused by uncertainty about whether the Soviet Union had been hijacked by a blood-soaked tyrant or still embodied the hope for social justice. The bitterness of disagreements over this question carried over into the 1940s and 1950s, with Wallace versus Truman and Hiss versus Chambers taking the place of Stalin versus Trotsky. So did the indiscriminate use of words like "dupe," "sellout," "turncoat," and "renegade."

For most of the fifty years between 1939 and 1989, these two leftist camps exchanged charges of dishonesty. In both, it was agreed that no decent person who had sufficient intelligence to grasp the issues and weigh the evidence could remain in the other. No honest and informed person, it was said, could have stayed in the Communist Party after the Moscow purge trials. No such person, other people said, could vote for Truman, the president who financed the capture and murder of the Communist leaders of the Greek resistance by the postwar Greek government. The anti-Communists did not see how anyone could think of the USSR as on the side of peace and freedom after the Communist takeover of Czechoslovakia in 1948. The anti-anti-Communists did not see how a self-proclaimed leftist could give information to the FBI. The terms in which each group described the other did not allow for the possibility of honest mistakes.

This sort of rhetoric is still with us. Consider Christopher Hitchens' book on George Orwell. Hitchens there recalls that Mary McCarthy "secretly feared" that Orwell's anti-Communism would, had he lived, have led him to support the war in Vietnam. Hitchens assured her that her fears were groundless. Orwell, he explained to her, "was for decolonization without conditions, and . . . saw clearly the imperial-successor role that the United States was ambitious to play."[1] Hitchens is sure that Orwell's anti-imperialism would have prevailed over his anti-Communism – that he would never have become a cold war liberal. I am not so sure. Like McCarthy, I can easily imagine Orwell's anti-Communism prevailing over his anti-imperialism. If he had lived for another twenty years, he might well have joined Sidney Hook, James Farrell, and many other ex-Trotskyists who urged the US to persist in its struggle with the Viet Cong.

Suppose Orwell had made that mistake. Or suppose that, ten years earlier, he had taken a different route into Spain, had fought on another front, had never served in a POUM unit, had accepted the Stalinist version of what happened in the streets of Barcelona, and so had never had occasion to write *Homage to Catalonia*. He might then, after World War II, have opposed Churchill's anti-Communism as fiercely as he did his pro-colonialism. Would either mistake have shown that he was deficient in either intelligence or honesty? Surely not. Yet Hitchens writes as if it was moral virtue that caused Orwell always to be on the right side, as if luck had had nothing to do with it.

Hitchens quotes Orwell's autobiographical claim that, from youth on, he had had "a power of facing unpleasant facts." Hitchens glosses this by saying that "a striking fact about Orwell, a tribute to his 'power of facing', is that he never underwent a Stalinist phase, never had to be cured or purged by sudden 'disillusionment.' "[2] That suggests that all those people who did undergo a Stalinist phase, or who admired Hitler or Mussolini, or otherwise swerved off course in their political choices, were deficient in the virtues which enabled Orwell always to be on the right side.

Hitchens seems committed to the idea that any honest and intelligent man will adopt political positions of which future historians will approve. He says, for example, that "one can reprint every single letter, book review and essay composed by Orwell without exposing him to any embarrassment."[3] In contrast, admirers of Shaw and Yeats are unhappy to have to reprint what these men said about Mussolini. Admirers of Sartre would like

---

[1] Christopher Hitchens, *Why Orwell Matters* (New York: Basic Books, 2002), 28.
[2] Ibid., 56.   [3] Ibid., 4.

not to have to reprint his description of anti-Communists like Raymond Aron as "scum." Embarrassment of this sort stems from the implicit view that the morally relevant facts were there for all to see, and that it was a moral flaw for men as intelligent as these not to have faced up to them. This view lies behind the left's fondness for words like "renegade" and "sellout," and more generally behind the priggishness for which leftist intellectuals are notorious. Such priggishness is a minor vice when compared to the heartlessness of rightist intellectuals, but it should not be encouraged. Books such as Hitchens' do encourage it.

Viewing political disagreement as a symptom of moral failure presupposes a moral psychology that goes back to the notion of sin as a free choice of evil, a deliberate turning away from the divine light. Kant inherited the notion of radical evil from this theological tradition. He combined it with the idea that being moral was a matter of obedience to principles whose truth was evident to all rational beings. Many contemporary moral philosophers still take seriously the idea that moral and political decisions are made by pondering practical syllogisms whose major premises are luminously clear principles and whose minor premises are plain empirical facts. These philosophers like to describe people of whose views they disapprove – racists and homophobes, for example – as "irrational." Irrationality, thought of as a blamable failure to exercise an innate faculty, has thus become the secular equivalent of sin. Both are thought of as a deliberate turning away from the light.

John Dewey regarded the Kantian way of thinking of morality as incorporating all that was worst in Platonism and Christianity. So he urged that we get rid of faculty psychology, the notion of radical evil, the morality–prudence distinction, and the model of the practical syllogism. Like Hegel, Dewey viewed moral principles not as self-evident truths but as rough summaries of past practices. He did not think that any particular empirical fact sufficed to determine any particular moral choice. He saw decisions about what to believe and what to do as episodes in an endless process of reweaving our networks of beliefs and desires. This process is rarely a matter of applying antecedent criteria.

On a Deweyan view, the best explanation of why Orwell was always on the right side is sheer dumb luck. Orwell happened to have been in the right places at the right times to have gotten switched on to the right political tracks, the ones that history has decided that it would be better if everybody had been on. Honesty is not a good explanation of Orwell's political choices, nor is dishonesty a good explanation of why T. S. Eliot rejected the manuscript of *Animal Farm*. If we think of moral choice as Dewey did, we shall stop saying such things as "No honest woman could have failed to see, by 1939, that Stalin was a mad tyrant" or "No honest man would have named names to the House Un-American Activities Committee."

We shall also stop repeating Auden's description of the 1930s as "a low dishonest decade." History tells us that Léon Blum and Stanley Baldwin tragically miscalculated the consequences of their decisions, but not that they acted basely. Blum, at least, was as honorable a man as has ever headed a government. His utterly disastrous mistakes were as honest as they come. Churchill was right, and Blum wrong, about the political choices that had to be made if fascism were not to triumph. History is on Churchill's side, but not because Churchill remained faithful to principle and Blum did not, nor because Churchill was more rational than Blum. Churchill, like Orwell, guessed right. He lucked out.

Louis Menand has noted (in correspondence) that "a huge emphasis has been placed on how *soon* one turned against the Soviet Union, as though taking a year or two longer than the next person to decide that Stalin was indeed the bad guy, or that even in the Trotskyist version Communism was the wrong road, made a person less reliable, [less] honest." Menand's remark made me squirm. That was because I remembered that, as a teenage student at the University of Chicago, I had enjoyed a snotty sense of inherited superiority to fellow-students whose parents had waited until the Moscow trials to break with the American Communist Party. That was a whole five years later than my own parents, who had broken in 1932. If I were able to share Hitchens' views, I would think of my mother and father as exceptionally clear-headed and honest. But in fact I think of them as lucky. They had occasion to work closely with the Party's leaders, as most fellow-travelers did not. So they learned things that other people only learned later.

The idea that, in the flux of political events, there is a particular moment at which the relevant empirical facts became obvious to all, so that only dishonesty can prevent one from seeing their implications, is as bad as the idea that crucial experiments in science necessitate scientific revolutions. The latter suggests that the professors at Pisa should have abandoned Aristotle as soon as Galileo's unequal weights landed simultaneously at the bottom of the tower, and Ptolemy as soon as soon as they looked at Jupiter's moons through his telescope. This is like thinking that in 1850 a glimpse of the mills of Lancashire or the mines of Picardy was sufficient to convince any rational human being to become a socialist, or that in 1950 revelations about the Gulag were sufficient to demonstrate that socialism was the road to serfdom.

Dewey thought that Platonist models of the decision-making process which reduced it to the application of pre-existing criteria should be set aside. He urged us to substitute the notion of "intelligence" for the Greek notion of "reason." The difference he had in mind is that between the thought processes of the skilled carpenter and those of the Euclidean geometer. One of the most influential of the American cold war liberals, Lionel Trilling, applauded Dewey's suggestion. Trilling expressed his own understanding of what Dewey was getting at when he wrote that "it is a long time since we have heard a man praised for his intelligence – that is, for the activity of his mind, for its centrality, its flexibility, its awareness of difficulty and complexity, and its readiness to confront and deal with difficulty and complexity."[4]

Trilling, who had hoped to become a novelist rather than a critic, thought that the novel was the paradigm example of the application of intelligence to human affairs. For the novelist is to the theorist as the carpenter is to the geometer. The novel, Trilling wrote, is "of all genres the most indifferent to manifest shapeliness and decorum, and the most devoted to substance, which it presumes to say is actuality itself; the genre which is least disposed to say that it is self-sufficient and unconditioned."[5] The geometer, like the rational decision theorist, hopes for shapeliness and decorum. So does the Kantian moral philosopher who hopes to reach what he calls "the only rational conclusion" about what is to be done – a conclusion backed by valid reasoning from self-evident major premises

---

4 Lionel Trilling, *The Last Decade: Essays and Reviews, 1965–1975* (New York: Harcourt, 1979), 230. This passage is from a paragraph in "Some Notes for an Autobiographical Lecture" which is preceded by the words "JOHN DEWEY," capitalized. The context is the account of the virtues of Columbia College in the 1920s, when he was an undergraduate. This is one of the relatively few references to Dewey in Trilling's work. As I have learned from an unpublished dissertation by Michael Kimmage, Trilling attended only a few of Dewey's lectures, and found them unintelligible. But he apparently read Dewey's *Ethics*, and came away from the experience believing that Dewey had learned from Hegel that in the modern world the crucial moral question is about what sort of person one wants to become. See *The Moral Obligation to be Intelligent: Selected Essays of Lionel Trilling*, ed. Leon Wieseltier (Farrar, Straus and Giroux, 2000), 310: "Dewey followed Hegel in this when, in his *Ethics*, he said that moral choice is not really dictated by the principle or the maxim that is applicable to the situation but rather by the 'kind of selfhood' that one wishes to 'assume.'" See also 8: "there are certain moral situations, Dewey says, where we cannot decide between the ends; we are forced to make our moral choices in terms of our preference for one kind of character or another." Trilling goes on to say that "The modern novel, with its devices for investigating the quality of character, is the aesthetic form almost specifically called forth to exercise the modern way of judgment." Trilling was criticized by Joseph Frank for misunderstanding Hegel, but his way of reading Hegel chimes with that of a leading contemporary Hegel scholar, Robert Pippin. In his *Henry James and Modern Moral Life* (Cambridge: Cambridge University Press, 2001), Pippin echoes Trilling's account of the relationship between between modernity and the modern novel.

5 Trilling, *The Last Decade*, 228.

conjoined with minor premises that any honest empirical inquirer can confirm. But if one gives up such hopes, one will see the story that one tells oneself about who one is and why one is acting as one does – the novel of one's life – as one among many possible stories that might be told. One will admit that honest men and women may differ about which of these stories rings true, and that all such stories have many loose threads.

A central character in the one novel that Trilling published, *The Middle of the Journey*, was modeled on Whittaker Chambers, a college acquaintance whose early brilliance had made a deep impression on him. Trilling was the most respected American man of letters of his generation, and Chambers was one of the most politically influential intellectuals of the day. Yet Trilling's novel about Chambers has received surprisingly little attention. One reason is that we have forgotten just how important Chambers was. Even before his accusations of espionage against Hiss were made public, Chambers had helped persuade American public opinion that, once Hitler had been disposed of, it would be necessary to fight Stalin. As foreign news editor of *Time* during a crucial year – mid-1944 to mid-1945 – he ruthlessly revised, or simply discarded, reports from foreign correspondents that contradicted or weakened the anti-Communist message that he wanted *Time* to broadcast.

Even more important than his editorship, however, was Chambers' success in convincing Henry Luce to enforce the hard anti-Communist line that all the Luce publications eventually adopted. When Chambers wrote a devastating account of the Yalta conference, Luce was not at all sure that it should be published. In 1945, he had the same honest doubts about whether we should be beastly to Stalin as did the various publishers who rejected Orwell's *Animal Farm*. Luce, like those publishers, still hoped that there might be a chance that the wartime cooperation between the USSR and the democracies could be extended into the postwar era. They did not want to do anything that might help foreclose this hope.

In the end Chambers' piece was published, but only over the infuriated objections of most of the other journalists who worked for Luce. In 1945, many members of the American media held the opinions that were to be expressed by Henry Wallace in his presidential campaign of 1948. The million votes that Wallace won in that year are a testimony to the division in American public opinion about Stalin and the nature of the postwar world. This division was especially marked among leftist intellectuals who were ashamed of America's treatment of the Soviet Union under Lenin, and who rightly feared that anti-Communism would be used by the Republicans as a pretext for repealing as much of the New Deal as possible.

Such people were very reluctant indeed to back the Truman Doctrine or to accept George Kennan's view of the need to contain the USSR. Chambers understood the state of mind of such proto-Wallaceites perfectly, did his best to change it, and had a great deal of success in doing so. Three years after Luce yielded to the pressure of complaints about Chambers from his fellow-staffers and took him off the foreign news desk, the magazine's views had become just what Chambers had wanted them to be. Within the Luce organization – the media powerhouse of the day – Chambers lost a battle but won a war.

Chambers' name became widely known, however, only in 1948, the year after Trilling's novel was published. That was the year in which he repeated, before the House Un-American Activities Committee, the story that he had told to the Assistant Secretary of State for Security, Adolf Berle, in 1939: a story about a Soviet espionage ring operating in Washington in the 1930s, one member of which was Alger Hiss. Many people who read Trilling's book after the Hiss case broke, and who had learned that the character Gifford Maxim was modeled on Chambers, went on to assume that the characters Arthur and Nancy Croome – the smug fellow-travelers – were modeled on Alger Hiss and his wife Priscilla. This assumption was false; Trilling had been unaware of Hiss' existence when he wrote the book. But the entirely fortuitous parallels between the two couples are striking.

Today Chambers is usually referred to with a sneer. A recent advertisement for Trilling's novel refers to him as a "turncoat." He is frequently described as a "professional apostate" or "professional ex-Communist" – epithets chosen to convey a suggestion that he was in it for the money or the fame, and was not an honest man. But Trilling, when asked by Hiss' attorney, Harold Rosenwald, to testify for the defense, replied that Chambers was a man of honor. Rosenwald reacted, Trilling reports, with "an outburst of contemptuous rage." Contemptuous, presumably, because the attorney had concluded that since Trilling was obviously not stupid, he must necessarily be dishonest. An honest mistake about Chambers and Hiss was, Rosenwald assumed, impossible.

Trilling made a point of reporting his conversation with Rosenwald, and of reaffirming his confidence in Chambers' moral character, when he wrote an introduction to a new edition of his little-read novel in 1975. This was twenty-eight years after its original publication, fourteen years after Chambers' death, and shortly before Trilling's own. Trilling wrote there that "Chambers had been engaged in espionage against his own country" and had later "named the comrades who shared his own [treason] including one whom for a time he cherished as a friend." However, he continued, "I hold that when this has been said of him, it is still possible to say that he was a man of honor."[6] I read this passage as a protest against the idea that every political mistake can be attributed to either stupidity or dishonesty. I take Trilling to have been arguing that such terms as these are much too coarse to do justice to the phenomena of divided loyalties and difficult moral choice – the sort of phenomena best studied in novels.

Trilling's description of Chambers as a man of honor was not popular. Even Diana Trilling thought that her husband had chosen his words poorly. No spy, she thought, could be a man of honor. A friend of Trilling's, Morris Dickstein, wrote him saying that if anyone deserved honor it was not an informer like Chambers, but someone like Lillian Hellman, who had refused to name names. In a reply that Dickstein has kindly made available to me, Trilling defended his characterization of Chambers. He pointed out that Hellman had no knowledge of espionage activities that could have endangered the country, but that Chambers did. He addressed the issue of divided loyalties by way of a criticism of E. M. Forster's famous dictum: "If I had to choose between betraying my country and betraying my friends, I hope that I should have the courage to betray my country."[7] Trilling thought that this general principle – always prefer friends to country – was as hopeless as its converse. He saw invocation of such principles as a cop-out, a way of avoiding the need to stay at the level of the concrete and complex – the level at which Dewey thought intelligence operated.

The Middle of the Journey is, among other things,[8] a plea for this kind of concreteness and complexity, for the work of what the Chambers figure, Gifford Maxim, sneeringly calls "the humanistic critical intelligence." John Laskell, the Trilling figure in the novel, is striving to differentiate himself both from Maxim's apocalyptic certainties and from the Croomes' priggish idealism. The Croomes have never questioned the Stalinist lies that, in those days, filled the pages of the *The Nation* and *The New Republic*.

---

[6] Introduction to Lionel Trilling, *The Middle of the Journey* (New York: New York Review Books Classics, 1975 edn), xix. The Introduction concludes with the sentence "In Whittaker Chambers there was much to be faulted, but nothing I know of him has ever led me to doubt his magnanimous intention." Parenthetical references to Trilling's novel inserted in the text are to this edition.

[7] Trilling to Dickstein, April 7, 1975 (unpublished).

[8] It is also a meditation on the realization of the proximity of death that comes with middle age, and on the inability of a certain kind of person to bear the thought of death. This side of the novel is prominent in the opening chapters, but is gradually submerged beneath an account of various characters' relations with the Communist Party. *The Middle of the Journey* is, on my reading, two books in one – one about sickness, death, and human finitude and one about the situation of the New York Intellectuals vis-à-vis the CPUSA. The two books are somewhat awkwardly joined at the hip on the first page of chapter 10 (272 in the 1975 edition), where Nancy Croome's Duchesse-de-Guermantes-like refusal to consider the possibility of Laskell's death is connected up with her inability to have doubts about the USSR.

Maxim, by contrast, is a disillusioned member of the underground Communist Party. At its behest, Laskell suspects, he has committed murder. Having broken with the Party, Maxim is now in fear of his life.

Though Laskell himself is not a Communist, but merely "a sincere liberal," useful on committees concerned with public housing (37), he nevertheless "has to check a feeling of revulsion" whenever he hears of someone leaving the Party (73). He has always assumed that the claim that the American Communist Party was run out of Moscow was merely a myth propagated by the reactionary press. But now Maxim's revelations are forcing him to question this assumption (14). By the time that he has nerved himself to tell the Croomes about Maxim's break, he has begun to wonder whether it is Maxim who has become paranoid or he himself who has been naïve (167–8). The reader can easily imagine that Laskell will, after the novel's end, follow the same trajectory as Trilling did – becoming a cold war liberal, voting for Truman rather than Wallace, and finding Chambers' charges against Hiss perfectly plausible.

Nancy Croome, however, has no intention of changing her mind about anything. She despises mere liberals. She had been willing to help Maxim in his undercover work for the Party, but now refuses to break bread with him (245). When Maxim says that he now cannot see a great difference between Communists and Nazis, the Croomes are able to relax, since they realize that they are dealing not with a political opinion, but with a mental disorder (255). The more the Croomes draw back from Maxim in horror and incredulity, however, the more Laskell comes to see Nancy and Arthur Croome as colder, harder and more dangerous than he had realized. In the end, Laskell says to himself that "I believe that Maxim is telling the truth because of what I have learned about the Croomes" (272). There was, he discovers, "a large vacancy in his thought – it was the place that the Party and the Movement had been. It was also the place where Nancy and Arthur had been" (273).

At the climax of the novel, Maxim, a self-dramatizing bully, explains to Laskell that Deweyan intelligence is obsolete, because the future belongs to people like himself and the Croomes – people of unyielding will. He and the Croomes, he explains, are at irreconcilable extremes – whereas Laskell is still trying to mediate intelligently between these extremes, trying to be a mature human being (353). "You are proud," he tells Laskell, "of that flexibility of mind . . . But it is too late for that – the Renaissance is dead . . . Maybe it will come again. But not for a long time, not until the Croomes and I have won, and established ourselves against the anarchy of the world" (355). He urges Laskell to perform what he calls "the supreme act of the humanistic critical intelligence – it perceives the cogency of the argument and acquiesces in the fact of its own extinction." Maxim replies that he does not acquiesce. Maxim replies that it does not matter whether he does or not. Laskell rejoins, as Orwell might have, that it is the only thing that matters (356).

The Croomes are predictably outraged by Maxim's claim that he and they resemble each other. But Trilling wrote his novel to make that resemblance clear. The last words Nancy Croome says to Laskell are: "What Maxim said last night – you don't believe that do you? About him and us being together against you. As if that could ever be true." Laskell replies "I hope it's not true," knowing perfectly well that it is (360). Maxim's bullying pontifications, still utterly self-assured even after having changed sides, and the Croomes' childlike refusal to listen to anything they do not want to hear, are two ways in which a lack of "humanistic critical intelligence" makes itself manifest.

For Maxim, as for Chambers, life is not worth living unless one is a solitary and heroic figure, standing alone against the horrors of the time and yet in touch with something omnipotent, ruthless, unpredictable, and yet redemptive – the Party, History, or God. When a colleague at *Time* asked Chambers how he stood the strain, he replied "I cannot really be beaten because on my side there is a Power."[9] The Croomes, like the Hisses, do not pretend to heroism, but they do have convictions that are invulnerable to objections. Chambers remembered that when he enumerated Stalin's crimes in order to persuade the Hisses to follow him out of the Party, Priscilla Hiss retorted that such a recital was merely "mental masturbation."

Maxim and Chambers know that certainty is impossible, but like Kierkegaard – one of Chambers' favorite authors – they think that the knight of faith has no need of, or desire for, certainty. Kierkegaardian, Nietzschean and Dostoievskian heroes know that the quest for certainty is a cop-out, and that absolute commitment has nothing to do with the ability to win arguments or convince opponents. The Croomes and the Hisses, like the complacent and priggish inhabitants of what Kierkegaard called "Christendom," know what is necessary to be saved, and they know that all decent, honest, intelligent persons also know this. They realize that there are people who have turned away from the light by breaking with the Party, but they see no reason to talk further with such people.

---

[9] Whittaker Chambers, *Witness* (Washington DC: Regnery, 1952), 479. See also 793–4, where Chambers explains that "the great body of the nation" had kept its mind open about the Hiss case, and that "it was they who . . . produced the forces that could win a struggle whose conspicuous feature is that it was almost without leadership. From the very outset, I was in touch with that enormous force, for which I was making the effort, and from which I drew strength."

People who try for what Maxim calls "humanistic critical intelligence" do their best to resist the temptation to think of their own moral identity as self-sufficient and unconditioned, rather than being one more creature of time and chance. Neither Maxim nor the Croomes will ever be able to acknowledge that they are such creatures. But the reader of the novel is led to imagine that Laskell will devote the remainder of his life to acquiring the sort of negative capability that permits one to live with moral uncertainty. *The Middle of the Journey* is, among other things, Trilling's attempt to defend himself against charges of being an indecisive petit-bourgeois wimp, a Woody Allen figure, never quite sure who he is or what is to be done. He knew that that was how Laskell looked to both Maxim and the Croomes. He wrote his novel to explain why people like Laskell and himself had nothing to be ashamed of.

If this reading of his novel is right, Trilling is saying that not only Maxim and Chambers, but also the Croomes and the Hisses, are people of honor, and that honor has little to do with one's choice of a political position. It also has little to do with whether one winds up a murderer, a traitor, or a liar – or with whether one is condemned by the judgment of history. I suspect that Trilling thought that Alger Hiss had no base motives, any more than Chambers did. Chambers' informing on his old friend was dictated by his beliefs about what was needed to save the world. So was Hiss' willingness to spend the last forty-eight years of his life repeating the same old lies: that he had never been a Communist, had never spied, and was the helpless victim of a vast conspiracy. Alfred Kazin, in a 1978 article called "Why Alger Hiss Can't Confess," said that several conversations with Hiss had convinced him of Hiss' "passionate patriotism." They left him realizing that Hiss saw his services to the New Deal and to Soviet intelligence as all of a piece. Both were products of his hopes for his country's future. Kazin predicted that Hiss "will go his grave believing that he was a better American than you or I."[10]

I think that Trilling was right in believing that both Chambers and Hiss had no base motives. They were as honest as Orwell, or as Trilling himself. Both were, at various times, spies and perjurers, but they spied and lied for the right sorts of reasons. They were serving the needs of humanity as they understood those needs. The moral is that being honest, being true to one's ideals, has nothing in particular to do with the story history will tell about you. For historians are more interested in the consequences of your actions

---

[10] Alfred Kazin, "Why Alger Hiss Can't Confess," reprinted in *Alger Hiss, Whittaker Chambers and the Schism in the American Soul*, ed. Patrick A. Swan (Wilmington, DE: ISI Books, 2002), 220.

than in your motives. Novelists, because they are equally interested in both, help us come to terms with the fact that the two may have little to do with one another. They thereby help free us from the ideas we have inherited from Christianity and from Kant – ideas that suggest that those who got on the wrong track have sinned against the light.

Trilling did not always hold firm to the Deweyan beliefs that I have attributed to him. In his hero-worshipping essay "George Orwell and the Politics of Truth" his treatment of Orwell resembles Hitchens'. "The moral tone of [Homage to Catalonia]," he gushes, "is uniquely simple and true." "If we ask what Orwell stands for," Trilling continues, "the answer is: the virtue of not being a genius, of confronting the world with nothing more than one's simple, direct, undeceived intelligence . . .". Orwell, he continues, is one of the few who "in addition to being good, have the simplicity and sturdiness and activity which allow us to say of them that they are virtuous men." Such passages remind us of how much Woody Allen would like to have been Humphrey Bogart, and of Trilling's remark that Hemingway was the only writer of his time whom he envied.[11] But they do not show Trilling at his best.

Orwell worked very hard to create a work that would seem uniquely simple and true. As Hemingway had, he cultivated simplicity and sturdiness like the fragile blossoms they are. He wanted his readers to respond just as Trilling and Hitchens actually did. Yet there is nothing objectionable, nothing hypocritical, in Orwell's and Hemingway's attempts to obtain such responses. From a Deweyan as from an Aristotelian point of view, these attempts are not a matter of pretending to a virtue you lack, but rather of gradually acquiring a virtue by performing actions characteristic of those who have already acquired it. One would only find such efforts hypocritical if one believed that virtues such as these cannot be the result of hard work, but are genuine only if they stem from a uniquely simple and direct relation to goodness – the sort of relation that Kant, but neither Aristotle nor Dewey, thought that human beings could achieve.

The fantasy that such directness is possible is embodied in Trilling's unhappy phrase "the politics of truth." That phrase suggests that all you have to do to avoid political mistakes is to be honest. But there is no such politics, any more than there is a science of truth. Galileo did not practice such a science. He did not cut through superstition and prejudice with the sword of intellectual righteousness. He just had some bright, and revolutionary, ideas that, as it happened, paid off.

[11] See Diana Trilling, *The Beginning of the Journey* (New York: Harcourt, Brace, 1993), 417.

Galileo has become, deservedly, one of the heroes of modern times, and Orwell, no less deservedly, one of the heroes of the twentieth century. Admiration for people such as these, who had the courage to buck the received opinion of the day, is entirely appropriate, and indeed necessary. For where there is no worship of heroes and heroines, there will be little moral idealism, and therefore little moral progress. But we should bear in mind what the late Bernard Williams said, in his celebrated essay "Moral Luck," about another hero: Gauguin. Gauguin abandoned his responsibilities and his family, and boldly set sail for the South Seas. We forgive him everything because the pictures he painted in Tahiti were superb.

But suppose, Williams says, that they had been hopelessly banal. Then Gauguin would have been the painterly equivalent of Alger Hiss – producing wretched canvases decade after decade, faithful to his vision yet unable to realize that the history of painting had passed him by. He would have resembled one of those brave and imaginative contemporaries of Leibniz who argued that Aristotle had been right and Galileo wrong, and tried, unsuccessfully, to turn back the scientific clock. Such people are examples of the irrelevance of honor, honesty and courage to the judgment of history. The history of politics, like the history of science, is written from the point of view of how things have come to look to us now.

Just as hero-worship is necessary for moral progress, so is disgust. But one can be disgusted by a person while granting, for what little that is worth, that his or her mistakes were honest ones. The abolitionists were disgusted by Lee's decision to fight to preserve slavery, but it never occurred to them to deny that Lee was a man of honor. Nobody would want to break bread with Eichmann or Suslov, but we can easily imagine that the stories these men told themselves about who they were and what they were doing had the same coherence as those that Orwell and Trilling told themselves about their lives, and as the ones we tell ourselves about ours.

Honesty and honorableness are measured by the degree of coherence of the stories people tell themselves and come to believe. Most people are able construct a novel of their own lives in which they appear as, if not heroes and heroines, at least good. That is what is true in Socrates' claim that no one consciously does evil. But if one thinks, as Christianity and Kant did, that people are bad only because they have deliberately turned away from the light, then one will see most of these stories as dishonest and self-deceptive. To think in that way is to infer, as Plato did, from the fact that coherence is not enough for goodness to the conclusion that there must be some recourse other than coherence – some bright star to steer by, visible to any honest mind.

Plato was wrong. The best we can do, when making moral or political choices, or when deciding between scientific theories or religious convictions, is to work out as coherent a story as we can. But doing that will not ensure that the judgment of history will be on our side. Whether sticking to our stories will make us objects of admiration or of disgust to future generations is entirely beyond our control. The officers who, honoring their oaths, refused to join the Stauffenberg plot to kill Hitler look very bad. Those who broke their oaths, and were tortured to death after the plot failed, look very good indeed. But there was no star on which either group fixed their gaze, and from which the other turned away.

The absence of such a star entails that honorable men and women are quite able to do disgusting things. It also entails that the judgment of history is quite likely to be wrong, since our remote descendants will also lack such a star. But it does not mean that we should, or that we can, stop making moral judgments. We can still say that, even if the Nazis had won and had been able to write all the history books, Stauffenberg would have done the right thing. Even though we suspect that the humanistic critical intelligence may soon become an historical curiosity, we should still rebuke our children when they show signs of becoming more like Gifford Maxim, or like Nancy Croome, than like John Laskell.

II

Philosophy's Place in Culture

5

Grandeur, profundity, and finitude

Philosophy occupies an important place in culture only when things seem to be falling apart – when long-held and widely cherished beliefs are threatened. At such periods, intellectuals reinterpret the past in terms of an imagined future. They offer suggestions about what can be preserved and what must be discarded. The ones whose suggestions have been most influential win a place on the list of "great philosophers." For example, when prayer and priestcraft began to be viewed with suspicion, Plato and Aristotle found ways for us to hold on to the idea that human beings, unlike the beasts that perish, have a special relation to the ruling powers of the universe. When Copernicus and Galileo erased the world-picture that had comforted Aquinas and Dante, Spinoza and Kant taught Europe how to replace love of God with love of Truth, and how to replace obedience to the divine will with moral purity. When the democratic revolutions and industrialization forced us to rethink the nature of the social bond, Marx and Mill stepped forward with some useful suggestions.

In the course of the twentieth century there were no crises that called forth new philosophical ideas. There was no intellectual struggle comparable in scale to the one that Andrew White famously described as the warfare between science and theology. Nor were there any social convulsions that rendered either Mill's or Marx's suggestions irrelevant. As high culture became more thoroughly secularized, the educated classes of Europe and the Americas became complacently materialist in their understanding of how things work. In the battle between Plato and Democritus – the one Plato described as waged between the gods and the giants – Western intellectuals have come down, once and for all, on the side of the giants. They also became complacently utilitarian and experimentalist in their evaluations of proposed social and political initiatives. They share the same utopian vision: a global commonwealth in which human rights are respected, equality of opportunity is assured, and the chances of human happiness are thereby increased. Political argument nowadays is about how this goal might best be reached.

This consensus among the intellectuals has moved philosophy to the margins of culture. Such controversies as those between Russell and Bergson, Heidegger and Cassirer, Carnap and Quine, Ayer and Austin, Habermas and Gadamer, or Fodor and Davidson have had little resonance outside the borders of philosophy departments. Philosophers' explanations of how the mind is related to the brain, or of how there can be a place for value in a world of fact, or of how free will and mechanism might be reconciled, do not intrigue most contemporary intellectuals. These problems, preserved in amber as the textbook "problems of philosophy," still capture the imagination of some bright students. But no one would claim that discussion of them is central to intellectual life. Solving those very problems was all-important for contemporaries of Spinoza, but when today's philosophy professors insist that they are "perennial," or that they remain "fundamental," nobody listens. Most intellectuals of our day brush aside claims that our social practices require philosophical foundations with the same impatience as they display when similar claims are made for religion.

But even though the struggle between the gods and the giants is over, two other controversies that Plato described are still alive. The first is the quarrel between philosophy and poetry – a quarrel that was revitalized by the romantic movement, and now takes the form of tension between C. P. Snow's "two cultures." This quarrel is about whether human beings are at their best – realize their special powers to the fullest – when they use reason to discover how things really are, or when they use imagination to transform themselves. The second is the quarrel that Plato described as between the philosophers and the sophists. This quarrel is between those who think there is an important virtue called "the love of truth" and those who do not.

The standoff between Nietzsche and Plato that dominates a great deal of recent philosophical writing epitomizes both quarrels. That opposition, unlike any of the more parochial ones I listed earlier, is still capable of gripping the imagination of intellectuals who are commonsensical materialists and utilitarians. It would be an exaggeration to say that it is at the center of contemporary life, but surely the best way for us philosophy professors to get the attention of people outside our own discipline is to raise the question of whether Plato was right that human beings can transcend contingency by searching for truth, or whether Nietzsche was right to treat both Platonism and religion as escapist fantasies.

The quarrel that the philosophers have with the poets is not the same as their quarrel with the sophists, for reasons that I shall come to shortly. But the poets and the sophists have a lot in common – especially their doubts about the idea that natural science should serve as a model for the rest of high culture. Both are suspicious of what I shall call "universalistic grandeur" – the sort of grandeur attained by mathematics and mathematical physics.

Both numbers and elementary particles display the imperturbability traditionally attributed to the divine. The study of both produces structures of great beauty, structures that are godlike in their aloofness, their indifference to human concerns. The same impulse that led Plato to think that what he called "the really real" must be more like a number than like a lump of dirt has led many recent philosophers to take modern physical science as the overarching framework within which philosophical inquiry is to be conducted. Thus we find Quine identifying the question "is there a fact of the matter?" with the question "does it make a difference to the elementary particles?" A host of other philosophers have devoted themselves to "naturalizing epistemology" and "naturalizing semantics." These are attempts to describe mind and language in terms which allow for the fact that what is thought and what is meant are supervenient on the behavior of physical particles. Whereas intellectuals in general are happy to agree that physical science tells you how things work, many contemporary philosophers are still Platonist enough to think that it does more than that. They think it tells you what is really real.

Philosophers of this sort often describe the battle they wage against colleagues whom they describe as "irrationalists," "deniers of truth," or "sophists" as a defense of science against its enemies. Many of these philosophers think of natural science as pre-Galilean intellectuals thought of religion – as the area of culture in which human beings are at their best, because most willing to acknowledge the claims of something that transcends the human. Hostility to science is, in their view, a form of spiritual degradation. Thus Bertrand Russell, at the beginning of the last century, reacted against the line of thought that William James called "pragmatism" and that his Oxford friend F. C. S. Schiller called "humanism," by writing as follows:

greatness of soul is not fostered by those philosophies which assimilate the universe to Man. Knowledge is a form of union of Self and not-Self; like all union, it is impaired by domination, and therefore by any attempt to force the universe into conformity with what we find in ourselves. There is a widespread philosophical tendency towards the view which tells us that Man is the measure of all things, that truth is man-made . . . This view . . . is untrue; but in addition to being untrue, it has the effect of robbing philosophic contemplation of all that gives it value . . .

The free intellect will see as God might see, without a here and now, without hopes and fears . . . calmly, dispassionately, in the sole and exclusive desire of know-ledge – knowledge as impersonal, as purely contemplative, as it is possible for man to attain.[1]

In our own day, Thomas Nagel shares Russell's contempt for those who believe that, as William James put it, "the trail of the human serpent is over all." Nagel describes what he calls "the outermost framework of all thoughts" as "a conception of what is objectively the case – what is the case without subjective or relative qualification."[2] In response to pragmatists and historicists who argue that all justification is by our lights – the lights of a particular time and place – Nagel replies that:

claims to the effect that a type of judgment expresses a local point of view are inher-ently objective in intent. They suggest a picture of the true sources of those judg-ments that places them in an unconditional context. The judgment of relativity or conditionality cannot be applied to the judgment of relativity itself . . . There may be some subjectivists, perhaps calling themselves pragmatists, who present subjec-tivism as applying even to itself. But then what they say does not call for a reply, since it is just a report of what the subjectivist finds it agreeable to say.[3]

Russell and Nagel share Plato's taste for universalist grandeur. They also share his conviction that there is no middle way between acknowledging the claims of the unconditional outermost framework of thought and simply saying whatever you find agreeable to say. Like Plato, they see human beings as facing a choice between striving for the universal and unconditional and giving free rein to unjustifiable, idiosyncratic desires. So the pragmatists' suggestion that mathematics and physics be thought of simply as useful for the improvement of man's estate, as tools for coping with our environment, strikes both Russell and Nagel as a symptom of moral slackness as well as of intellectual error.

I have attempted in previous writings to defend James' replies to Russell, and to restate the defense of Protagoras mounted by Schiller, by tying prag-matism together with romanticism. But it is important to emphasize the difference between a pragmatist and the kind of romantic who buys into the Platonic reason–passion distinction and then exalts passion at the expense of reason. The pragmatists have little use for either the reason–passion or the objective–subjective distinction. So in this chapter I shall contrast the two quarrels I have been discussing: the one between

---

[1] Bertrand Russell, *The Problems of Philosophy* (Buffalo, NY: Prometheus Books, 1988), ch. XV, 160 and passim.   [2] Thomas Nagel, *The Last Word* (Oxford: Oxford University Press, 2001), 16.
[3] Ibid., 14–15.

philosophy and poetry and the one between neo-Platonists such as Russell and Nagel and neo-sophists like myself.

To bring out the difference, I shall invoke two distinctions that Juergen Habermas drew in his book *The Philosophical Discourse of Modernity* – distinctions I have found invaluable in trying to tell a story about the history of modern philosophy. The first is the one Habermas makes between what he calls "subject-centered reason" and "communicative reason." Subject-centered reason is a Platonic invention: it consists in a purported connaturality between the mind of each human being and the nature of things. Plato described this connaturality in terms of the soul's pre-existence in an immaterial world. Descartes, Russell, and Nagel presuppose it when they claim that all we have to do to reach a transcultural and ahistorical outermost framework of thought is to substitute conceptual clarity for conceptual confusion.

What Habermas calls "communicative rationality," on the other hand, is not a natural human endowment, but a set of social practices. It is found, in some measure, wherever people are willing to hear the other side, to talk things over, to argue until areas of agreement are found, and to abide by the resulting agreements. To think of reason as subject-centered is to believe that human beings possess a faculty that enables them to circumvent conversation – to side-step opinion and head straight for knowledge. To replace subject-centered reason with communicative rationality is to see truth as what is likely to emerge from free and imaginative conversation. It is to think of knowledge as the achievement of consensus rather than as a mental state that enjoys a closer relation to reality than does opinion.

To agree with Habermas that reason is communicative and dialogical rather than subject-centered and monological is to substitute responsibility to other human beings for responsibility to a non-human standard. It is to lower our sights from the unconditional above us to the community around us. This substitution enables us to accept with equanimity Kuhn's suggestion that scientists are better thought of as solving puzzles than as gradually disclosing the true nature of things. It helps us limit ourselves to hopes for small, finite, fleeting successes, and to give up the hope of participation in enduring grandeur.

So much for Habermas' first distinction. His second is between remaining loyal to rationality and seeking what he calls "an other to reason." Habermas uses the latter term to characterize such things as mystic insight, poetic inspiration, religious faith, imaginative power, and authentic self-expression – sources of conviction that have been put forward as superior to reason.

Like Descartes' clear and distinct ideas, each of these others to reason is put forward as a short cut around conversation, leading straight to truth. If you are in touch with such an other, you do not need to converse with other human beings. If you have something like what Kierkegaard called "faith," or if you can engage in what Heidegger called "Denken," it will not matter to you whether or not other people can be persuaded to share your beliefs. It would debase the relevant "other to reason" to force those beliefs into the conversational arena, to make them compete in the marketplace of ideas.

Habermas has suggested that I go too far when I deny that universal validity is a goal of inquiry. He thinks of my repudiation of this goal, and my enthusiasm for what Heidegger called *Welterschliessung* – world-disclosure – as unfortunate concessions to Romanticism, and as putting me in bad company. But I regard Habermas' insistence that we retain the ideal of universal validity as an unfortunate concession to Platonism. By hanging on to it, it seems to me, Habermas remains in thrall to the philosophical tradition that burdened us with the idea of reason as a human faculty that is somehow attuned to the really real.

Going all the way with Habermas' project of replacing a subject-centered conception of reason with a communicative conception would, it seems to me, leave us without any need or any use for the notion of universal valid-ity.[4] For it would let one think of rational inquiry as having no higher goal than solving the transitory problems of the day. Habermas and I both distrust metaphysics. But whereas he thinks that we must find a metaphysics-free interpretation of the notion of universal validity in order to avoid the seductions of Romanticism, I think that that notion and metaphysics stand or fall together.

One way to express our disagreement is to say that I cast Habermas in the role in which he casts Hegel – as someone who almost reaches the correct philosophical position but fails to take the last crucial step. One of the central points Habermas makes in *The Philosophical Discourse of Modernity* is that Hegel almost, but not quite, broke the hold of subject-centered conceptions of rationality. He came very close to replacing it, once and for all, with what Terry Pinkard has called "the doctrine of the social-ity of reason." That doctrine holds that an individual human being cannot be rational all by herself, for the same reasons that she cannot use language all by herself. For unless and until we take part in what Robert Brandom

---

[4] I rehearse my disagreements with Habermas about the utility of the notion of universal validity in "Universalism and Truth," in *Rorty and his Critics*, ed. Robert Brandom (Oxford: Blackwell, 2000).

calls "the game of giving and asking for reasons," we remain unthinking brutes.

Habermas thinks that if Hegel had managed to carry through on this proto-Wittgensteinian line of thought we might have been spared the aggressive post-Hegelian anti-rationalisms of Kierkegaard, Bergson, Nietzsche, Heidegger, Sartre, Foucault, and others. But for Hegel to have taken the plunge he would have had to drop the idea of absolute knowledge. He would have had to turn his back on Parmenides, Plato, and the quest for the kind of grandeur that becomes possible only when doubt is eliminated, when no participant in the conversation has anything left to say, and so history – and perhaps time as well – can come to an end. To do that, Hegel would have had to give up the confluence of the divine and the human at which his System aimed. He would have had to rest content with the idea that the conversation of humankind would go its unpredictable way for as long as our species lasts – solving particular problems as they happen to arise, and, by working through the consequences of those solutions, generating new problems.

One way to follow up on Habermas' criticism of Hegel is to say that Hegel took on the impossible task of reconciling the Romantic idea that the human future might become unimaginably different – unimaginably richer – than the human past, with the Greek idea that time, history, and diversity are distractions from an eternal oneness. As with Goethe, much of Hegel's greatness lies in his having heightened the tensions between the temporal and the eternal, and between the Classic and the Romantic, rather than in his success at synthesizing them. It is as if the cunning of reason used Hegel to intensify this tension, thereby warning us against attempting any such synthesis.

John Dewey, the greatest of the Left Hegelians, heeded this warning. Dewey had no use either for theodicy or for the ideal of absolute knowledge. He was interested only in helping people solve problems, and had no wish for either grandeur or profundity. His abandonment of both goals has resulted in his being dismissed as a bourgeois bore, which was pretty much the way Russell regarded him. Both Russell and Heidegger thought Dewey incapable of rising to the spiritual level on which philosophy should be conducted.

One reason that Dewey is my philosophical hero is that I think it would be a good idea for philosophers to bourgeoisify themselves, to stop trying to rise to the spiritual level at which Plato and Nietzsche confront each other. Indeed, it would be best if they would stop thinking in terms of levels altogether, cease to imagine themselves ascending to heights or plumbing depths. In order to develop this point, I turn now from the universalist metaphor of ascent to an overarching framework that transcends the merely human to the romantic metaphor of descent to the very bottom of the human soul.

One of Dewey's most trenchant critics, Arthur Lovejoy, was also a distinguished historian of ideas. In the latter capacity, he urged that it was time to put aside the hackneyed opposition between classicism and romanticism – to treat it as an overused, worn-out, historiographical device. In a celebrated essay, Lovejoy listed a large number of intellectual movements that had been labeled "romanticism," and showed not only that nothing bound them together, but that some of them stood in direct opposition to one another.

Isaiah Berlin is one of the few historians of ideas who have had the courage to challenge Lovejoy on his own ground and to insist that he was, in this instance, mistaken. "There *was* a romantic movement," Berlin insists. "It did," he continues, "have something that was central to it; it did create a great revolution in consciousness, and it is important to discover what this is."[5] Berlin revivifies the notion of romanticism by opposing it not to classicism but to universalism. He thereby transforms it into one term of a philosophical, rather than a literary, contrast. He calls universalism the "backbone of the main Western tradition," and says that it was that backbone that romanticism "cracked."[6] Romanticism, Berlin says, was "the deepest and most long-lasting of all changes in the life of the West."[7]

Prior to the late eighteenth century, Berlin claims, Western thinkers were pretty much agreed on three doctrines: First, all genuine questions can be answered. Second, all these answers can be discovered by public means – means which, as Berlin says, "can be learnt and taught to other persons." Third, all these answers are compatible with one another. They all fit together into One Truth. As Berlin nicely puts it, Western thinkers viewed human life as the attempt to solve a jigsaw puzzle. He describes what I have called their obsession with universalist grandeur as follows:

There must be some way of putting the pieces together. The all-wise being, the omniscient being, whether God or an omniscient earthly creature – whichever way you like to conceive of it – is in principle capable of fitting all the pieces together into one coherent pattern. Anyone who does this will know what the world is like: what things are, what they have been, what they will be, what the laws are that govern them, what man is, what the relation of man is to things, and therefore what man needs, what he desires, and how to obtain it.[8]

---

[5] Isaiah Berlin, *The Roots of Romanticism* (Princeton, NJ: Princeton University Press, 2001), 20.
[6] Ibid., 21.   [7] Ibid., xiii.   [8] Ibid., 23.

Berlin's own philosophical writings are built around his conviction that the pieces will not, in fact, fit together. The theme of his best-known essay, "Two Concepts of Liberty," is that some goods are incompatible with one another. No matter what sociopolitical setup we come to agree on, something will be lost. Somebody will get hurt. This is a view with which Dewey would have entirely agreed.

As Berlin tells the story, the French Revolution forced us to face up to incompability. The unity of Truth cannot be reconciled with the fact that "Danton . . . a sincere revolutionary who committed certain errors, did not deserve to die, and yet Robespierre was perfectly right to put him to death."[9] The romantic reaction to this paradox, Berlin says, was to attach the highest importance to such values as "integrity, sincerity, readiness to sacrifice one's life to some inner light, dedication to some ideal for which it is worth both living and dying."[10] Seen from a Platonist point of view, this amounted to giving passion supremacy over rationality, authenticity over conversability.

Berlin sums up the romantic reaction against the assumption that there is always one right answer to the question "what is to be done?" by saying that what Hegel called "the collision of good with good" is "due not to error, but to some kind of conflict of an unavoidable kind, of loose elements wandering about the earth, of values which cannot be reconciled. What matters is that people should dedicate themselves to these values with all that is in them."[11]

Pragmatism differs from romanticism in taking seriously the collision of good with good while remaining dubious about total dedication and passionate commitment. Pragmatists think that Danton and Robespierre – and, for that matter, Antigone and Creon – should have tried harder to make some sort of deal. The Platonist tradition insists that collisions of good with good are always illusory, because there is always one right thing to do. Pieces of the puzzle that obstinately refuse to fit are to be discarded as mere appearance. But for pragmatists intellectual and moral conflict is typically a matter of beliefs that have been acquired in the attempt to serve one good purpose getting in the way of beliefs that were developed in the course of serving another good purpose. The thing to do, they say, is not to figure out what is real and what is merely apparent, but to find some compromise that will let both sides achieve at least some of the good they originally hoped for. This usually means redescribing the situation that gave rise to the various problems, finding a way of thinking about it that

9 Ibid., 13.   10 Ibid., 8.   11 Ibid., 13.

both sides might be able to live with. Since pragmatists agree with James that the true is the good in the way of belief, and since they take the conflict of good with good as inevitable, they do not think that univeralist grandeur and finality will ever be attained. Ingenious compromises between old goods will produce new sets of aspirations and new projects, and new collisions between those aspirations and projects, forever. We shall never escape what Hegel called "the struggle and labor of the negative," but that is merely to say that we shall remain finite creatures, the children of specific times and specific places.

Plato's idea that "the Good" is the name of a something perfectly unified, something like the Parmenidean One, helped him see all the goods he cherished as compatible with one another. The author of both love poems and mathematical proofs, he wanted to see both as serving a single purpose. If we put the *Phaedrus* together with the *Republic*, we can see Plato as trying to fit his attraction to the young men to whom he dedicated his poems, his love for Socrates, and his hopes for a just city together with his passion for demonstrative certainty. By, as Nietzsche put it, insisting that only the rational can be beautiful, and by identifying true beauty with ultimate reality, he succeeded in convincing himself that the ugly collision of good with good could be set aside as mere appearance.

On Berlin's account, the imperturbable grandeur of the new and radiant world that Plato claimed to have discerned dominated the imagination of the West up until the romantic movement. Thanks to the thinkers of philosophy's heroic age, such as Spinoza and Kant, the ideal of universalist grandeur was able to survive the secularization of high culture. For these philosophers suggested ways of retaining the jigsaw-puzzle view of inquiry even after we had become Democriteans in our understanding of how things work. They suggested ways in which Truth might remain One, how it might still be regarded both as an appropriate object of erotic striving and as an invulnerable ally.

The romantic movement did its best to break apart what Plato thought he had fitted together. It mocked Plato's attempt to fuse mathematical certainty and erotic ecstasy. It refused to think that the particular person or city or book one loves with all one's heart and soul and mind is simply a temporary disguise adopted by something eternal and infinite, something not itself subject to contingency or defeat. It abandoned the idea of an all-encompassing framework which would eventually reveal itself to all who tried hard to think objectively. To quote Berlin again:

What romanticism did was to undermine the notion that in matters of value, politics, morals, aesthetics there are such things as objective criteria which operate between human beings, such that anyone who does not use these criteria is simply either a liar or a madman, which is true of mathematics and physics.[12]

Romanticism, in other words, undermined the assumption common to Plato, Kant, and Habermas: that there is such a thing as "the better argument" – better not by reference to its ability to convince some particular audience, but because it possesses universal validity. The idea that there is one right thing to do or to believe, no matter who you are, and the idea that arguments have intrinsic goodness or badness, no matter who is asked to evaluate them, go hand in hand. Pragmatists discard both ideas. My basic disagreement with Habermas concerns his attempt to retain the notion of the intrinsically better argument while adopting a theory of the sociality of reason. These two seem to me, as I think they did to Dewey, like oil and water.

If we agree with Berlin that the romantics exploded the jigsaw-puzzle view of inquiry, then we become willing to admit that inquiry need have no higher goal than the solving of problems when they arise. But Berlin, like Dewey, recognized that the Platonist hope of speaking with an authority that is not merely that of a certain time and place had survived within the bosom of romanticism, and engendered what Habermas calls "others to reason." Berlin's treatment of the universalism–romanticism contrast helps us see that one of the most important ideas the romantics took over from the ontotheological tradition was that of "the infinite."

"Infinite" is an ambiguous term that univeralists and romantics use in different ways. Universalism's idea of the infinite is of something that encompasses everything else, and thus something against which nothing else has any power. To say that God is infinite is to say that nothing outside him can affect him, much less deter him from his purposes. Romanticism's idea of infinity is different. It is the essentially reactive idea of removing all constraints, and in particular all the limitations imposed by the human past, all those which are built into the ways we currently talk and think. The romantic idea of infinity has more to do with the figure of Prometheus than with that of Socrates. It is the idea of perfect freedom decoupled from that of perfect knowledge and of affiliation with the invulnerable.

Berlin uses the terms "depth" and "profundity" to describe the romantic version of the infinite. Here is a passage in which he expatiates on the sense that the romantics gave these terms:

When I say that Pascal is more profound than Descartes . . . or that Kafka is a more profound writer than Hemingway, what exactly am I trying unsuccessfully to convey by means of this metaphor? . . . According to the romantics – and this is

[12] Ibid., 140.

one of their principal contributions to understanding in general – what I mean by depth, although they do not discuss it under that name, is inexhaustibility, unembraceability . . . [I]n the case of a work that is profound the more I say the more remains to be said. There is no doubt that, although I attempt to describe what their profundity consists in, as soon as I speak it becomes quite clear that, no matter how long I speak, new chasms open. No matter what I say I always have to leave three dots at the end.[13]

Plato thought that conceptualization and argument would eventually bring one to a full stop, to a point beyond which no new chasms opened. His hope that argument will eventually bring us to a point where it will be unnecessary to leave three dots at the end epitomizes the jigsaw-puzzle view of the human situation – the view that there is a grand overall meaning to human life in general, rather than merely small transitory meanings that are constructed by individuals and communities and abandoned by their successors.

The romantics became convinced that conceptualization and argumentation would always leave three dots at the end, and then concluded that it is the poet, or, more generally, the imaginative genius, who will save us from finitude, rather than the Socratic dialectician. Berlin says that Friedrich Schiller introduced, "for the first time in human thought," the notion that "ideals are not to be discovered at all, but to be invented; not to be found but to be generated, generated as art is generated."[14] Simultaneously, Shelley was telling Europe that the poet glimpses the gigantic shadows that futurity casts upon the present. For both, the poet does not fit past events together in order to provide lessons for the future, but rather shocks us into turning our backs on the past and incites the hope that our future will be wonderfully different.

So much for Berlin's account of the romantic revolt against universalism. When this revolt was modulated into a philosophical key the result was a series of attempts to unveil an other to reason. Philosophers made such attempts because they thought of *depth* as providing a kind of legitimacy that would substitute for the legitimacy that resides in universal agreement. Agreement is, for many of the romantics, as more recently for Foucault, simply a way of procuring conformity to current beliefs and institutions. Depth does not produce agreement, but for romantics it trumps agreement.

In the dialectic that runs through the last two centuries of philosophical thought, and that Habermas summarizes in his *Philosophical Discourse*, the

---

[13] Ibid., 102–3.   [14] Ibid., 87.

universalists decry each new other to reason as endangering both rationality and human solidarity. The romantics rejoin that what has been called rationality are merely disguised attempts to eternalize custom and tradition. The universalists rightly say that to abandon the quest for intersubjective agreement is to abandon the restraints on power which have made it possible to achieve some measure of social justice. The romantics say, with equal plausibility, that to accept the idea that only what everybody can agree on can be regarded as true is to surrender to the tyranny of the past over the future.

Formulating the opposition in these terms brings me to my central thesis: that pragmatism, and its defense of Protagorean anthropocentrism, should be viewed as an alternative both to rationalism and to the idea that we can have recourse to an other to reason. The pragmatist response to the dialectic Habermas summarizes in *The Philosophical Discourse of Modernity* is to say that talk of universal validity is simply a way of dramatizing the need for intersubjective agreement, while romantic ardor and romantic depth are simply ways of dramatizing the need for novelty, the need to be imaginative.

Neither need should be elevated over, or allowed to exclude, the other. So, instead of asking epistemological questions about sources of knowledge, or metaphysical questions about what there is to be known, philosophers might be content to do what Dewey tried to do: help their fellow-citizens balance the need for consensus and the need for novelty. Suggesting how to achieve such balance is not, of course, something that philosophy professors are better at than members of other academic disciplines. To suggest ways of achieving such balance is the work of anyone with ambitions to reshape the surrounding culture. That is why carrying through on F. C. S. Schiller's humanism – his attempt to rehabilitate Protagoras' claim that man is the measure of all things – would mean giving up the idea that there is a special sort of activity called "philosophizing" that has a distinctive cultural role.

On the view of culture I am suggesting, intellectual and moral progress is achieved by making claims that seem absurd to one generation into the common sense of the later generations. The role of the intellectuals is to effect this change by explaining how the new ideas might, if tried out, solve, or dissolve, problems created by the old ones. Neither the notion of universal validity nor that of a privileged access to truth are necessary to accomplish this latter purpose. We can work toward intersubjective agreement without being lured by the promise of universal validity. We can introduce and recommend new and startling ideas without attributing them to a privileged source. What both Platonist universalists and other-to-reason romantics find most exasperating in pragmatism is its suggestion that we shall never be either purified or transfigured by drawing upon such a source, and will never do more than tinker with ourselves.

If one thinks that experimentalist tinkering is all we shall ever manage, then one will be suspicious of both universalist metaphors of grandeur and romantic metaphors of depth. For both suggest that a suggestion for further tinkering can gain strength by being tied in with something that is not, in Russell's words, merely of here and now – something like the intrinsic nature of reality or the uttermost depths of the human soul. By contrast, Berlin's view that the best we can do in politics is to iron out as many conflicts as possible exhibits the same pragmatist attitude as Kuhn's view that the best we can do in science is to resolve anomalies as they arise. But for thinkers like Russell and Nagel, universal agreement on the desirability of a political institution or the truth of a scientific theory is not, as it is for pragmatists, just a happy social circumstance, but also a sign that we are getting closer to the true nature of man or of nature.

Romantics who relish metaphors of depth are better able than universalists to resist the lures of the jigsaw-puzzle view of reality and of the correspondence theory of truth. But they often do make the mistake of which Habermas accuses them: they neglect their responsibility for making imaginative suggestions plausible by explaining how the new institution or the new theory might solve problems that the old institutions or theories could not handle. The romantic often tells us that what is needed is authenticity rather than argument, as if the fact that she has had a new idea were enough to exempt her from the responsibility of explaining the utility of that idea.

Thus when Christ is described as the way, the truth and the life, or when Heidegger tells us that Hitler is the present and future reality of Germany, the claim is that our old ideas, our old problems, and our old projects, should simply be shelved, in order that our minds may be completely taken over by the new. Instead of being awed by superhuman grandeur, we are to be awed by Promethean daring. Instead of being told that we have been elevated to the level of unchanging Truth, we are told that we have finally been put in touch with our deepest self.

If we abandon metaphors of height, we shall see neither the ability to attain universal agreement on some updated version of Newton's *Principia*, nor the need for universal respect for the provisions of the Helsinki Declaration on Human Rights, as an indication that these documents somehow correspond to reality. Both the prospect of a fully unified system of scientific explanation and that of a world civilization in which human rights are respected are inspiring. But inspirational value is obviously not a reliable indicator of validity. Both the appeal to something overarching and invulnerable and the appeal to something ineffable and exhaustibly deep, are advertising slogans, public relations gimmicks – ways of gaining our attention.

If we could come to see such appeals as gimmicks, we might become able to dispense with words like "intrinsic," "authentic," "unconditional," "legitimate," "basic," and "objective." We could get along with such banal expressions of praise or blame as "fits the data," "sounds plausible," "would do more harm than good," "offends our instincts," "might be worth a try," and "is too ridiculous to take seriously." Pragmatists who find this sort of banality sufficient think that no inspired poet or prophet should argue for the utility of his ideas from their putative source in some other to reason. Nor should any defender of the status quo argue from the fact of intersubjective agreement to the universality and necessity of the belief about which consensus has been reached. But one can still value intersubjective agreement after one has given up both the jigsaw-puzzle view of things and the idea that we possess a faculty called "reason" that is somehow attuned to the intrinsic nature of reality. One can still value novelty and imaginative power even after one has given up the romantic idea that the imagination is so attuned.

I shall conclude by returning to the contrast between the days when philosophy was central to intellectual life and our own time. The main reason for philosophy's marginalization, as I said earlier, is the same as the reason why the warfare between science and theology looks quaint – the fact that nowadays we are all commonsensically materialist and utilitarian. But there is a further reason. This is that the quarrels which, in the course of the nineteenth and twentieth centuries, gradually replaced the warfare between the gods and the giants – the quarrels between philosophy and poetry and between philosophy and sophistry – have themselves become tedious.

The intellectuals of recent times have grown weary of watching philosophical fashion swing back and forth between enthusiasts for enduring grandeur such as Russell and Nagel and celebrants of ineffable profundity like Bergson and Heidegger. It has become harder to persuade them that the fate of civilization depends either on avoiding the excesses of scientific rationalism or on guarding against the frivolous irrationalism of the littérateurs. The arguments about relativism between pragmatists like myself and those who denounce us as "deniers of truth" excite only very languid interest. The idea that the philosophical foundations of our culture need attention or repair now sounds silly, since it is a long time since anybody thought that it had foundations, philosophical or otherwise. Only the philosophy professors still take seriously the Cartesian idea of a "natural order of reasons," an ahistorical and transcultural inferential structure that dictates the priority of the questions philosophers ask to the questions other intellectuals ask.

Perhaps the best way to describe the diminishing interest in philosophy among the intellectuals is to say that the infinite is losing its charm. We are becoming commonsensical finitists – people who believe that when we die we rot, that each generation will solve old problems only by creating new ones, that our descendants will look back on much that we have done with incredulous contempt, and that progress toward greater justice and freedom is neither inevitable nor impossible. We are becoming content to see ourselves as a species of animal that makes itself up as it goes along. The secularization of high culture that thinkers like Spinoza and Kant helped bring about has put us in the habit of thinking horizontally rather than vertically – figuring out how we might arrange for a slightly better future rather than looking up to an outermost framework or down into ineffable depths. Philosophers who think all this is just as it should be can take a certain rueful satisfaction in their own steadily increasing irrelevance.

6

Philosophy as a transitional genre

REDEMPTIVE TRUTH

Questions such as "Does truth exist?" or "Do you believe in truth?" seem fatuous and pointless. Everybody knows that the difference between true and false beliefs is as important as that between nourishing and poisonous foods. Moreover, one of the principal achievements of recent analytic philosophy is to have shown that the ability to wield the concept of "true belief" is a necessary condition for being a user of language, and thus for being a rational agent.

Nevertheless, the question "Do you believe in truth or are you one of those frivolous postmodernists?" is often the first one that journalists ask intellectuals whom they are assigned to interview. That question now plays the role once played by the question "Do you believe in God, or are you one of those dangerous atheists?" Literary types are frequently told that they do not love truth sufficiently. Such admonitions are delivered in the same tones in which their predecessors were reminded that the fear of the Lord is the beginning of wisdom.

Obviously, the sense of the word "truth" invoked by that question is not the everyday one. Nobody is worried about a mere nominalization of the adjective "true." The question "Do you believe that truth exists?" is shorthand for something like "Do you think that there is a natural terminus to inquiry, a way things really are, and that understanding what that way is will tell us what to do with ourselves?"

Those who, like myself, find themselves accused of postmodernist frivolity do not think that there is such a terminus. We think that inquiry is just another name for problem-solving, and we cannot imagine inquiry into how human beings should live, into what we should make of ourselves, coming to an end. For solutions to old problems will produce fresh problems, and so on forever. As with the individual, so with both the society and the species: each stage of maturation will overcome previous dilemmas only by creating new ones.

I shall use the term "redemptive truth" for a set of beliefs which would end, once and for all, the process of reflection on what to do with ourselves. Redemptive truth, if it existed, would not be exhausted by theories about how things interact causally. It would have to fulfill a need that religion and philosophy have attempted to satisfy. That is the need to fit everything – every thing, person, event, idea, and poem – into a single context, a context that will somehow reveal itself as natural, destined, and unique. It would be the only context that would matter for purposes of shaping our lives, because it would be the only one in which those lives appear as they truly are. To believe in redemptive truth is to believe that there is something that stands to human life as elementary physical particles stand to the four elements – something that is the reality behind the appearance, the one true description of what is going on.

Hope that such a context can be found is one version of what Heidegger called the hope for authenticity – the hope to become one's own person rather than merely the creation of one's education or one's environment. As Heidegger emphasized, to achieve authenticity in this sense is not necessarily to *reject* one's past. It may instead be a matter of reinterpreting that past so as to make it more suitable for one's own purposes. But it is essential to have glimpsed one or more alternatives to the purposes that most people take for granted, and to have chosen among these alternatives – thereby, in some measure, creating yourself. As Harold Bloom tells us, the point of reading a great many books is to become aware of a great number of alternative purposes, and the point of *that* is to become an autonomous self.[1] Autonomy, in this non-Kantian and distinctively Bloomian sense, is pretty much the same thing as Heideggerian authenticity. It is the distinctive trait of the intellectual.

I shall define an intellectual as someone who yearns for Bloomian autonomy, and is lucky enough to have the money and leisure to do something about it: to visit different churches or gurus, go to different theatres or museums, and, above all, to read a lot of different books. Most human beings, even those who have the requisite money and leisure, are not intellectuals. If they read books it is not because they seek redemption but either because they wish to be entertained or distracted, or because they want to become better able to carry out some antecedent purpose. They do not read books to find out what purposes to have. The intellectuals do.

---

[1] Harold Bloom, *How to Read and Why* (New York: Scribner, 2000).

FROM RELIGION THROUGH PHILOSOPHY TO LITERATURE

Equipped with these definitions of "redemptive truth" and "intellectual," I can now state my thesis. It is that the intellectuals of the West have, since the Renaissance, progressed through three stages: they have hoped for redemption first from God, then from philosophy, and now from literature. Monotheistic religion offers hope for redemption through entering into a new relation to a supremely powerful non-human person. Belief in the articles of a creed may be only incidental to such a relationship. For philosophy, however, true belief is of the essence: redemption by philosophy would consist in acquiring a set of beliefs that represent things in the one way they truly are. Literature, finally, offers redemption through making the acquaintance of as great a variety of human beings as possible. Here again, as with religion, true belief may be of little importance.

From within a literary culture, religion and philosophy appear as literary genres. As such, they are optional. Just as an intellectual may opt to read many poems but few novels, or many novels but few poems, so he or she may read much philosophy, or much religious writing, but relatively few poems or novels. The difference between the literary intellectuals' readings of *all* these books and other readings of them is that the inhabitant of a literary culture treats books as human attempts to meet human needs, rather than as acknowledgments of the power of a being that is what it is apart from any such needs. "God" and "Truth" are, respectively, the religious and the philosophical names for that sort of being.

The transition from religion to philosophy began with the revival of Platonism in the Renaissance, the period in which humanists began asking the same questions about Christian monotheism that Socrates had asked about Hesiod's pantheon. Socrates had suggested to Euthyphro that the real question was not whether one's actions were pleasing to the gods, but rather which gods held the correct views about what actions ought to be done. When that latter question was once again taken seriously, the road lay open to Kant's conclusion that even the Holy One of the Gospels must be judged in the light of one's own conscience.

The transition from a philosophical to a literary culture began shortly after Kant, about the time that Hegel warned us that philosophy paints its gray on gray only when a form of life has grown old. That remark helped the generation of Kierkegaard and Marx realize that philosophy was never going to fill the redemptive role that Hegel himself had claimed for it. Hegel's supremely ambitious claims for philosophy were counter-productive. His System was no sooner published than it began to be read as a *reductio ad absurdum* of a certain form of intellectual life.

Since Hegel's time, the intellectuals have been losing faith in philosophy. This amounts to losing faith in the idea that redemption can come in the form of true beliefs. In the literary culture which has been emerging during the last two hundred years, the question "Is it true?" has yielded to the question "What's new?" Heidegger thought that that change was a decline, a shift from serious thinking to mere gossipy curiosity.[2] On the account I am offering, however, this change is an advance. It represents a desirable replacement of bad questions like "What is Being?", "What is really real?", and "What is man?" with the sensible question "Does anybody have any new ideas about what we human beings might manage to make of ourselves?"

In its pure form, undiluted by philosophy, religion is a relation to a non-human person. This relation may be one of adoring obedience, or ecstatic communion, or quiet confidence, or some combination of these. But it is only when religion has become mingled with philosophy that this non-cognitive redemptive relation to a person begins to be mediated by a creed. Only when the God of the philosophers has begun to replace the God of Abraham, Isaac, and Jacob is correct belief thought to be essential to salvation.

For religion in its uncontaminated form, argument is no more important than is belief. To become a New Being in Christ is, as Kierkegaard insisted, not the same sort of thing as being forced to grant the truth of a proposition in the course of Socratic reflection, or as the outcome of Hegelian dialectic. Insofar as religion requires belief in a proposition, it is, as Locke said, belief based on the credit of the proposer rather than backed by argument. But beliefs are irrelevant to the special devotion of the illiterate believer to Demeter, or to the Virgin of Guadelupe. It is this irrelevance that intellectuals like St. Paul, Kierkegaard, and Karl Barth – spiritual athletes who relish the thought that their faith is a folly to the Greeks – hope to recapture.

To take seriously the idea that redemption can come in the form of true beliefs, one must believe both that the life that cannot be successfully argued for is not worth living, and that persistent argument will lead all inquirers to the same set of beliefs. Religion and literature, insofar as they are uncontaminated by philosophy, share neither of these convictions.

[2] See the discussions of *das Gerede* and *die Neugier* in sections 35–6 of *Sein und Zeit*. Martin Heidegger, *Sein und Zeit* (Tübingen: Max Niemeyer Verlag, 1967), 167–73.

Uncontaminated religion may be monotheistic in the sense that a community may think it essential to worship only one particular god. But the idea that there can *be* only one god, that polytheism is contrary to reason, is one that can only take hold after philosophy has convinced us that every human being's reflections must lead to the same outcome.

As I am using the terms "literature" and "literary culture", a culture which has substituted literature for both religion and philosophy finds redemption neither in a non-cognitive relation to a non-human person nor in a cognitive relation to propositions, but in non-cognitive relations to other human beings, relations mediated by human artifacts such as books and buildings, paintings and songs. These artifacts provide a sense of alternative ways of being human. This sort of culture drops a presupposition common to religion and philosophy – that redemption must come from one's relation to something that is not just one more human creation.

Kierkegaard rightly said that philosophy began to set itself up as a rival to religion when Socrates suggested that our self-knowledge was a knowledge of God – that we had no need of help from a non-human person, because the truth was already within us. But literature began to set itself up as a rival to philosophy when people like Cervantes and Shakespeare began to suspect that human beings were, and ought to be, so diverse that there is no point in pretending that they all carry a single truth deep in their bosoms. Santayana pointed to this seismic cultural shift in his essay "The Absence of Religion in Shakespeare."[3] That essay might equally well have been called "The Absence of either Religion or Philosophy in Shakespeare" or simply "The Absence of Truth in Shakespeare."

I suggested earlier that "Do you believe in truth?" can be given both sense and urgency if it is reformulated as "Do you think that there is a single set of beliefs which can serve a redemptive role in the lives of all human beings, which can be rationally justified to all human beings under optimal communicative conditions, and which will thus form the natural terminus of inquiry?" To answer "yes" to this reformulated question is to take philosophy as the guide of life. It is to agree with Socrates that there are beliefs that are both susceptible of rational justification and capable of showing us what to do with our lives. The premise of philosophy is that there is a way things really are – a way humanity and the rest of the universe are and always will be, independent of any merely contingent human needs and interests.

---

[3] George Santayana, "The Absence of Religion in Shakespeare" (1900) in *Interpretations of Poetry and Religion*, ed. William G. Holzberger and Herman J. Saatkamp, Jr. (Cambridge, MA: MIT Press, 1990), 91–101.

It is not clear that Homer, or even Sophocles, could have made sense of this suggestion. Before Plato dreamt them up, the constellation of ideas necessary to make it intelligible was not available. Cervantes and Shakespeare understood Plato's suggestion, but they distrusted his motives. Their distrust led them to play up diversity and downplay commonality – to underline the differences between human beings rather than to look for a common human nature. This change of emphasis weakens the grip of the Platonic assumption that all these different sorts of people should be arranged in a hierarchy, judged on the basis of their relative success at attaining a single goal. Initiatives like Cervantes' and Shakespeare's helped create a new sort of intellectual – one who does not take the availability of redemptive truth for granted, and is not much interested in whether either God or Truth exist.

This change helped create today's high culture, one to which religion and philosophy have become marginal. To be sure, there are still numerous religious intellectuals, and even more philosophical ones. But bookish youngsters in search of redemption nowadays look first to novels, plays, and poems. The sort of books which the eighteenth century thought of as marginal have become central. The authors of *Rasselas* and of *Candide* helped bring about, but could hardly have foreseen, a culture in which the novel has become the central vehicle of moral instruction.

For members of the literary culture, redemption is to be achieved by getting in touch with the present limits of the human imagination. That is why a literary culture is always in search of novelty, rather than trying to escape from the temporal to the eternal. It is a premise of this culture that though the imagination has present limits, these limits are capable of being extended forever.[4] The imagination endlessly consumes its own artifacts. It is as subject to time and chance as are the flies and the worms, but while it endures and preserves the memory of its past, it will continue to transcend its previous limits.

The sort of person I am calling a "literary intellectual" thinks that a life that is not lived close to the present limits of the human imagination is not worth living. For the Socratic idea of self-examination and self-knowledge, the literary intellectual substitutes the idea of enlarging the self by becoming acquainted with still more ways of being human. She thinks that the more books you read, the more ways of being human you have considered, the more human you become – the less tempted by dreams of an escape from time and chance, the more convinced that we humans have nothing

4 I enlarge on this point in "Pragmatism and romanticism," 105–19 of this volume.

to rely on save one another. The great virtue of the literary culture is that it tells young intellectuals that the only source of redemption is the human imagination, and that this fact should occasion pride rather than despair.

From the point of view of this culture, philosophy was a transitional stage in the development of increased self-reliance. Philosophy's attempt to replace God with Truth requires the conviction that a set of beliefs which can be justified to all human beings will also fill all the needs of all human beings. But that idea was an inherently unstable compromise between the masochistic urge to submit to the non-human and the need to take proper pride in our humanity. Redemptive truth is an attempt to find something which is not made by human beings but to which human beings have a special, privileged relation not shared by the animals. The intrinsic nature of things is like a god in its independence of us, and yet – so Socrates and Hegel tell us – self-knowledge will suffice to get us in touch with it. One way to see the quest for knowledge of such a quasi-divinity is as Sartre saw it: it is a futile passion, a foredoomed attempt to become a for-itself-in-itself. But it would be better to see philosophy as one of our greatest imaginative achievements, on a par with the invention of the gods.

Philosophers have often described religion as a primitive and insufficiently reflective attempt to philosophize. But, as I said earlier, a fully self-conscious literary culture would think of both religion and philosophy as largely obsolete, yet glorious, literary genres. They are genres in which it is now becoming increasingly difficult to write, but their replacements might never have emerged had they not been read as swerves away from religion, and later as swerves away from philosophy. Religion and philosophy were stepping-stones, stages in a continuing process of maturation.

THE CULMINATION OF PHILOSOPHY: IDEALIST AND MATERIALIST METAPHYSICS

In the hope of making this account of philosophy as a transitional genre more plausible, I shall say something about the two great movements in which philosophy culminated. Philosophy began to come into its own when the thinkers of the Enlightenment no longer had to hide themselves behind the sort of masks worn by Descartes, Hobbes, and Spinoza, and were able to be openly atheistic. These masks could be dropped after the French Revolution. That event, by making it plausible that human beings might build a new heaven and a new earth, made God seem far less necessary than before.

That newfound self-reliance produced two great metaphysical systems. First came the metaphysics of German idealism, and second, the reaction against idealism which was materialist metaphysics, the apotheosis of the results of natural science. The first movement belongs to the past. Materialist metaphysics, however, is still with us. It is, in fact, pretty much the only version of redemptive truth presently on offer. It is philosophy's last hurrah, its last attempt to avoid being demoted to the status of a literary genre.

This is not the place to recapitulate the rise and fall of German idealism, nor to eulogize what Heidegger called "the greatness, breadth, and originality of that spiritual world." It suffices for my present purposes to say that Hegel, the most original of the idealists, believed himself to have given the first satisfactory proof of the existence of God, and the first satisfactory solution to the traditional theological problem of evil. He was, in his own eyes, the first fully successful natural theologian – the first to reconcile Socrates with Christ by showing that the Incarnation was not an act of grace on God's part but rather a necessity. "God," Hegel said, "had to have a Son" because eternity is nothing without time, God nothing without man, Truth nothing without its historical emergence.

In Hegel's eyes, the Platonic hope of escape from the temporal to the eternal was a primitive, albeit necessary, stage of philosophical thinking – a stage that the Christian doctrine of Incarnation has helped us outgrow. Now that Kant has opened the way to seeing mind and world as interdependent, Hegel believed, we are in a position to see that philosophy can bridge the Kantian distinction between the phenomenal and the noumenal, just as Christ's stay on earth overcame the distinction between God and man.

Idealist metaphysics seemed both true and demonstrable to some of the best minds of the nineteenth century. Josiah Royce, for example, wrote book after book arguing that Hegel was right: simple armchair reflection on the presuppositions of common sense, exactly the sort of philosophizing that Socrates practiced and commended, will lead you to recognize the truth of pantheism as surely as reflection on geometrical diagrams will lead you to the Pythagorean Theorem. But the verdict of the literary culture on this metaphysics was nicely formulated by Kierkegaard when he said that if Hegel had written at the end of his books that "this was all just a thought experiment" he would have been the greatest thinker who ever lived, but that, as it was, he was merely a buffoon.[5]

---

[5] S. Kierkegaard, *Papers and Journals: A Selection*, trans. Alastair Hannay (London: Penguin, 1996), 182.

I would rephrase Kierkegaard's point as follows: if Hegel had been able to stop thinking that he had given us redemptive truth, and had claimed instead to have given us something *better* than redemptive truth – namely a way of holding all the previous products of the human imagination together in a single vision – he would have been the first philosopher to admit that a better cultural product than philosophy had come on the market. He would have been the first self-consciously to replace philosophy with literature, just as Socrates and Plato were the first self-consciously to replace religion with philosophy. But instead Hegel presented himself (at least part of the time) as having discovered Absolute Truth, and men like Royce took his idealism with a seriousness which now strikes us as both endearing and ludicrous.[6] So it was left to Nietzsche, in *The Birth of Tragedy*, to suggest that the premise common to Socrates and Hegel should be rejected, and that the invention of the idea of self-knowledge was a great imaginative achievement that had outlived its usefulness.

Between Hegel's time and Nietzsche's, however, there arose the second of the great metaphysical systems. It bore the same relation to Democritus and Lucretius that German idealism had borne to Parmenides and Plotinus. It tried to put natural science in the place of both religion and Socratic reflection – to see empirical inquiry as providing exactly what Socrates thought it could never give us: redemptive truth.

By the middle of the nineteenth century, it had become clear that mathematics and empirical science were going to be the only areas of culture in which one might conceivably hope to get unanimous, rational agreement – the only disciplines able to provide beliefs unlikely to be overturned as history rolled along. They were the only sources of cumulative results, and thus of plausible candidates for the status of insight into the way things are in themselves. Unified natural science still seems to many intellectuals to be the answer to Socrates' prayers.

On the other hand, pretty much everybody in the nineteenth century had come to agree with Hume that Plato's model of cognitive success – mathematics – was never going to offer us anything redemptive. Only a few flaky neo-Pythagoreans still saw mathematics as having more than practical and aesthetic interest. So nineteenth-century positivists drew the moral that the only other source of rational agreement and unshakable truth, empirical science, just *had* to have a redemptive function. Since philosophy had always taught that an account that bound everything together into a

---

6 I discuss Royce's treatment of Hegel, and contrast it with Dewey's, Sellars' and Brandom's in "Some American Uses of Hegel," in *Das Interesse des Denkens: Hegel aus heutiger Sicht*, ed. Wolfgang Welsch and Klaus Urewig (Paderborn, Fink Verlag, 2003).

coherent whole would have redemptive value, and since the collapse of idealist metaphysics had left materialism as the only account left standing, the positivists concluded that natural science was all the philosophy we would ever need. (Or at least that, as Quine once put it, philosophy of natural science is philosophy enough.)

This project of giving redemptive status to empirical science still appeals to two sorts of present-day intellectuals. The first is the kind of philosopher who insists that natural science attains objective truth in a way that no other portion of culture does. These philosophers usually insist that the natural scientist is the paradigmatic possessor of intellectual virtues, notably the love of truth, which are scarcely to seek among the inhabitants of the literary culture. The second is the kind of scientist who announces that the latest work in his discipline has deep philosophical implications: that advances in evolutionary biology or cognitive science, for example, do more than tell us how things work and what they are made of.[7] They also tell us, these scientists say, something about how to live, about human nature, about what we really are.

I shall discuss these two groups of people separately. The problem with the attempt by philosophers to treat the empirical scientist as a paradigm of intellectual virtue is that the astrophysicists' love of truth seems no different from that of the classical philologist or the archive-oriented historian. All these people are trying hard to get something right. So, for that matter, are the master carpenter, the skilled accountant, and the careful surgeon. The need to get it right is central to all these people's sense of who they are, of what makes their lives worthwhile.

It is certainly the case that without people whose lives are centered around this need we should never have had much in the way of civilization. The free play of the imagination is possible only because of the substructure literal-minded people have built. No artisans, no poets. No engineers to provide the technology of an industrialized world, few people with sufficient money to send their children off to be initiated into a literary culture. But there is no reason to take the contributions of the natural scientist to this substructure as having a moral or philosophical significance that is lacking in those of the carpenter, the accountant, and the surgeon.

John Dewey thought that the fact that the mathematical physicist enjoys greater prestige than the skilled artisan is an unfortunate legacy of the Platonic–Aristotelian distinction between eternal truths and empirical

---

7   I discuss this sort of attempt to replace philosophy with science in "Philosophy-envy," *Daedelus* (Fall 2004), 18–24.

truth, the elevation of leisured contemplation above sweaty practicality. His point might be restated by saying that the prestige of the scientific theorist is an unfortunate legacy of the Socratic idea that what we can all, as a result of rational debate, agree to be true is a reflection of something more than the fact of agreement – the idea that intersubjective agreement under ideal communicative conditions is a token of correspondence to the way things really are.

The current debate among analytic philosophers about whether truth is a matter of correspondence to reality, and the parallel debate over Kuhn's denial that science is asymptotically approaching the really real, are disputes between those who see empirical science as fulfilling at least some of Plato's hopes and those who think that those hopes should be abandoned. The former philosophers take it as a matter of unquestionable common sense that adding a brick to the edifice of knowledge is a matter of more accurately aligning thought and language with the way things really are. Their philosophical opponents take this so-called common sense to be merely what Dewey thought it: a relic of the religious hope that redemption can come from contact with something non-human and supremely powerful. To abandon the latter idea, the idea that links philosophy with religion, would mean acknowledging both the ability of scientists to add bricks to the edifice of knowledge and the practical utility of scientific theories for prediction while insisting on the irrelevance of both achievements to searches for redemption.

These debates among the analytic philosophers have little to do with the activities of the second sort of people – the ones I have labeled "materialist metaphysicians," a group that includes scientists who think that the public at large should take an interest in the latest discoveries about the genome, or cerebral localization, or child development, or quantum mechanics. Such scientists are good at dramatizing the contrast between the old scientific theories and the shiny new ones, but they are bad at explaining why we should care about the difference. They are like critics of art and literature who are good at pointing to the differences between the paintings and poems of a few years ago and those being produced now, but bad at explaining why these changes are important.

There is, however, a difference between such critics and the sort of scientists I am talking about. The former usually have the sense to avoid the mistake Clement Greenberg made when he claimed that what fills the art galleries this year is what all the ages have been leading up to, and that there is an inner logic to the history of the products of the imagination that has now reached its destined outcome. But the scientists still retain the idea that the latest product of the scientific imagination is not merely an improvement on what was previously imagined, but is also closer to the intrinsic nature of things. That is why they found Kuhn's suggestion that they think of themselves as problem-solvers so insulting. Their rhetoric remains "We have substituted Reality for Appearance!" rather than "We have solved some long-standing problems!" or "We have made it new!"

The trouble with this rhetoric is that it puts a glossy metaphysical varnish on a useful scientific product. It suggests that we have not only learned more about how to predict and control our environment and ourselves but also done something more – something of redemptive significance. But the successive achievements of modern science exhausted their philosophical significance when they made clear that there are no spooks – that a causal account of the relations between spatiotemporal events did not require the operation of non-physical forces.

Modern science, in short, has helped us see that if you want a metaphysics, then a materialistic metaphysics is the only one to have. But it has not given us any reason to think that we need a metaphysics. The need for metaphysics lasted only as long as the hope for redemptive truth lasted. But by the time that materialism triumphed over idealism, this hope had waned. So the reaction of most contemporary intellectuals to gee-whiz announcements of new scientific discoveries is "That's nice, but is it really so important?" This reaction is not, as C. P. Snow thought, a matter of pretentious and ignorant littérateurs condescending to honest, hard-working empirical inquirers. It is the perfectly sensible reaction of someone who is puzzled about ends and is offered information only about means.

The literary culture's attitude toward materialist metaphysics is, and should be, something like this: whereas both Plato's and Hegel's attempts to give us something more interesting than physics were laudable attempts to find a redemptive discipline to put in the place of religion, a materialist metaphysics is just physics getting above itself. Modern science is a gloriously imaginative way of describing things, brilliantly successful for the purpose for which it was developed – namely, predicting and controlling phenomena. But it should not pretend to have the sort of redemptive power claimed by its defeated rival, idealist metaphysics.

Questions of the "Is it really so important?" sort began to be put to scientists by the literary intellectuals of the nineteenth century. These thinkers were gradually learning, as Nietzsche was to put it, to see science through the optic of art, and art through that of life. Nietzsche's master Emerson was one such figure, and Baudelaire another. Although many of these intellectuals thought of themselves as having transcended romanticism, they nevertheless could agree with Schiller that the further maturation of mankind will be achieved through what Kant called "the aesthetic" rather than through what he called "the ethical." They could also endorse Shelley's claim that the great task of human emancipation from priests and tyrants could have been accomplished without "Locke, Hume, Gibbon, Voltaire and Rousseau" but that

> it exceeds all imagination to conceive what would have been the moral condition of the world if neither Dante, Petrarch, Boccaccio, Chaucer, Shakespeare, Calderon, Lord Bacon nor Milton, had ever existed; if Raphael and Michael Angelo had never been born; if the Hebrew poetry had never been translated, if a revival of the study of Greek literature had never taken place, if no monuments of ancient sculpture had been handed down to us, and if the poetry and the religion of the ancient world had been extinguished together with its belief.[8]

What Shelley said of Locke and Hume he might also have said of Galileo, Newton, and Lavoisier. What each of them said was well argued, useful, and true. But the sort of truth that is the product of successful argument cannot, Shelley thought, improve our moral condition. Of Galileo's and Locke's productions we may reasonably ask "Yes, but is it true?" But there is little point, Shelley rightly thought, in asking this question about Milton. "Objectively true," in the sense of "such as to gain permanent assent from all future members of the relevant expert culture," is not a notion that will ever be useful to literary intellectuals, for the progress of the literary imagination is not a matter of accumulating *results*.

We philosophers who are accused of not having sufficient respect for objective truth – the ones whom the materialist metaphysicians like to call "postmodern relativists" – think of objectivity as intersubjectivity. So we can happily agree that scientists achieve objective truth in a way that littérateurs do not. But we explain this phenomenon sociologically rather than philosophically – by pointing out that natural scientists are organized into expert cultures in a way that literary intellectuals should not try to organize themselves. You can have an expert culture if you agree on what you want to get, but not if you are wondering what sort of life you ought to desire. We know what purposes scientific theories are supposed to serve. But we are not now, and never will be, in a position to say what purposes novels, poems, and plays are supposed to serve. For such books continually redefine our purposes.

---

[8] Percy Bysshe Shelley, *Shelley's Poetry and Prose*, ed. Donald Reiman and Sharon Powers (New York: Norton, 1977), 695.

THE LITERARY CULTURE AND DEMOCRATIC POLITICS

I shall close by turning to the relation of the literary culture to politics. The quarrel between those who see the rise of that culture as a good thing and those who distrust it is largely a quarrel about what sort of high culture will do most to create and sustain the climate of tolerance that flourishes best in democratic societies.

Those who argue that a science-centered culture is best for this purpose set the love of truth over against hatred, passion, prejudice, superstition, and all the other forces of unreason from which Socrates and Plato claimed that philosophy could save us. But those on the other side of the argument are dubious about the Platonic opposition between reason and unreason. They see no need to relate the difference between tolerant conversability and stiff-necked unwillingness to hear the other side to a distinction between a higher part of ourselves that enables us to achieve redemption by getting in touch with non-human reality and another part which is merely animal.

The strong point of those who think that a proper respect for objective truth, and thus for science, is important for sustaining a climate of tolerance and good will is that argument is essential to both science and democracy. Both when choosing between alternative scientific theories and when choosing between alternative pieces of legislation, we want people to base their decisions on arguments – arguments that start from premises which can be made plausible to anyone who cares to look into the matter.

The priests rarely provided such arguments, nor do the literary intellectuals. So it is tempting to think of a preference for literature over science as a rejection of argument in favor of oracular pronouncements – a regression to something uncomfortably like the pre-philosophical, religious stage of Western intellectual life. Seen from this perspective, the rise of a literary culture looks like the treason of the clerks.

But those of us who rejoice in the emergence of the literary culture can counter this charge by saying that although argumentation is essential for projects of social cooperation, redemption is an individual, private, matter. Just as the rise of religious toleration depended on making a distinction between the needs of society and the needs of the individual, and on saying that religion was not necessary for the former, so the literary culture asks us to disjoin political deliberation from projects of redemption. This means acknowledging that private hopes for authenticity and autonomy should be left at home when the citizens of a democratic society foregather to deliberate about what is to be done.

Making this move amounts to saying: the only way in which science is relevant to politics is that the natural scientists provide a good example of social cooperation, of an expert culture in which argumentation flourishes. They thereby provide a model for political deliberation – a model of honesty, tolerance, and trust. This ability is a matter of procedure rather than results, which is why gangs of carpenters or teams of engineers can provide as good a model as does the Royal Society. The difference between reasoned agreement on how to solve a problem that has arisen in the course of constructing a house or a bridge and reasoned agreement on what physicists sometimes call "a theory of everything" is, in this context, irrelevant. For whatever the last theory of everything tells us, it will do nothing to provide either political guidance or individual redemption.

The claim I have just made may seem arrogant and dogmatic, for it is certainly the case that some results of empirical inquiry have, in the past, made a difference to our self-image. Galileo and Darwin expelled various varieties of spooks by showing the sufficiency of a materialist account. They thereby made it much easier for us to move from a religious high culture to a secular, merely philosophical one. So my argument on behalf of the literary culture depends on the claim that getting rid of spooks, of causal agency that does not supervene on the behavior of elementary particles, has exhausted the utility of natural science for either redemptive or political purposes.

I do not put this claim forward as a result of philosophical reasoning or insight, but merely as a prediction about what the future holds in store. A similar prediction led the philosophers of the eighteenth century to think that the Christian religion had done about all that it could for the moral condition of humanity, and that it was time to put religion behind us and to put metaphysics, either idealist or materialist, in its place. When literary intellectuals assume that natural science has nothing to offer us except an edifying example of tolerant conversability, they are doing something analogous to what the *philosophes* did when they said that even the best of the priests had nothing to offer us save edifying examples of charity and selflessness. Reducing science from a possible source of redemptive truth to a model of rational cooperation is the contemporary analogue of the reduction of the Gospels from a recipe for attaining eternal happiness to a compendium of sound moral advice. That was the sort of reduction that Kant and Jefferson recommended, and that liberal Protestants of the last two centuries have gradually achieved.

To put this last point another way: both the Christian religion and materialist metaphysics turned out to be self-consuming artifacts. The need for religious orthodoxy was undermined by St. Paul's insistence on the primacy of love. Christians gradually realized that a religion of love could not ask everyone to recite the same creed. The need for a metaphysics was undermined by the ability of modern science to see the human mind as an exceptionally complex nervous system and thus to see itself in pragmatic rather than metaphysical terms. Science showed us how to see empirical inquiry as the use of this extra physiological equipment to gain steadily greater mastery over the environment, rather than as a way of replacing appearance with reality. Just as the eighteenth century became able to see Christianity not as a revelation from on high but as continuous with Socratic reflection, so the twentieth century became able to see natural science not as revealing the intrinsic nature of reality but as continuous with the sort of practical problem-solving that engineers are good at.

To give up the idea that there is an intrinsic nature of reality to be discovered either by the priests, or the philosophers, or the scientists, is to disjoin the need for redemption from the search for universal agreement. It is to give up the search for an accurate account of human nature, and thus for a recipe for leading the Good Life for Man. Once these searches are given up, expanding the limits of the human imagination steps forward to assume the role that obedience to the divine will played in a religious culture, and the role that discovery of what is really real played in a philosophical culture. But this substitution is no reason to give up the search for a single utopian form of political life – the Good Global Society.

7

Pragmatism and romanticism

At the heart of pragmatism is the refusal to accept the correspondence theory of truth and the idea that true beliefs are accurate representations of reality. At the heart of romanticism is the thesis of the priority of imagination over reason – the claim that reason can only follow paths that the imagination has broken. These two movements are both reactions against the idea that there is something non-human out there with which human beings need to get in touch. In this chapter I want to trace the connections between James' and Dewey's repudiation of what Heidegger called "the Western ontotheological tradition" and Shelley's claim that poetry "is at once the center and the circumference of knowledge."

I shall begin with the quest for the really real. Common sense distinguishes between the apparent color of a thing and its real color, between the apparent motions of heavenly bodies and their real motions, between non-dairy creamer and real cream, and between fake Rolexes and real ones. But only those who have studied philosophy ask whether real Rolexes are *really* real. No one else takes seriously Plato's distinction between Reality with a capital R and Appearance with a capital A. That distinction is the charter of metaphysics.

Parmenides jump-started the Western philosophical tradition by dreaming up the notion of Reality with a capital R. He took the trees, the stars, the human beings, and the gods and rolled them all together into a well-rounded blob called "the One." He then stood back from this blob and proclaimed it the only thing worth knowing about, but forever unknowable by mortals. Plato was enchanted by this hint of something even more august and unapproachable than Zeus, but he was more optimistic. Plato suggested that a few gifted mortals might, by modeling themselves on Socrates, gain access to what he called "the really real." Ever since Plato, there have been people who worried about whether we can gain access to Reality, or whether the finitude of our cognitive faculties makes such access impossible.

Nobody, however, worries about whether we have cognitive access to trees, stars, cream, or wristwatches. We know how to tell a justified belief about such things from an unjustified one. If the word "reality" were used simply as a name for the *aggregate* of all such things, no problem about access to it could have arisen. The word would never have been capitalized. But when it is given the sense that Parmenides and Plato gave it, nobody can say what would count as a justification for a belief about the thing denoted by that term. We know how to correct our beliefs about the colors of physical objects, or about the motions of planets, or the provenance of wristwatches, but we have no idea how to correct our metaphysical beliefs about the ultimate nature of things. Metaphysics is not a discipline, but a sort of intellectual playspace.

The difference between ordinary things and Reality is that as we learned how to use the word "tree" we automatically acquired lots of true beliefs about trees. As Donald Davidson has argued, most of our beliefs about such things as trees have to be true. For if somebody thinks that trees are typically blue in color, and that they never grow higher than two feet, we shall conclude that whatever she may be thinking about, it is not trees. Davidson's point was that there have to be many commonly accepted truths about a thing before we can raise the question of whether any particular belief about it is erroneous. Once that question has been raised, any of those commonly accepted truths can be put in doubt, though obviously not all of them at once. One can only dissent from common sense about a thing if one is willing to accept most of the rest of what common sense has to say about it. Otherwise, one would not be able to say what one was talking about.

When it comes to Reality, however, there is no such thing as common sense. Unlike the case of trees, there are no platitudes accepted by both the vulgar and the learned. In some intellectual circles, you can get general agreement that the ultimate nature of Reality is atoms and void. In others, you can get a consensus that it is an immaterial, non-spatiotemporal, divine being. The reason why quarrels among metaphysicians about the nature of Reality seem so ludicrous is that each of them feels free to pick a few of her favorite things and to claim ontological privilege for them.

Ontology remains popular because we are still reluctant to yield to the Romantic's argument that the imagination sets the bounds of thought. At the heart of both philosophy's ancient quarrel with poetry and the more recent quarrel between the scientific and the literary cultures is the fear of both philosophers and scientists that the imagination may indeed go all the way down. This fear is entirely justified, for the imagination is the source of language, and thought is impossible without language. Revulsion against this claim has caused philosophers to become obsessed by the need to achieve an access to reality unmediated by, and prior to, the use of language.[1] So before we can rid ourselves of ontology we are going to have to get rid of the hope for such non-linguistic access. This will entail getting rid of the idea of the human mind as divided into a good part that puts us in touch with the really real and a bad part that engages in self-stimulation and auto-suggestion.

To get rid of this cluster of bad ideas we need to think of reason not as a truth-tracking faculty but as a social practice – the practice of enforcing social norms on the use of marks and noises, thereby making it possible to use words rather than blows as a way of getting things done. To be rational is simply to conform to those norms. This is why what counts as rational in one society may count as irrational in another. The idea that some societies are more rational than others presupposes that we have some access to a source of normativity other than the practices of the people around us. The hope to attain such access is another form of the hope to escape from language by achieving non-linguistic access to the real.

We should try to think of imagination not as a faculty that generates mental images but as the ability to change social practices by proposing advantageous new uses of marks and noises. To be imaginative, as opposed to being merely fantastical, one must both do something new and be lucky enough to have that novelty adopted by one's fellows – incorporated into their ways of doing things. The distinction between fantasy and imagination is between novelties that do not get taken up and put to use by one's fellows and those that do. People whose novelties we cannot appropriate and utilize we call foolish, or perhaps insane. Those whose ideas strike us as useful we hail as geniuses. That is why people like Socrates and Nietzsche often seemed like lunatics to some of their contemporaries and like heroes to others.

On the account of human capacities I am sketching, the use of persuasion rather than force is an innovation comparable to the beaver's dam. Language is a social practice that began when it dawned on some genius that we could use noises, rather than physical compulsion – persuasion rather than force – to get other humans to cooperate with us. Language got off the ground not by people giving names to things they were already thinking about, but by proto-humans using noises in innovative ways, just

---

[1] I discuss this point in the concluding pages of "Wittgenstein and the linguistic turn," 160–75 of this volume.

as the proto-beavers got the practice of building dams off the ground by moving sticks and mud around in innovative ways. Language was, over the millennia, enlarged and rendered more flexible. This was done not by adding the names of abstract objects to those of concrete objects, but by finding ways to use marks and noises in ways not directly connected with environmental exigencies. The distinction between the concrete and the abstract is simply the distinction between expressions that are useful for making perceptual reports and those unsuitable for such use. Which expressions are which varies with circumstance.

On this view, expressions like "gravity" and "inalienable human rights" should not be thought of as names of entities whose nature remains mysterious, but as noises and marks, the use of which by various geniuses have given rise to bigger and better social practices. Intellectual and moral progress is not a matter of getting closer to an antecedent goal, but of surpassing the past. The arts and the sciences improved over the millennia because our more ingenious ancestors did novel things not only with seeds, clay and metallic ores, but with noises and marks. On the pragmatist view I am putting forward, what we call "increased knowledge" should not be thought of as increased access to the Real, but as increased ability to *do* things – to take part in social practices that make possible richer and fuller human lives. This increased richness is not the effect of a magnetic attraction exerted on the human mind by the really real, nor by reason's ability to penetrate the veil of appearance. It is a relation between the human present and the human past, not a relation between the human and the non-human.

The view that I have just summarized has often been called "linguistic idealism." But that term confuses idealism, which is a metaphysical thesis about the ultimate nature of reality, with romanticism, which is a thesis about the nature of human progress. The latter is the view that Shelley put forward when he wrote that "the imagination is the chief instrument of the good," a dictum that John Dewey was to quote with approval.

William James summarized the romantic view of progress in the following passage:

Mankind does nothing save through initiatives on the part of inventors, great or small, and imitations by the rest of us – these are the sole factors active in human progress. Individuals of genius show the way, and set the patterns, which common people then adopt and follow. *The rivalry of the patterns is the history of the world.*[2]

[2] William James, "Essays, Comments, and Reviews," in *The Works of William James*, ed. Frederick Burkhardt (Cambridge, MA: Harvard University Press, 1987), 109.

James is echoing Emerson's essay "Circles." "The life of man," Emerson writes there,

is an ever-expanding circle, which, from a ring imperceptibly small, rushes on all sides outwards to new and larger circles, and that without end. The extent to which this generation of circles, wheel without wheel, will go, depends on the force or truth of the individual soul . . . Every ultimate fact is only the first of a new series . . . *There is no outside, no enclosing wall, no circumference to us.* [Emphasis added.] The man finishes his story – how good! how final! How it puts a new face on all things! He fills the sky. Lo! On the other side rises also a man and draws a circle around the circle we had just pronounced the outline of the sphere. Then already is our first speaker not man, but only a first speaker. His only address is forthwith to draw a circle outside of his antagonist . . . In the thought of tomorrow there is a power to upheave all thy creed, all the creeds, all the literatures of the nations . . . Men walk as prophecies of the next age.[3]

The most important claim Emerson makes in this essay is that there is no enclosing wall called "the Real." There is nothing outside language to which language attempts to become adequate. Every human achievement is simply a launching pad for a greater achievement. We shall never find descriptions so perfect that imaginative redescription will become pointless.

As James echoed Emerson, so Emerson was echoing Shelley and Coleridge. They too had urged that men should walk as prophecies of the next age, rather than in the fear of God or in the light of Reason. Shelley, in his "Defence of Poetry," deliberately and explicitly enlarged the meaning of the term "Poetry." That word, he said, "may be defined as 'the expression of the Imagination.'" In this wider sense, Shelley continued, poetry is "connate with the origin of man"[4] and is "the influence which is moved not, but moves".[5] It is "something divine . . . at once the center and the circumference of knowledge; it is that which comprehends all science, and that to which science must be referred. It is at the same time the root and blossom of all other systems of thought."[6] Just as the Enlightenment had capitalized and deified Reason, so Shelley and other Romantics capitalized and deified Imagination.

Nietzsche was, like Dewey and James, an admirer of Emerson's. Between the three of them, the romantic view of progress began to get disentangled from the idealists' claim that the intrinsic nature of reality is Spirit rather than Matter. But Nietzsche's contribution was particularly vital. It had been

---

[3] Ralph Waldo Emerson, *Essays and Lectures* (New York: Library of America, 1983), 405.
[4] Percy Bysshe Shelley, "Defence of Poetry," in *Shelley's Poetry and Prose*, ed. Donald Reiman and Sharon Powers (New York: Norton, 1977), 480.   [5] Ibid., 508.   [6] Ibid., 503.

easy for people like Coleridge to run together romanticism with idealist metaphysics – a temptation to which Emerson himself occasionally succumbed. For a metaphysics of Spirit seemed the natural concomitant of the claim that there is no description of things that cannot be transcended and replaced by another, more imaginative description. But in *The Birth of Tragedy* Nietzsche restaged the quarrel between poetry and philosophy. By treating Socrates as one more mythmaker rather than as someone who employed reason to break free of myth, he let us see Parmenides and Plato as all-too-strong poets.

Nietzsche's way of looking at the philosophical tradition that those two had initiated made it possible to see both German idealism and British empiricism as outgrowths of the urge to find unmediated access to the real. Nietzsche helped us think of this urge as the product of a cowardly unwillingness to acknowledge our finitude. He portrayed both movements as hoping to find something unredescribable, something that would trump poetry.

In his later work, Nietzsche echoed Schiller and Shelley when he urged us to become "the poets of our own lives" (*die Dichter unseres Lebens*). But he wanted to go further. He says over and over again that the world in which those lives are lived is a creation of the human imagination. In *The Gay Science* he summarized his criticism of Socrates and Plato in the following passage:

[The higher human being deludes himself]: he calls his nature contemplative and thereby overlooks the fact that he is also the actual poet and ongoing author of life [*der eigentlich Dichter und Fortdichter des Lebens*] . . . It is we, the thinking-sensing ones [*die Denkend-Empfindenden*] who really and continually make something that is not yet there: the whole perpetually growing world of valuations, colours, weights, perspectives, scales, affirmations, and negations. This poem that we have invented is constantly internalized, drilled, translated into flesh and reality, indeed, into the commonplace, by the so-called practical human beings (our actors). Only we have created the world that concerns human beings![7]

A conservative interpretation of this passage would treat it as saying that although of course nature is not made by us, it has no significance for us until we have topped it up. We overlay nature with another world, the world that concerns us, the only world in which a properly human life can be led. The senses give both us and the animals access to the natural world, but we humans have superimposed a second world by internalizing a poem, thereby making the two worlds seem equally inescapable. Outside of the

---

[7] Friedrich Nietzsche, *The Gay Science*, trans. Walter Kaufmann (New York: Random House, 1974), section 301.

natural sciences, reason works within the second world, following paths that the imagination has cleared. But inside those sciences, nature itself shows the way.

That conservative interpretation might have satisfied Emerson. It provides a plausible gloss on Shelley's claim that the poets are the unacknowledged legislators of the world. It is consistent with the view of the relation between the cognitive, the moral, and the aesthetic that Schiller offered in *Letters on the Aesthetic Education of Mankind*. Nevertheless, that interpretation is insufficiently radical. It does not take account of Nietzsche's polemics against the Reality–Appearance distinction – against the idea, common to the Greeks and to the majority of contemporary analytic philosophers, that there *is* a way that nature is in itself, apart from human needs and interests.

He says in the *Nachlass*, for example, that "The dogmatic idea of 'things that have a constitution in themselves' is one with which one must break absolutely."[8] He spells out his point by saying:

That things possess a constitution in themselves quite apart from interpretation and subjectivity, is a quite idle hypothesis; it presupposes that interpretation and subjectivity are not essential, that a thing freed from all relationships would still be a thing.[9]

In passages such as this one Nietzsche brushes aside the common-sense claim that there is a way Reality is independent of the way human beings describe it. He was equally contemptuous of the more sophisticated Kantian idea that an unknowable non-spatiotemporal thing-in-itself lurks behind the phenomenal world. Nietzsche's teaching does, however, bear some resemblance to Hegel's claim that Nature is but a moment in the developing self-consciousness of Spirit. Nietzsche would certainly second Hegel's insistence that we not conceive of knowledge as a medium for getting in touch with Reality, but instead think of it as a way in which Spirit enlarges itself. But Nietzsche differs from Hegel in rejecting the idea of a natural terminus to the progress of this self-consciousness – a final unity in which all tensions are resolved, in which appearance is put behind us and true reality revealed.[10] Unlike Hegel, and like Emerson, Nietzsche is making a purely negative point. He is not saying that Spirit alone is really real, but that we should stop asking questions about what is really real.

---

[8] Friedrich Nietzsche, *The Will to Power*, trans. Walter Kaufmann (New York: Random House, 1968), 558. [9] Ibid., 560.

[10] Some recent commentators on Hegel give him a radically non-metaphysical reading. They doubt whether Hegel is committed either to the notion of "the intrinsic nature of reality" or to this sort of eschatology. They may be right. I do not trust my own grasp of Hegel sufficiently to feel any certainty about this.

Nietzsche never developed this view in any detail, nor did he succeed in making it perspicuous. It is, as many commentators have pointed out, impossible to reconcile with many other things that he said. It is obviously incompatible, for example, with his repeated suggestion that he himself is the first post-Platonic thinker to be free from illusion. The only criticism of his predecessors which Nietzsche can consistently make is, once again, the accusation of cowardice: they were all too timid to break out of the Platonic account of the human situation, too hesitant to sketch a larger circle than the one Plato had drawn. Nor can Nietzsche's prophecy of a post-metaphysical age be squared with the passages in the later writings in which Nietzsche seems to be claiming that the Will to Power is the only thing that is really real. Those are the passages that Heidegger seized upon in order to caricature Nietzsche as "the last metaphysician," the proponent of an inverted Platonism.

Despite Nietzsche's own inconsistencies, the romantic anti-Platonism he put forward in the passages I have quoted is a coherent philosophical position. It can be buttressed and clarified by bringing Nietzsche together with the work of various twentieth-century analytic philosophers. In what follows, I shall be rehearsing some arguments put forward by Wittgenstein, and some others developed by Sellars, Davidson, and Brandom. I think that these arguments help give a plausible sense both to the romanticist claim that nature itself is a poem that we humans have written – that reason can only follow paths that the imagination has broken, only rearrange elements that the imagination has created.

The analytic philosophers I have listed are united in their repudiation of empiricism. They debunk the idea that animals and human beings take in information about the world through their sense organs. They deny that the senses provide a solid and unchanging core around which the imagination weaves wispy and ephemeral circles. On their account, the senses do not enjoy a special relation to reality that distinguishes their deliverances from those of the imagination.

The idea that they do enjoy such a relation goes back to Plato's analogy between the mind and a wax tablet, which Aristotle refashioned into the doctrine that the sensory organs take on the qualities of the sensed object. Ever since, it has sounded plausible to describe sense-perception as a process of tucking something that was outside the organism inside the organism – either by way of identity, as in Aristotle, or by way of representation, as in Lockean empiricism and contemporary cognitive science. On the latter account, there is a big difference between a mechanism like a thermostat that simply responds to changes in the environment and an organism with a nervous system capable of containing *representations* of the environment. The thermostat just reacts. The organism acquires information.

On the anti-empiricist view, a view that I think Nietzsche would have welcomed had he encountered it, there is no difference between the thermostat, the dog, and the pre-linguistic infant except the differing degrees of complexity of their reactions to environmental stimuli. The brutes and the infants are capable of discriminative responses, but not of acquiring information. For there is no such thing as the acquisition of information until there is language in which to formulate that information. Information came into the universe when the first hominids began to justify their actions to one another by making assertions and backing up those assertions with further assertions. There is information only where there is inferential justification. Before the practice of giving and asking for reasons developed, the noises these hominids made to each other did not convey information in any more interesting sense than that in which the motion of ambient molecules conveys information to the thermostat, or the digestive enzymes convey information to the contents of the stomach.

To accept this alternative account of sense-perception means abandoning the traditional story about language-learning – one in which language got its start by people giving names to what they were already thinking about. For on this account all awareness that is more than the ability to respond differentially to varied stimuli is, as Wilfrid Sellars said, "a linguistic affair." The brutes, the sunflowers, the thermostats, and the human infants can produce differential responses, but awareness, information, and knowledge are possible only after the acquisition of language.

On the view common to Sellars and Wittgenstein, to possess a concept is to be familiar with the use of a linguistic expression. Whereas empiricists think of concepts as mental representations, Sellars and Wittgenstein have no use for what Quine called "the idea idea." Abandoning that idea means treating the possession of a mind as the possession of certain social skills – the skills required to give and ask for reasons. To have a mind is not to have a movie theatre inside the skull, with successive representations of the surroundings flashing on the screen. It is the ability to use persuasion to get what one wants.

Before there were conversational exchanges, on this view, there were neither concepts, nor beliefs, nor knowledge. For to say that a dog knows its master, or a baby its mother, is like saying that a lock knows when the right key has been inserted, or that a computer knows when it has been given the right password. To say that the frog's eye tells something to the frog's brain is like saying that screwdriver tells something to the screw. The line between mechanism and something categorically distinct from mechanism comes when organisms develop social practices that permit those organisms to consider the relative advantages and disadvantages of alternative descriptions of things. Mechanism stops, and freedom begins, at the point where we go metalinguistic – the point at which we can discuss which words best describe a given situation. Knowledge and freedom are coeval.

On the romantic view I am commending, the imagination is the source of freedom because it is the source of language. It is, as Shelley put it, root as well as blossom. It is not that we first spoke a language that simply reported what was going on around us, and later enlarged this language by imaginative redescription. Rather, imaginativeness goes all the way back. The concepts of redness and roundness are as much imaginative creations as those of God, of the positron, and of constitutional democracy. Getting the word "red" into circulation was a feat on a par with Newton's persuading people to start using the term "gravity." For nobody knew what redness was before some early hominids began talking about the differences in the colors of things, just as nobody knew what gravity was before Newton began describing an occult force that helped account both for ballistic trajectories and for planetary orbits. It took imaginative genius to suggest that everybody make the same noise at the sight of blood, of certain maple leaves in autumn, and of the western sky at sunset. It was only when such suggestions were taken seriously and put into practice that hominids began to have minds.

As for the concept "round," it was not obvious that the full moon and the trunks of trees had anything in common before some genius began to use a noise that we would translate as "round." Nothing at all was obvious, because obviousness is not a notion that can be applied to organisms that do not use language. The thermostats, the brutes, and the pre-linguistic human infants do not find anything obvious, even though they all respond to stimuli in predictable ways. The notion of pre-linguistic obviousness is inseparable from the Cartesian story about the spectator sitting in a little theatre inside the skull, watching representations come and go, giving them names as they pass. This story is the one Sellars ridiculed when he described the empiricists' picture of a child mind confronting the manifold of sense. "This one," this child's mind says to itself in its private little language, "stands out clearly. Here! and here! No, that can't be it! Aha! a splendid specimen. By the methods of Mill! That *must* be what mother calls 'red'!" [11]

---

[11]   Wilfrid Sellars, "Is there a Synthetic A Priori?" in *Science, Perception and Reality* (London: Routledge, 1963), p. 309.

On the Lockean account the pre-linguistic child already knows the difference between colors and shapes, and between red and blue, before having learned any words. The contrasting view is suggested by Nietzsche in another passage from the *Nachlass*. There he writes, "In a world in which there is no being, a certain calculable world of identical cases must first be created."[12] He would have done better to have written "in a world in which there is no knowledge" rather than "in a world in which there is no being." If we do rewrite in that way, we can read him as saying that you cannot have knowledge without identifiable things, and that there is no such thing as identification until people can use terms such as "same shape," and "different color." We only begin to have knowledge when we can formulate such thoughts as that this thing has a different color than that, but the same shape. The empiricist tradition attributes the ability to have this thought to brutes and pre-linguistic infants. The anti-empiricist view I am offering says that there is no more reason to attribute it to them than to attribute the thought "It is cooler than it used to be" to a thermostat.

Imagination, in the sense in which I am using the term, is not a distinctively human capacity. It is, as I said earlier, the ability to come up with socially useful novelties. This is an ability Newton shared with certain eager and ingenious beavers. But giving and asking for reasons *is* distinctively human, and is coextensive with rationality. The more an organism can get what it wants by persuasion rather than force, the more rational it is. Ulysses, for example, was more rational than Achilles. But you cannot use persuasion if you cannot talk. No imagination, no language. No linguistic change, no moral or intellectual progress. Rationality is a matter of making allowed moves within language games. Imagination creates the games that reason proceeds to play. Then, exemplified by people like Plato and Newton, it keeps modifying those games so that playing them is more interesting and profitable. Reason cannot get outside the latest circle that imagination has drawn. In this sense, imagination has priority over reason.

The Nietzschean view I have been sketching is often described as the doctrine that everything is "constituted" by language, or that everything is "socially constructed," or that everything is "mind-dependent." But these terms are hopelessly misleading. Words like "constitution" and "construction" and "dependence," in the language games that are their original homes, refer to causal relations. They are invoked to explain how something came into existence or can continue to exist. We say, for example, that

---

[12] Nietzsche, *The Will to Power*, 568.

the USA was constituted out of the thirteen original colonies, that wooden houses are constructed by carpenters, and that children depend on their parents for their support.

But philosophers who say, misleadingly, that redness, like gravity, is constituted by language, or that roundness, like gender, is a social construction, do not mean to suggest that one sort of entity was brought into existence by another sort. They are not offering an absurd hypothesis about causal relations. Such relations only hold within what Nietzsche called "a certain calculable world of identical cases" – a world of identifiable objects. We can investigate causal relations once we have identified such objects, but there is no point in asking where the world that contains such objects comes from. You can ask sensible paleontological questions about where trees and beavers came from, and sensible astrophysical questions about where stars came from, but you cannot give a sense to the question of where spatiotemporal objects in general came from.

Plato, in the *Timaeus*, did pose that bad question, and Augustine and later Christian theologians thought they could answer it. Kant transposed the question into a new key, and answered it by telling an imaginative story about how ineffable intuitions – which are produced by the non-causal interaction of the thing-in-itself with the self-in-itself – get whipped into spatiotemporal shape by the transcendental ego. The blatant internal incoherence of Kant's story soon gave idealism a bad name. But the Nietzschean view I have been outlining eschews any such story while nevertheless preserving what was true in idealism – namely, the thesis that there is no preconceptual cognitive access to objects. Our only cognitive access to beavers, trees, stars, our own subjectivity, or the transcendental ego lies in our ability to wield such expressions as "beaver," "tree," "star," "subjectivity," and "transcendental ego."

Kant's mistake was to formulate a thesis about the inseparability of identifiable things from our identifying descriptions of them – about the impossibility of getting between words and their objects – as a thesis about where these things came from. Hegel, by substituting absolute for transcendental idealism, avoided this mistake. But Hegel phrased many of his doctrines in terms of the Platonic–Cartesian distinction between material and immaterial being, and he seems to have been inspired by the hope of transcending the finite human condition – reaching a realm beyond time and chance. So Hegelianism – perhaps the most imaginative and original achievement of the Western philosophical tradition – gradually succumbed to positivistic criticism. The historicism that Hegel took from Herder had to be reformulated by post-Nietzschean philosophers such as Heidegger before it could be disentangled from Hegel's awkward but persistent attempts at eschatology.

Defenders of the Platonic tradition often interpret views of the sort I am putting forward as claiming that nothing was red or round before the first hominids began to converse, and that mountains came into existence only when they began to use a noise meaning "mountain." But this is a caricature. Wittgenstein's anti-empiricist point is not about when things came into existence but about how language and thought did. Naming, as he put it, requires a lot of stage setting in the language: it is no use pointing to a red and round ball, uttering "red," and expecting the baby to grasp that you are directing its attention to a color rather than to a shape. Wittgenstein seems to have been the first to remark that the empiricist picture of language-learning requires us to think of babies as talking to themselves in Mentalese, the language that Sellars' child was thinking in when it figured out what mother called "red."

The issue about pre-linguistic awareness that pits Wittgenstein, Sellars, Davidson, and Brandom against Fodor and other philosophers who pin their hopes on cognitive science may seem remote from the question of the priority of the imagination. But I think that is in fact decisive for the question of whether Nietzsche was right to think of the world as our poem rather than as something that communicates information about itself to us through our sense-organs. How we answer that question goes a long way toward deciding whether we will think of the progress human beings have made in the last few millennia as a matter of expanding our imaginations, or an increased ability to represent reality accurately.

Nietzsche thought that Plato's success in putting the term "really real" into circulation was a great imaginative achievement. But the answer to a great poem is a still better poem, and that is what Nietzsche thought of himself as writing. He asked us to treat "the true world" as a fable, a myth concocted by Parmenides and Plato. The problem, he said, is not that it is a fable, but that it is one that has exhausted its utility. We should not say that the hope of knowing the intrinsic nature of Reality was an illusion, because, as Nietzsche rightly says, when we give up the notion of a true world we give up that of an illusory world as well. The difference between a good old poem and a new better poem is not the difference between a bad representation of Reality and a better one. It is the difference between a smaller circle and a bigger one.

I am convinced that Nietzsche wrote the better poem. As I see it, the romantic movement marked the beginning of the attempt to replace the tale told by the Greek philosophers with a better tale. The old story was about how human beings might manage to get back in touch with something from which they had somehow become estranged – something that is not itself a human creation, but stands over and against all such creations. The new story is about how human beings continually strive to overcome the human past in order to create a better human future.

Plato said that we should try to substitute logic for rhetoric, the application of criteria for imaginative power. By tracing an argumentative path back to first principles, Plato thought, we can attain the goal that he described as "reaching a place beyond hypotheses." When we have reached that goal we shall be immune to the seductive effects of redescription, for we shall have established the sort of "ostensive tie" between ourselves and the really real that, on the empiricist view, visual perception establishes with colors and shapes. Just as we cannot deny the evidence of our senses – cannot make ourselves believe that something is blue when our eyes tell us that it is red – so the Platonic philosopher cannot make himself doubt what he sees when he reaches the top of Plato's divided line. But for the poets logical argumentation – conformity to the rules of deductive validity – is just one rhetorical technique among others. Nietzsche and Wittgenstein both suggest substituting Emerson's metaphor of endlessly expanding circles for Plato's metaphor of ascent to the indubitable.

When he used the figure of the divided line to symbolize the ascent from opinion to knowledge, and when he used the allegory of the cave for the same purpose, Plato was implicitly recognizing that the only way to escape from redescription was to attain a kind of knowledge that was not discursive – a kind that did not rely on choice of a particular linguistic formulation. To reach truth that one cannot be argued out of is to escape from the linguistically expressible to the ineffable. Only the ineffable – what is not describable at all – cannot be described differently.

When Nietzsche says that a thing conceived apart from its relationships would not be a thing, he should be read as saying that since all language is a matter of relating some things to other things, what is not so related cannot be talked of. Language establishes relationships by, for example, tying blood in with sunsets and full moons with tree trunks. Lack of describability means lack of relations, so our only access to the indescribable must be the sort of direct awareness that the empiricist has of redness and that the mystic has of God. Much of the history of Western philosophy, from Plotinus and Meister Eckhart down to Husserl and Russell, is the history of the quest for such direct awareness.

As I have already said, Nietzsche viewed this quest as a symptom of cowardice – of inability to bear the thought that we shall always live and move and have our being within a cloud of words, words that are no more than the creation of finite human creatures in response to finite human needs. If pragmatism is of any importance – if there is any difference between pragmatism and Platonism that might eventually make a difference to practice – it is not because it got something right that Platonism got wrong. It is because accepting a pragmatist outlook would change the cultural ambience for the better. It would complete the process of secularization by letting us think of the desire for non-linguistic access to the real as as hopeless as that for redemption through a beatific vision. Taking this extra step toward acknowledging our finitude would give a new resonance to Blake's dictum that "All deities reside in the human breast."[13] Yeats alluded to, and improved upon, Blake when he wrote "Whatever flames upon the night / Man's own resinous heart has fed."[14]

[13] William Blake, "The Marriage of Heaven and Hell."
[14] William Butler Yeats, "Two Songs from a Play."

8

Analytic and conversational philosophy

The distinction between "analytic" and "continental" philosophy is very crude, but it does provide a rough-and-ready way to start sorting out the philosophy professors. To tell which pigeonhole to put a professor in, look at the books and journal issues on her shelves. If she has quite a lot of books by and about Hegel and Heidegger, and none by Davidson or Rawls, she will probably be content to be described as continental, or at least not to be described as analytic. If her desk is strewn with marked-up offprints from *The Journal of Philosophy*, *The Philosophical Quarterly*, and *Philosophical Review*, she can safely be typed as analytic.

Sometimes, however, you meet a philosophy professor who takes part in the debates conducted in those journals and also can discourse learnedly on, for example, the adequacy of Habermas' account of the motives for Heidegger's "turn." Quite a few people, both Anglophones and non-Anglophones, can easily turn from Rawls to Carl Schmitt, or from Derrida to Wittgenstein, or from Foucault to Christine Korsgaard. But this ability is still confined to a relatively small fraction of the world's philosophers.

The main reason such ambidexterity is rare is that students trying to shape themselves into plausible job candidates for teaching positions in philosophy only have time to read so much. They can please only so many potential employers. In most European countries, candidates for such positions have to learn quite a lot of intellectual history before they go on the market. They cannot afford to look blank when somebody asks them what they think about the relation between Hobbes and Machiavelli, or about Nietzsche's preference for Sophocles over Socrates. In Anglophone countries, they can. But they cannot afford to be ignorant of the issues being debated in recent volumes of the leading Anglophone philosophy journals – or at least some particular subset of these issues.

No matter how much intellectual curiosity a student has, and however much she might like to have views about Kierkegaard as well as about Kripke, or about David Lewis as well as Schelling, there just is not enough time. So if she develops ambidexterity, it will often be only in later life – usually after she gets tenure. Then she can afford to start following her nose rather than pleasing interviewers or senior colleagues.

As long as these differences between how to get jobs in various places persist, philosophy will continue to be "split" along roughly analytic-vs.-continental lines. But it is not clear that this split is anything to worry about. The academic study of philosophy has, like the academic study of literature and unlike that of the natural sciences, always been fairly parochial. Just as graduate training in the study of literature is typically study of a single national literature, so graduate training in philosophy is typically study of the books and issues currently being discussed in the philosophy departments of the student's own country.

Few Germans took the time to read Léon Brunschvig during a period when no French student of philosophy could afford to be ignorant of him, or Croce when his Hegel book was being read by every philosopher in Italy. In the 1930s in the US, most philosophy students at Harvard read quite different books than those that were being read by their counterparts in Heidelberg, Pisa, Oxford, or even Columbia. A student's notion of the frontiers of philosophy – of the urgent issues – will be quite different depending on the country, and indeed the particular university, in which she receives her training.

The majority of philosophy professors, in every country, never move far beyond the horizons that were set for them by their teachers. So if one's teachers at Michigan assure one that Derrida is a charlatan, or if one's teachers at Tübingen suggest that formal semantics is just a mystification and cognitive science just a boondoggle, one may well believe these propositions for the rest of one's life. Ideally, we philosophers are supposed to be constantly questioning our own presuppositions. In fact, we are no better at doing so than anybody else. Most analytic philosophers feel a vague contempt for continental philosophy without ever having read much of it. Many continental philosophers sneer at analytic philosophy without trying to figure out what the analytic philosophers think they are doing.

But if the analytic–continental split is just the most conspicuous example of familiar, and pretty much inevitable, academic parochialism, why should it be so much more productive of distrust and contempt than the "split" between astrophysics and physical chemistry, or between civil and criminal legal practice, or between Italian and German literature? Why not view it simply as a matter of different people being attracted by different specialties within a single discipline?

The answer is that the differences in professional formation that I have described give rise to different accounts of what philosophy professors are good for, and of philosophy's place in culture. People trained in one way acquire a very different self-image than people trained in the other way. The contempt they frequently feel for people whose training was different results from a suspicion that those people are freeloaders, profiting from the prestige of a discipline whose nature and function they fail to understand.

The biggest difference in self-image is that the model of the natural sciences remains much more important for most analytic philosophers than it is for most continental philosophers. Much of what is done by philosophers in France and Germany looks to analytic philosophers like, at best, "mere" intellectual history – something quite different from the kind of problem-solving that is the philosopher's proper business. Much of what is published in *Nous, Mind,* and *The Journal of Philosophy* looks like bombination in a pseudo-scientific vacuum to most people teaching philosophy in Spain, Japan, Poland, and Brazil. They view the rather miscellaneous group of issues that the analytic philosophers group under the heading "metaphysics and epistemology" as, for the most part, examples of what Berkeley called "kicking up the dust and then complaining that they cannot see." Discussion of those topics, which constitute what the Anglophones call "the core areas" of philosophy, strike them as quite irrelevant to the interests that initially led them to study philosophy.

The question of whether philosophy should think of itself as a science, like that of whether it can be assimilated to intellectual history, might seem discussable without reference to substantive philosophical doctrines. But in fact metaphilosophical issues – issues about what, if anything, philosophy is good for and about how it is best pursued – are inseparable from issues about the nature of knowledge, truth, and meaning. In what follows I shall outline one such issue, in order to show how different responses to it might produce, and be produced by, different metaphilosophical views.

The issue is: is there such an activity as "conceptual analysis," or can philosophers do no more than describe usage and, perhaps, make recommendations for change in usage? One's answer to this question will determine whether one thinks that Wittgenstein was right to give up on the idea of a systematic theory of meaning, and Quine right to suggest that the very notion of "meaning" was a hangover of Aristotelian essentialism. If they were right, it is hard to hang on to the idea that "conceptual clarity" is a goal of philosophical inquiry. We cannot repudiate the analytic–synthetic and language–fact distinctions and still distinguish between "conceptual" and other issues.

Metaphilosophical issues hover in the wings of debates over whether the content of an assertion varies from utterer to utterer and from audience to audience. If it does not, if something remains invariable – the concepts expressed by the words that make up the sentence – then perhaps there really are entities with intrinsic properties which philosophical analysis can hope to pin down. But if content does vary in this way, then concepts are like persons – never quite the same twice, always developing, always maturing. You can change a concept by changing usage, but you cannot get a concept right, once and for all.

Robert Brandom has argued that treating concepts on the model of persons is central both to Hegel's thought and to pragmatism.[1] Brandom's own inferentialist philosophy of language is built around the claim that the content of a sentence is in constant flux, and none the worse for that. On his view, the inferences drawn from and to assertions made with the sentence constitute the only content the sentence has. Inferential proprieties are not built into the structure of the language, but are always up for grabs as individuals and communities go about revising their patterns of behavior, linguistic and non-linguistic.[2] Adopting Brandom's view would force one to give up the notion that concepts such as "knowledge" or "morality or "mind" or "justice" have permanent, structural, features that philosophers can discern, and that the vulgar may not have noticed.

In the absence of that notion, it is hard to see the history of philosophy as most analytic philosophers would prefer to see it – as a continuing examination of the same data as were examined by Plato and Aristotle, in the hope of finally getting knowledge, or morality, or mind, or justice, *right*. The hope to get *something* right, once and for all, just as natural scientists do, is very precious to most analytic philosophers. Those whose self-image is built around that hope accuse philosophers who think that there are no

---

[1] See Robert Brandom, "Some Pragmatist Themes in Hegel's Idealism: Negotiation and Administration in Hegel's Account of the Structure and Content of Conceptual Norms," *European Journal of Philosophy* 7, no. 2 (1999), 164–89. Brandom identifies "the idealist thesis" as the view that "the structure and unity of the *concept* is the same as the structure and unity of the *self*" (164).

[2] See Robert Brandom, *Making it Explicit* (Cambridge, MA: Harvard University Press, 1944), 587: "The relativity of explicit inferential endorsements to the deontic repertoires of various scorekeepers reflects the underlying relativity of the inferential endorsements implicit in the concepts expressed by particular words, according to various scorekeepers. A word – 'dog', 'stupid', 'Republican' – has a different significance in my mouth than it does in yours, because and insofar as what follows from its being applicable, its consequences of application, differ for me, in virtue of my different collateral beliefs [and similarly for circumstances of application – consider 'murder', 'pornographic', 'lyrical'.]"

stable entities called "concepts" or "meanings" of reducing philosophy to "mere conversation."

In my case, at least, this accusation is quite correct (or would be if "mere" were omitted). Because I do not think that philosophy is ever going to be put on the secure path of a science, nor that it is a good idea to try to put it there, I am content to see philosophy professors as practicing cultural politics. One of the ways they do this is by suggesting changes in the uses of words and by putting new words in circulation – hoping thereby to break through impasses and to make conversation more fruitful. I am quite willing to give up the goal of getting things right, and to substitute that of enlarging our repertoire of individual and cultural self-descriptions. The point of philosophy, on this view, is not to find out what anything is "really" like, but to help us grow up – to make us happier, freer, and more flexible. The maturation of our concepts, and the increasing richness of our conceptual repertoire, constitute cultural progress.

As an example of a change in usage that might facilitate philosophical controversy, I suggest we drop the term "continental" and instead contrast analytic philosophy with *conversational* philosophy. This change would shift attention from the differences between the job requirements imposed on young philosophers in different regions of the world to the issue I have just sketched: whether there is something that philosophers can get right.

The term "getting it right," I would argue, is appropriate only when everybody interested in the topics draws pretty much the same inferences from the same assertions. That happens when there is consensus about the aim of inquiry in the area, and when a problem can be pinned down in such a way that everybody concerned is clear about what it would take to solve it. Common sense provides such consensus on many of the topics we discuss, and expert cultures provide it for many others. Within such cultures there is agreement, for example, on when a gene has been located, a chemical compound analyzed into its component elements, or a theorem proved. The members of such cultures all use the relevant referring expressions ("gene," "element," "proof") in pretty much the same way. They are also pretty much agreed about what exists, for shared confidence in the existence of a certain sort of entity is indistinguishable from consensus on the utility of certain referring expressions.[3]

---

[3]   Brandom has discussed the nature of existence in *Making it Explicit* at 440ff. I gloss his views on this topic, and apply them to a special case, in "Cultural politics and the question of the existence of God," 3–26 of this volume. Some philosophers (including, alas, Quine) think that ontological questions should be distinguished from questions of utility. Anti-metaphysicians like Brandom and myself, however, have no use for the notion of "ontological commitment," nor for the project of, as Quine put it, "limning the true and ultimate structure of reality."

Analytic philosophy as a whole is not, and has never been, an expert culture characterized by such long-term, near-universal consensus. What consensus has existed has been local and transitory. The problems about which the full professors in analytic philosophy departments wrote their dissertations often look merely quaint to their newly hired junior colleagues. The spectacle of the hungry analytic generations treading each other down is, to my mind, the strongest argument in favor of conversational philosophy. The failure of the analytic philosophers to develop a transgenerational problematic is the best reason to think that the slogan "let's get it right!" needs to be replaced by something like "let's try something different!"

Contemplating this failure helps one realize that philosophy is what is left over after one has bracketed both common sense and all the various expert cultures.[4] It was never supposed to be such a culture. Whenever it has attempted to become one it has degenerated into scholasticism, into controversies which are of no interest to anyone outside the philosophical profession. The idea that either literary criticism or philosophy should become an expert culture is a result of unfortunate attempts to squeeze these areas of culture into a university system tailored to the needs of lawyers, physicians, and natural scientists.[5]

Once one gives up on the notion that certain things are "natural explananda" – topics of concern to any reflective mind at any era and in any society – one will cease to read Kant, Hegel, Wittgenstein, Austin, or Brandom either as "doing" metaphysics or epistemology or semantics or as trying to get reality or knowledge or meaning *right*. One will instead think of them as expressing impatience with a certain familiar mind set, and as attempting to entrench a new vocabulary, one which uses old words in new ways.

Hegel was expressing impatience with the vocabulary used by philosophers who, like Kant, insisted on the irreducibility of the subject–object distinction. In order to persuade people to stop talking in Cartesian and Kantian ways, he offered a wholesale redescription of knowledge, of moral

---

4   For a good account of the distinction between philosophers and members of expert cultures, see Isaiah Berlin, "Does Political Theory Still Exist?" included in a collection of his essays edited by Henry Hardy: *The Proper Study of Mankind* (New York: Farrar, Straus and Giroux, 1998), 59–90. See especially the arguments leading up to Berlin's claim that "One of the surest hallmarks of a philosophical question . . . is that we are puzzled from the very outset, that there is no automatic technique, no universally recognized expertise, for dealing with such questions" (62).

5   This is not to deny that a specialized course of reading is necessary in order to produce, or to appreciate, original work in either philosophy or literary criticism. But there is a difference between being learned and being "scientific," in a sense of the latter term which is narrower than the German *wissenschaftlich* – a sense in which physics is taken as the paradigmatic science.

and intellectual progress, and of many other things. He gave many of the old terms used to discuss these matters new, specifically Hegelian, senses. The later Wittgenstein was expressing impatience with his own *Tractatus* and with the philosophical mind set shared by Moore and Russell. Austin trashed Ayer because he got impatient with his Oxford colleagues' attempts to find something worth saving in British empiricism. Brandom is not saying: everybody has been getting concepts wrong, and I am getting them right. He is saying something more like: representionalist accounts of semantic content have become familiar, and the problems they raise increasingly tedious, so let us try an inferentialist account and see whether things go better. *The Phenomenology of Spirit* and *Making it Explicit*, like *Philosophical Investigations* and *Sense and Sensibilia*, are not books of which it is useful to ask "What exactly do they get right?" – nor even "What are they *trying* to get right?" It is more useful to ask: would it help to start talking that way?

Whereas the analytic–continental distinction is primarily a geographic and sociological one, the analytic–conversational distinction which I should like to substitute distinguishes between differing self-images – images produced by adopting differing metaphilosophical attitudes. These, in turn, are both cause and effect of the answers one gives to such first-order philosophical questions as those concerning the nature of concepts.

I prefer conversational to analytic philosophy, so defined, because I prefer philosophers who are sufficiently historicist as to think of themselves as taking part in a conversation rather than as practicing a quasi-scientific discipline. Despite my admiration for, and sedulous borrowing from, the writings of many analytic philosophers, I am dubious about analytic philosophy as disciplinary matrix. The problem is that philosophers shaped by that matrix tend to take for granted that the problems that they were taught to discuss in graduate school are, simply by virtue of that very fact, important. So they are tempted to evaluate other philosophers, past and present, by the relevance of their work to those problems. This sort of professional deformation seems to me more damaging than any disability characteristic of conversational philosophers.

One reason why there is a rough correlation between a philosophy professor's geographical location and her self-image is that conversational philosophy is more popular in those countries in which Hegel is a required text for advanced students of philosophy. It is less popular in countries in which the historicism he introduced into philosophy is viewed with suspicion. In those countries, students still tend to go straight from Kant to Frege. Skipping Hegel helps them to retain the Kantian idea that there are permanent structures of thought, or consciousness, or rationality, or language or *something*, for philosophers to reveal, and about which the vulgar may well be confused. Those who believe in such structures tend to think of analytic philosophy as continuous with the Descartes-to-Kant sequence. They treat the Hegel–Nietzsche–Heidegger sequence as an unfortunate divagation, one that can safely be neglected.

In contrast, philosophers who have spent a lot of time thinking about those latter three figures are usually sympathetic to Hegel's suggestion that philosophy is its time held in thought. They are inclined to think that philosophy makes progress not by solving problems but by replacing old problems with new problems – problems created by one use of words with problems created by another use of words. This historicist outlook makes them dubious about Wittgenstein's suggestion that philosophy's goal is "*complete* clarity" – an unproblematic grasp of the way things really are, one which will give philosophy perpetual peace (not just Aristotelian philosophy, or Cartesian philosophy, or Fregean philosophy, but philosophy itself). Philosophy, they suspect, cannot cease as long as there is cultural change – as long as the arts, the sciences, and politics come up with things that do not seem happily described when the old words are used in the old ways. It also makes them suspicious of Wittgenstein's incautious use of the term "nonsense," and sympathetic to his alternative suggestion that everything has a sense if you give it a sense. So they see their task not as replacing nonsense with sense but rather as replacing a sensible and coherent use of certain terms with something even better.[6]

Substituting analytic–conversational for analytic–continental as a description of the most salient split among today's philosophy professors might help us resist the temptation to treat this split either as dividing those who love truth and reason from those who prefer dramatic effects and rhetorical triumphs, or as dividing the unimaginative clods from the free spirits. It is better understood as a split between two quite different ways of thinking of the human situation – a split as deep as that between religious and secular outlooks. This split has been deepening ever since Hegel challenged Kant's version of the Platonic idea that philosophy could be like mathematics – that it could offer conclusive demonstrations of truths about structural features of human life, rather than simply summaries of the way human beings have conducted their lives so far.

---

[6] For more on this point, see "Wittgenstein and the linguistic turn," included in this volume at 60–175.

Those who are on the neo-Kantian side of this split take for granted that Plato was right to postulate a permanent ahistorical matrix for human thought: to attempt to cut things at their joints by making such distinctions as knowledge–opinion, reality–appearance, reason–passion, and logic–rhetoric. Those on the other side follow Hegel in thinking that those distinctions and many others (e.g. mind–body, subjective–objective, transcendental–empirical, realist–anti-realist, representationalist–inferentialist, Kantian–Hegelian, analytic–conversational) are temporary expedients that will sooner or later become obsolete.

Hegelians think that blurring old distinctions is one of the most effective ways to make the future an improvement over the past. Whereas the neo-Kantians like to quote Bishop Butler's maxim "a thing is what it is and no other thing," the neo-Hegelians think that a thing (and, a fortiori, an academic discipline) is what it is by virtue of its relations to everything else, just as a word has the use it does because of the way all the other words in the language are used. All such relations are in constant flux.

Those who take this view of both things and words (which might be called "relationalism" but is usually called "holism") include many people who think of themselves as working, as they put it, "within the analytic tradition." (Brandom himself is an obvious example.) But the majority of people who would so describe themselves still distrust holism deeply. These include not just most Anglophone teachers of philosophy but most of the non-Anglophones who belong to such organizations as the European Society for Analytic Philosophy. They correctly perceive that a thoroughgoing holism will sooner or later lead to a conversational view of philosophy, and thereby lead it away from the sciences and in the direction of the humanities. They regard proper philosophical professionalism as inseparable from some form of atomism – some account of philosophy's method and subject-matter which will make it possible to preserve Plato's image of cutting things at the joints.

Those who would like to preserve that image include not just people self-identified as "analytic," but also many of the European and Asian philosophy teachers who have little use for what Anglophones describe as "metaphysics and epistemology." Some of these people cling to the conviction that transcendental phenomenology has finally put philosophy on the secure path of a science. But many who have long since given up on Husserl are still convinced that there is something "out there" to be gotten right – something, for example, that Heidegger was trying to get right when he talked about the *die ontologische Differenz*, and that Derrida was still trying to get right when he talked about *différance*. They still believe in something like a fixed, ahistorical, framework of human existence that philosophers should try to describe with greater accuracy. They just think that the Anglophones have been looking for this framework in the wrong places.

Neo-Hegelian holists like myself do not think that the sociological conditions outlined above, the ones that permit one usefully to talk about getting an entity right, are fulfilled in the case of *différance*, or of any other specifically philosophical topic. So we prefer to describe Heidegger and Derrida as offering us imaginative neologisms that help us hold our time in thought. We see no need to distinguish sharply between the imaginative creations offered by philosophers and those offered by non-philosophers. So we do not worry about which academic department should take responsibility for the study of Hegel, Freud, Heidegger, Nietzsche, or Derrida.

This insouciance leads us to seek out the company of intellectual historians and students of literature, since they too often find these latter figures of interest. We do so not because we think that the humanities offer truth and the natural sciences do not, but because study of the history of philosophy leads us to try to fit that history into a larger historical context. The history of algebraic topology or of molecular biology does not, we presume, require such contextualization. But the history of philosophy, like the history of the novel, does. Whereas the neo-Kantians think that one can be a well-trained philosopher without any particular knowledge of literary or political history, we disagree. Just as the value of a philosopher's work, in our eyes, is not a matter of its relation to *die Sache selbst*, but to the work of other philosophers, so the value of philosophy itself is a matter of its relation not to a subject-matter but to the rest of the conversation of humankind.

The differing emphasis we neo-Hegelians place on history is paralleled by the differing values we place on metaphilosophical discussion. Neo-Kantians are always trying to get away from metaphilosophy and, as they often put it, "get down to *doing* some philosophy." For us, on the other hand, discussing what philosophy has been and might be is as respectable a way of doing philosophy as, for example, discussing how to give referentially opaque contexts their proper place in a semantic theory.

Both discussions are part of the same conversation, because to understand why referential opacity matters one has to think about why the founders of analytic philosophy wanted what they wanted and took the stands they did – what the point of an extensionalist semantics was supposed to be. Whereas neo-Kantians think that introducing a student to the problems that opaque contexts pose for formal semantics is enough to give her a good start on doing some good philosophy, neo-Hegelians think that students who have never reflected on what a semantic theory might be good for are undesirably unconversable. These students are in danger of writing dissertations whose half-life may be very short, and which will be ignored, or even mocked, by the next generation. Historical and metaphilosophical self-consciousness, we think, is the best precaution against barren scholasticism.

III

Current Issues Within Analytic Philosophy

9

A pragmatist view of contemporary analytic philosophy

This chapter has two parts. In the first I discuss the views of my favorite philosopher of science, Arthur Fine. Fine has become famous for his defense of a thesis whose discussion seems to me central to contemporary philosophy – namely, that we should be neither realists nor antirealists, that the entire realism–antirealism issue should be set aside. On this point he agrees with my favorite philosophers of language, Donald Davidson and Robert Brandom. I see the increasing consensus on this thesis as marking a breakthrough into a new philosophical world. In this new world, we shall no longer think of either thought or language as containing representations of reality. We shall be freed both from the subject–object problematic that has dominated philosophy since Descartes and from the appearance–reality problematic that has been with us since the Greeks. We shall no longer be tempted to practice either epistemology or ontology.

The second, shorter, portion of the chapter consists of some curt, staccato, dogmatic theses about the need to abandon the intertwined notions of "philosophical method" and of "philosophical problems." I view the popularity of these notions as an unfortunate consequence of the overprofessionalization of philosophy that has disfigured this area of culture since the time of Kant. If one adopts a non-representationalist view of thought and language, one will move away from Kant in the direction of Hegel's historicism.

Historicism has no use for the idea that there are recurrent philosophical problems that philosophers have employed various methods to solve. This description of the history of philosophy should, I think, be replaced by an account on which philosophers, like other intellectuals, make imaginative suggestions for a redescription of the human situation; they offer new ways of talking about our hopes and fears, our ambitions and our prospects. Philosophical progress is thus not a matter of problems being solved, but of descriptions being improved.

I

Arthur Fine's famous article "The Natural Ontological Attitude" begins with the sentence "Realism is dead." In a footnote to that article, Fine offers a pregnant analogy between realism and theism.

In support of realism there seem to be only those "reasons of the heart" which, as Pascal says, reason does not know. Indeed, I have long felt that belief in realism involves a profound leap of faith, not at all dissimilar from the faith that animates deep religious convictions . . . The dialogue will proceed more fruitfully, I think, when the realists finally stop pretending to a rational support for their faith, which they do not have. Then we can all enjoy their intricate and sometimes beautiful philosophical constructions (of, e.g., knowledge, or reference, etc.) even though to us, the nonbelievers, they may seem only wonder-full castles in the air.[1]

In an article called "Pragmatism as Anti-authoritarianism,"[2] I tried to expand on Fine's analogy. I suggested that we see heartfelt devotion to realism as the Enlightenment's version of the religious urge to bow down before a non-human power. The term "Reality as it is in itself, apart from human needs and interests," is, in my view, just another of the obsequious Names of God. In that article, I suggested that we treat the idea that physics gets you closer to reality than morals as an updated version of the priests' claim to be in closer touch with God than the laity.

As I see contemporary philosophy, the great divide is between representationalists, the people who believe that there is an intrinsic nature of non-human reality that humans have a duty to grasp, and anti-representationalists. I think F. C. S. Schiller was on the right track when he said that "Pragmatism . . . is in reality only the application of Humanism to the theory of knowledge."[3] I take Schiller's point to be that the humanists' claim that human beings have responsibilities only to one another entails giving up both representationalism and realism.

Representationalists are necessarily realists, and conversely. For realists believe both that there is one, and only one, Way the World Is In Itself, and that there are "hard" areas of culture in which this Way is revealed. In these areas, they say, there are "facts of the matter" to be discovered, though in softer areas there are not. By contrast, anti-representationalists believe that scientific, like moral, progress is a matter of finding ever more effective ways to enrich human life. They make no distinction between hard and soft

---

[1] Arthur Fine, "The Natural Ontological Attitude," in his *The Shaky Game: Einstein, Realism and the Quantum Theory* (Chicago: University of Chicago Press, 1986), 116n.

[2] *Revue Internationale de Philosophie* 53, no. 207 (1999), 7–20.

[3] F. C. S. Schiller, *Humanism: Philosophical Essays*, 2nd edn (London: Macmillan, 1912), xxv.

areas of culture, other than the sociological distinction between less and more controversial topics. Realists think of anti-representationalists as anti-realists, but in doing so they confuse discarding the hard–soft distinction with preaching universal softness.

Intellectuals cannot live without pathos. Theists find pathos in the distance between the human and the divine. Realists find it in the abyss separating human thought and language from reality as it is in itself. Pragmatists find it in the gap between contemporary humanity and a utopian human future in which the very idea of responsibility to anything except our fellow-humans has become unintelligible, resulting in the first truly humanistic culture.

If you do not like the term "pathos," the word "romance" would do as well. Or one might use Thomas Nagel's term: "the ambition of transcendence." The important point is simply that both sides in contemporary philosophy are trying to gratify one of the urges previously satisfied by religion. History suggests that we cannot decide which form of pathos is preferable by deploying arguments. Neither the realist nor her anti-representationalist opponent will ever have anything remotely like a knockdown argument, any more than Enlightenment secularism had such an argument against theists. One's choice of pathos will be settled, as Fine rightly suggests, by the reasons of one's heart.

The realist conviction that there just must be a non-human authority to which humans can turn has been, for a very long time, woven into the common sense of the West. It is a conviction common to Socrates and to Luther, to atheistic natural scientists who say they love truth and fundamentalists who say they love Christ. I think it would be a good idea to reweave the network of shared beliefs and desires that makes up Western culture in order to get rid of this conviction. But doing so will take centuries, or perhaps millennia. This reweaving, if it ever occurs, will result in everybody becoming commonsensically verificationist – in being unable to pump up the intuitions to which present-day realists and theists appeal.

To grasp the need to fall back on reasons of the heart, consider the theist who is told that the term "God," as used in the conclusion of the cosmological argument, is merely a name for our ignorance. Then consider the realist who is told that his explanation for the success of science is no better than Molière's doctor's explanation of why opium puts people to sleep. Then consider the pragmatist who is told, perhaps by John Searle, that his verificationism confuses epistemology and ontology. All three will probably be unfazed by these would-be knockdown arguments. Even if they admit that their opponent's point admits of no refutation, they will remark, complacently and correctly, that it produces no conviction.

It is often said that religion was refuted by showing the incoherence of the concept of God. It is said, almost as often, that realism has been refuted by showing the incoherence of the notions of "intrinsic nature of reality" and "correspondence," and that pragmatism is refuted by pointing out its habit of confusing knowing with being. But no one accustomed to employ a term like "the will of God" or "mind-independent World" in expressing views central to her sense of how things hang together is likely to be persuaded that the relevant concepts are incoherent. Nor is any pragmatist likely to be convinced that the notion of something real but indescribable in human language or unknowable by human minds can be made coherent. A concept, after all, is just the use of a word. Much-used and well-loved words and phrases are not abandoned merely because their users have been forced into tight dialectical corners.

To be sure words and uses of words do get discarded. But that is because more attractive words or uses have become available. Insofar as religion has been dying out among the intellectuals in recent centuries, it is because of the attractions of a humanist culture, not because of flaws internal to the discourse of theists. Insofar as Fine is right that realism is dying out among the philosophers, this is because of the attractions of a culture that is more deeply and unreservedly humanist than that offered by the arrogant scientism that was the least fortunate legacy of the Enlightenment.

For all these reasons, I do not want to echo Fine's charge that the realist, like the theist, lacks "rational support" for his beliefs. The notion of "rational support" is not apropos when it comes to proposals to retain, or to abandon, intuitions or hopes as deep-lying as those to which theists, realists, and anti-representationalists appeal. Where argument seems always to fail, as James rightly says in "The Will to Believe," the reasons of the heart will and should have their way. But this does not mean that the human heart always has the same reasons, asks the same questions, and hopes for the same answers. The gradual growth of secularism – the gradual increase in the number of people who do not find theism what James called "a live, momentous and forced option" – is testimony to the heart's malleability.

Only when the sort of cultural change I optimistically envisage is complete will we be able to start doing what Fine suggests – enjoying such intricate intellectual displays as the *Summa Contra Gentiles* or *Naming and Necessity* as aesthetic spectacles. Someday realism may no longer be "a live, momentous and forced option" for us. If that day comes, we shall think of questions about the mind-independence of the real as having the quaint charm of questions about the consubstantiality of the Persons of the Trinity. In the sort of culture that I hope our remote descendants may inhabit, the philosophical literature about realism and antirealism will have been aestheticized in the way that we moderns have aestheticized the medieval disputations about the ontological status of universals.

Michael Dummett has suggested that many traditional philosophical problems boil down to questions about which true sentences are made true by "facts" and which are not. This suggestion capitalizes on one of Plato's worst ideas: the idea that we can divide up the culture into the hard areas, where the non-human is encountered and acknowledged, and the softer areas in which we are on our own. The attempt to divide culture into harder and softer areas is the most familiar contemporary expression of the hope that there may be something to which human beings are responsible other than their fellow-humans. The idea of a hard area of culture is the idea of an area in which this responsibility is salient. Dummett's suggestion that many philosophical debates have been, and should continue to be, about which sentences are bivalent amounts to the claim that philosophers have a special responsibility to figure out where the hard stops and the soft begins.

A great deal of Fine's work is devoted to casting doubt on the need to draw any such line. Among philosophers of science, he has done the most to deflate Quine's arrogant quip that philosophy of science is philosophy enough. His view that science is not special, not different from the rest of culture in any philosophically interesting way, chimes with Davidson's and Brandom's attempt to put all true sentences on a referential par, and thereby to erase further the line between the hard and the soft. Fine, Davidson, and Brandom have helped us understand how to stop thinking of intellectual progress as a matter of increasing tightness of fit with the non-human world. They help us picture it instead as our being forced by that world to reweave our networks of belief and desire in ways that make us better able to get what we want. A fully humanist culture, of the sort I envisage, will emerge only when we discard the question "Do I know the real object, or only one of its appearances?" and replace it with the question "Am I using the best possible description of the situation in which I find myself, or can I cobble together a better one?"

Fine's "NOA papers"[4] fit together nicely with Davidson's claim that we can make no good use of the notion of "mind-independent reality" and with Brandom's Sellarsian attempt to interpret both meaning and reference

---

[4] These papers include, in addition to "The Natural Ontological Attitude" and "And Not Anti-realism Either" (both in Fine's *The Shaky Game*), the "Afterword" to *The Shaky Game* and "Unnatural Attitudes: Realist and Instrumentalist Attachments to Science," *Mind* 95 (April 1986), 149–79.

as functions of the rights and responsibilities of participants in a social practice. The writings of these three philosophers blend together, in my imagination, to form a sort of manifesto for the kind of anti-representationalist
movement in philosophy whose humanistic aspirations I have outlined.

Occasionally, however, I come across passages, or lines of thought, in
Fine's work that are obstacles to my syncretic efforts. The following passage
in Fine's "The Natural Ontological Attitude" gives me pause:

> When NOA counsels us to accept the results of science as true, I take it that we
> are to treat truth in the usual referential way, so that a sentence (or statement) is
> true just in case the entities referred to stand in the referred-to relations. Thus
> NOA sanctions ordinary referential semantics and commits us, via truth, to the
> existence of the individuals, properties, relations, processes, and so forth referred
> to by the scientific statements that we accept as true.[5]

Reading this passage leaves me uncertain of whether Fine wants to read
all the sentences we accept as true – the ones accepted after reading works
of literary criticism as well as after reading scientific textbooks – as true
"just in case the entities referred to stand in the referred-to relations."
Davidson is clearer on this point. He thinks that the sentence "Perseverance
keeps honor bright" is true in this way, the same way that "The cat is on
the mat," "F=MA," and every other true sentence is true. But Davidson
thinks this in part because he does not think that reference has anything to
do with ontological commitment. The latter is a notion for which he has
no use, just as he has no use for the distinction between sentences made
true by the world and those made true by us.

Fine, alas, does seem to have a use for ontological commitment. Indeed,
I suspect he drags in "ordinary referential semantics" because he thinks that
the deployment of such a semantics might help one decide what ontological commitments to have. But it would accord better with the overall drift
of Fine's thinking if he were to discard that unfortunate Quinean idea
rather than attempting to rehabilitate it. NOA, Fine says, "tries to let
science speak for itself, and it trusts in our native ability to get the message
without having to rely on metaphysical or epistemological hearing aids."[6]
So why, I am tempted to ask Fine, would you want to drag in a semiotic
hearing aid such as "ordinary referential semantics"? Fine recommends that
we stop trying to "conceive of truth as a substantial something," something
that can "act as limit for legitimate human aspirations."[7] But if we accept
this recommendation, will we still want to say, as Fine does, that we are
"committed, via truth, to the existence" of this or that?

---

[5] Fine, "NOA," 130.   [6] Fine, "And Not Anti-realism Either," 63.   [7] Ibid.

As support for my suggestion that the notion of ontological commitment is one Fine could get along nicely without, let me cite another of his instructive remarks about the analogy between religion and realism. Fine's answer to the question "Do you believe in X?," for such X's as electrons and dinosaurs and DNA, is "I take the question of belief to be whether to accept the entities or instead to question the science that backs them up."[8] Then, in response to the objection "But does not 'believe in' mean that they really and truly exist out there in the world?," Fine says that he is not sure it does. He points out that "those who believe in the existence of God do not think that is the meaning [they attach to their claim] at least not in any ordinary sense of 'really and truly out there in the world.'"

I take the point of the analogy to be that unquestioningly and unphilosophically religious people need not distinguish between talking about God as they do and believing in God. To say that they believe in God and that they habitually and seriously talk the talk are two ways of saying the same thing. Similarly, for a physicist to assert that to say that she believes in electrons and to say that she does not question the science behind electron-talk are two ways of asserting the same thing. The belief cannot count as a reason for the unquestioning attitude, nor conversely.

When Kant or Tillich ask the pious whether they are perhaps really talking about a regulative ideal or a symbol of ultimate concern rather than about the existence of a being, the pious are quite right to be annoyed and unresponsive. Physicists should be equally irritated when asked whether they think that statements about electrons are true or merely empirically adequate. The theist sees no reason why he need resort to natural theology, or analyses of the meaning of "is," or distinctions between the symbolic–existential and the factual–empirical. For he takes God-talk into his life in exactly the way in which a physicist takes electron-talk into hers – the same way we all take dollars-and-cents talk into ours.

It accords with the overall humanist position I outlined earlier to say there are no acts called 'assent' or 'commitment' we can perform that will put us in a relation to an object different than that of simply talking about that object in sentences whose truth we have taken into our lives.

The idea of ontological commitment epitomizes a confusion between existential commitment on the one hand and a profession of satisfaction with a way of speaking or a social practice on the other. An existential commitment, as Brandom nicely says in *Making it Explicit*, is a claim to be able to provide an address for a certain singular term within the "structured

---

[8] Fine, "Afterword," 184.

space provided mapped out by certain canonical designators."[9] To deny the existence of Pegasus, for example, is to deny that "a continuous spatiotemporal trajectory can be traced out connecting the region of spacetime occupied by the speaker to one occupied by Pegasus." To deny that Sherlock Holmes' Aunt Fanny exists is to deny that she can be related to the canonical designators in Conan Doyle's text in the way that Moriarty and Mycroft can. And so on for other addresses for singular terms, such as those provided for the complex numbers by the structured space of the integers.

Putting the matter Brandom's way highlights the fact that metaphysical discourse, the discourse of ontological commitment, does not provide us with such a structured space. For no relevant designators are agreed upon to be canonical. This discourse is, instead, one in which we express our like or dislike, our patience or impatience with, various linguistic practices.

As a safeguard against linking up referential semantics with ontological commitment, it is useful to bear in mind Davidson's insistence that we should not treat reference as "a concept to be given an independent analysis or interpretation in terms of non-linguistic concepts."[10] Reference is rather, he says, a "posit we need to implement a theory of truth."[11] For Davidson, a theory of truth for a natural language "does not explain reference, at least in this sense: it assigns no empirical content directly to relations between names or predicates and objects. These relations are given a content indirectly when the T-sentences are."[12] If one assumes that a theory that permits the deduction of all the T-sentences is all we need in the way of what Fine calls "ordinary referential semantics," then reference no longer bears on ontological commitment. The latter notion will seem otiose to anyone who takes the results of both physics and literary criticism in (as Fine puts it) "the same way as we accept the evidence of our senses."

Perhaps, however, Fine would agree both with Davidson about the nature of the notion of reference and with me about the need to treat literary criticism and physics as producing truth – and reference – of exactly the same sort. That he would is suggested by his saying that those who accept NOA are "being asked not to distinguish between kinds of truth or modes of existence or the like, but only among truths themselves in terms of centrality, degrees of belief, and the like."[13]

This last quotation chimes with Fine's remark that "NOA is basically at odds with the temperament that looks for definite boundaries demarcating

[9] Robert Brandom, *Making it Explicit* (Cambridge, MA: Harvard University Press, 1994), 444.
[10] Donald Davidson, *Inquiries into Meaning and Truth* (Oxford: Oxford University Press, 1984), 219.
[11] Ibid., 222.   [12] Ibid.   [13] Fine, "NOA," 127.

science from pseudo-science, or that is inclined to award the title 'scientific' like a blue ribbon on a prize goat."[14] It chimes also with the last paragraph of his recent Presidential Address to the APA, in which he says that "the first false step in this whole area is the notion that science is special and that scientific thinking is unlike any other."[15] If we carry through on these remarks by saying that there is no more point in using notions like "reference" and "ontological attitude" in connection with physics than in connection with literary criticism, then we shall think that nobody should ever worry about having more things in her ontology than there are in heaven and earth. To stop dividing culture into the hard and the soft areas would be to cease to draw up two lists: the longer containing nominalizations of every term used as the subject of a sentence, and the shorter containing all the things there are in heaven and earth.

Before leaving the topics of reference and ontological commitment, let me remark that the passage I quoted about "ordinary referential semantics" has been seized upon by Alan Musgrave to ridicule Fine's claim to have a position distinct from that of the realist.[16] Musgrave would have had less ammunition, I think, if Fine had not only omitted this passage but had been more explicit in admitting that NOA is, as Jarrett Leplin has lately said, "not an alternative to realism and antirealism, but a preemption of philosophy altogether, at least at the metalevel."[17] Leplin is right to say that Fine's "idea that 'scientific theories speak for themselves,' that one can 'read off' of them the answers to all legitimate philosophical questions about science, cannot be squared with the rich tradition of philosophical debate among scientists over the proper interpretation of theories." So I think that Fine should neither take the Einstein–Bohr debate at face value, nor try to rehabilitate notions like "ontological commitment." He should grant to Leplin that "Philosophy of science in the role of interpreter and evaluator of the scientific enterprise, and realism in particular, as such a philosophy of science, are superfluous."[18] We felt the need for such an interpreter, evaluator, and public-relations man only so long as we thought of natural science as privileged by a special relation to non-human reality, and of the natural scientists as stepping into the shoes of the priests.

---

[14] Fine, "And Not Anti-realism Either," 62.

[15] Arthur Fine, "The Viewpoint of No One in Particular," *Proceedings And Addresses of the American Philosophical Association* 72 (November 1998), 19.

[16] See Alan Musgrave's "NOA's Ark – Fine for Realism," in *The Philosophy of Science*, ed. David Papineau (Oxford: Oxford University Press, 1996), 45–60.

[17] Jarrett Leplin, *A Novel Defense of Scientific Realism* (New York and Oxford: Oxford University Press, 1997), 174.   [18] Ibid., 139.

II

So much for my broad-brush account of the wonderful new philosophical prospects that I see Fine, Davidson, and Brandom opening up. Now I want to explain why anyone who enjoys these prospects should be suspicious of the notion of "philosophical method" and of the idea that philosophy has always dealt, and will always deal, with the same recalcitrant problems. I shall offer sixteen metaphilosophical theses that sum up my own suspicions.

Thesis One: A recent "call for papers" for a big philosophical conference refers to "The analytic methodology which has been so widely embraced in twentieth century philosophy [and which] has sought to solve philosophical problems by drawing out the meaning of our statements." Such descriptions of twentieth-century philosophy are ubiquitous, but they seem to me seriously misleading. "Drawing out the meaning of our statements" is a pre-Quinean way of describing philosophers' practice of paraphrasing statements in ways that further their very diverse purposes. It would be pointless to think of the disagreements between Carnap and Austin, Davidson and Lewis, Kripke and Brandom, Fine and Leplin, or Nagel and Dennett as arising from the differing meanings that they believe themselves to have found in certain statements. These classic philosophical standoffs are not susceptible of resolution by means of more careful and exacting ways of drawing out meanings.

Thesis Two: The philosophers I have just named belong to, or at least were raised in, a common disciplinary matrix – one in which most members of Anglophone philosophy departments were also raised. Philosophers so raised do not practice a common method. What binds them together is rather a shared interest in the question, "What happens if we transform old philosophical questions about the relation of thought to reality into questions about the relation of language to reality?"

Thesis Three: Dummett is wrong in thinking that such transformations suggest that philosophy of language is first philosophy. His picture of the rest of philosophy as occupied with the analysis of "specific types of sentence or special forms of expression,"[19] analyses that can be guided or corrected by discoveries about the nature of meaning made by philosophers of language, has no relevance to the actual arguments that analytic philosophers invoke.

---

[19] Michael Dummett, "Can Analytical Philosophy Be Systematic, and Ought it to Be?" in his *Truth and other Enigmas* (Cambridge, MA: Harvard University Press, 1978), 442.

Thesis Four: The diverse answers to the question of the relation between language and reality given by analytic philosophers do indeed divide up along some of the same lines that once divided realists from idealists. But Dummett is wrong to think that this earlier division was marked by disagreement about which sentences are made true by the world and which by us. Rather, the division between Bain and Bradley, or between Moore and Royce, was one between representationalist atomists and non-representationalist holists. The latter are the people whom Brandom refers to as his fellow-inferentialists. They include all the people traditionally identified as "idealists," just as the representationalists include all those traditionally identified as "empiricists."

Thesis Five: Anti-representationalists do not use a different method than representationalists, unless one uses the term "method" synonymously with "research program," or "leading idea," or "basic insight," or "fundamental motivation." Such uses are misleading. The term "method" should be restricted to agreed-upon procedures for settling disputes between competing claims. Such a procedure was what Ayer and Carnap on the one side, and Husserl on the other, thought had recently been discovered. They were wrong. Nagel and Dennett no more appeal to such a procedure than did Cassirer and Heidegger. Neither logical analysis nor phenomenology produced anything like the procedure for settling philosophical quarrels that the founders envisaged.

Thesis Six: When "method" is used in this restricted sense, as meaning "neutral decision procedure," there is no such thing as either philosophical or scientific method. There are only local and specific agreements on procedure within such specific expert cultures as stellar spectroscopy, modal logic, admiralty law, possible-world semantics, or Sanskrit philology. There is no method shared by geologists and particle physicists but not employed by lawyers and literary critics. Nor is there any method shared by Kripke and Davidson, or by Nagel and Dennett, that is more peculiarly philosophical than ordinary argumentative give-and-take – the kind of conversational exchange that is as frequent outside disciplinary matrices as within them.

Thesis Seven: The idea that philosophy should be put on the secure path of a science is as bad as the idea, mocked by Fine, of awarding prizes for scientificity as one awards blue ribbons to prize goats. It is one thing to say that philosophers should form a distinct expert culture, but quite another to suggest that they ought to be more like mathematicians than like lawyers, or more like microbiologists than like historians. You can have an expert culture without having an agreed-upon procedure for resolving disputes. Expertise is a matter of familiarity with the course of a previous conversation, not a matter of ability to bring that conversation to a conclusion by attaining general agreement.

Thesis Eight: If twentieth-century analytic philosophy gets favorable reviews in the writings of intellectual historians of the twenty-second century, this will not be because those historians are impressed by its exceptional clarity and rigor. It will be because they have seen that following up on Frege's suggestion that we talk about the statements rather than about thoughts made it possible to frame the old issue between representationalist atomists and non-representationalist holists in a new way. Representation in the relevant sense is a matter of part-to-part correspondence between mental or linguistic and non-mental or non-linguistic complexes. That is why it took what Bergmann called the "linguistic turn" to get the issue into proper focus. For thoughts do not have discrete parts in the right way, but statements do. Frege's dictum that words only have meanings in the contexts of sentences will be seen by future intellectual historians as the beginning of the end for representationalist philosophy.

Thesis Nine: The issue between the non-representationalists and the representationalists is not a matter of competing methods. Nor is the issue about whether a proper graduate education in philosophy should include reading Hegel and Heidegger or mastering symbolic logic. Both are matters of what one thinks it important and interesting to talk about. There is not now, and there never will be, a method for settling disputes about what is interesting and important. If one's heart leads one toward realism, then one will take representationalism and research programs for analyzing complexes into simples seriously. If it leads one elsewhere, one probably will not.

Thesis Ten: The idea of method is, etymology suggests, the idea of a road that takes you from the starting point of inquiry to its goal. The best translation of the Greek *meth' odō* is "on track." Representationalists, because they believe that there are objects that are what they are apart from the way they are described, can take seriously the picture of a track leading from subject to object. Anti-representationalists cannot. They see inquiry not as crossing a gap but as a gradual reweaving of individual or communal beliefs and desires under the pressure of causal impacts made by the behavior of people and things. Such reweaving dissolves problems as often as it solves them. The idea that the problems of philosophy stay the same but the method of dealing with them changes begs the metaphilosophical question at issue between representationalists and non-representationalists. It is much easier to formulate specific "philosophical problems" if, with Kant, you think that there are concepts that stay fixed regardless of historical change rather than, with Hegel, that concepts change as history moves along. Hegelian historicism and the idea that the philosopher's job is to draw out the meanings of our statements cannot easily be reconciled.

Thesis Eleven: Anti-representationalists are sometimes accused, as Fine has been by Leplin and I have been by Nagel, of wanting to walk away from philosophy. But this charge confuses walking away from a certain historically determined disciplinary matrix with walking away from philosophy itself. Philosophy is not something anybody can ever walk away from; it is an amorphous blob that will englobe anyone attempting such an excursion. But unless people occasionally walk away from old disciplinary matrices as briskly as Descartes and Hobbes walked away from Aristotelianism, or Carnap and Heidegger from neo-Kantianism, decadent scholasticism is almost inevitable.

Thesis Twelve: Sometimes those who walk away from worn-out disciplinary matrices offer new philosophical research programs, as Descartes and Carnap did. Sometimes they do not, as in the cases of Montaigne and Heidegger. But research programs are not essential to philosophy. They are of course a great boon to the professionalization of philosophy as an academic specialty. But greater professionalization should not be confused with intellectual progress, any more than a nation's economic or military might should be confused with its contribution to civilization.

Thesis Thirteen: Professionalization gives an edge to atomists over holists and thus to representationalists over non-representationalists. For philosophers who have theories about the elementary components of language or of thought and about how these elements get compounded look more systematic, and thus more professional, than philosophers who say that everything is relative to context. The latter see their opponents' so-called elementary components as simply nodes in webs of changing relationships.

Thesis Fourteen: The big split between "continental" and "analytic" philosophy is largely due to the fact that historicism and anti-representationalism are much more common among non-Anglophone philosophers than among their Anglophone colleagues. It is easy to bring Davidson together with Derrida and Gadamer, or Brandom together with Hegel and Heidegger. But it is less easy to find common ground between somebody distinctively "continental" and Searle, Kripke, Lewis, or Nagel. It is this difference in substantive philosophical doctrine, rather than any difference between "methods," that makes it unlikely that the split will be healed.

Thesis Fifteen: Philosophical progress is not made by patiently carrying out research programs to the end. Such programs all eventually trickle into the sands. It is made by great imaginative feats. These are performed by people like Hegel or Wittgenstein who tell us that a picture has been holding us captive. Many people on both sides of the analytic–continental split are spending much of their time waiting for Godot. They hope someone will do for us what *Philosophical Investigations* or *Being and Time* did for our predecessors – wake us from what we belatedly realize to have been dogmatic slumber.

Thesis Sixteen: Waiting for a guru is a perfectly respectable thing for us philosophers to do. It is waiting for the human imagination to flare up once again, waiting for it to suggest a way of speaking that we had not thought of before. Just as intellectuals cannot live without pathos, they cannot live without gurus. But they can live without priests. They do not need the sort of guru who explains that his or her authority comes from a special relation to something non-human, a relation gained by having found the correct track across an abyss.

10

Naturalism and quietism

Philosophy is an almost invisible part of contemporary intellectual life. Most people outside of philosophy departments have no clear idea of what philosophy professors are supposed to contribute to culture. Few think it worth the trouble to inquire.

The lack of attention that our discipline receives is sometimes attributed to the technicality of the issues currently being discussed. But that is not a good explanation. Debates between today's philosophers of language and mind are no more tiresomely technical than were those between interpreters and critics of Kant in the 1790s.

The problem is not the style in which philosophy is currently being done in the English-speaking world. It is rather that many of the issues discussed by Descartes, Hume, and Kant had cultural resonance only as long as a significant portion of the educated classes still resisted the secularization of moral and political life.[1] The claim that human beings are alone in the universe, and that they should not look for help from supernatural agencies, went hand-in-hand with the admission that Democritus and Epicurus had been largely right about how the universe works. The canonically great

---

[1] The most important change produced by secularism was a shift from thinking of morality as a matter of unconditional prohibitions to seeing it as an attempt to work out compromises between competing human needs. This change is well described in a famous article by Elizabeth Anscombe called "Modern Moral Philosophy." She contrasts hard, unconditional, prohibitions of such things as adultery, sodomy, and suicide with the soft, squishy consequentialism advocated by, as she says, "every English academic moral philosopher after [Sidgwick]." That consequentialism is, Anscombe says, "quite incompatible with the Hebrew-Christian ethic": Elizabeth Anscombe, *Ethics, Religion and Politics* (Minneapolis University of Minnesota Press, 1981), 34.

In the United States we are currently experiencing a return to the the latter ethic – a revolt of the masses against the consequentialism of the intellectuals. The current red-state vs. blue-state clash is a flareup of the old struggle about the secularization of culture. But almost nobody now looks to philosophy for help with this struggle. In the seventeenth and eighteenth centuries, they did. Writers like Spinoza and Hume did a great deal to advance the secularist cause. In the course of the nineteenth and twentieth centuries, however, the baton was passed to art and literature. Novels whose characters discussed moral dilemmas without reference to God or Scripture took the place of moral philosophy.

modern philosophers performed a useful service by suggesting ways of dealing with the triumph of mechanistic materialism.

But as the so-called "warfare between science and theology" gradually tapered off, there was less and less useful work for philosophers to do. Just as medieval scholasticism became tedious once Christian doctrine had been synthesized with Greek philosophy, so a great deal of modern philosophy began to seem pointless after most intellectuals either abandoned their religious faith or found ways of rendering it compatible with modern natural science. Although rabble-rousers can still raise doubts about Darwin among the masses, the intellectuals – the only people on whom philosophy books have any impact – have no such doubts. They do not require either a sophisticated metaphysics or a fancy theory of reference to convince them that there are no spooks.

After the intellectuals had become convinced that empirical science, rather than metaphysics, told us how things work, philosophy had a choice between two alternatives. One was to follow Hegel's lead and to become a combination of intellectual history and cultural criticism – the sort of thing offered by Heidegger and Dewey, as well as by such people as Adorno, Strauss, Arendt, Berlin, Blumenberg, and Habermas. This way of doing philosophy flourishes mainly in the non-Anglophone philosophical world, but it is also found in the books of American philosophers such as Robert Pippin.

The other alternative was to imitate Kant by developing an armchair research program, thereby helping philosophy win a place in universities as an autonomous academic discipline. What was needed was a program that resembled Kant's in having no place for observation, experiment, or historical knowledge. German neo-Kantians and British empiricists agreed that the core of philosophy was inquiry into something called "Experience" or "Consciousness." An alternative program was launched by Frege and Peirce, this one purporting to investigate something called "Language" or "the Sign."

Both programs assumed that, just as matter can be broken down into atoms, so can experience and language. The first sort of atoms include Lockean simple ideas, Kantian unsynthesized intuitions, sense-data, and the objects of Husserlian *Wesenschau*. The second include Fregean senses, Peircean signs, and Tractarian linguistic pictures. By insisting that questions concerning the relation of such immaterial atoms to physical particles were at the core of their discipline, philosophers in Anglophone countries shoved social philosophy, intellectual history, culture criticism, and Hegel to the periphery.

Yet there have always been holists – philosophers who were dubious about the existence of either atoms of consciousness or atoms of significance. Holists often become skeptics about the existence of shadowy surrogates for Reality such as "Experience," "Consciousness," and "Language." Wittgenstein, the most celebrated of these skeptics, came close to suggesting that the so-called "core" areas of philosophy serve no function save to keep an academic discipline in business.

Skepticism of this sort has come to be labeled "quietism." Brian Leiter, in his introduction to a recently published collection titled *The Future for Philosophy*, divides the Anglophone philosophical world into "naturalists" and "Wittgensteinian quietists." The latter, he says, think of philosophy as "a kind of *therapy*, dissolving philosophical problems rather than solving them."[2] "Unlike the Wittgensteinians," Leiter continues, "the naturalists believe that the problems that have worried philosophers (about the nature of the mind, knowledge, action, reality, morality, and so on) are indeed real."[3]

I think Leiter's account of the standoff between these two camps is largely accurate. He has identified the deepest and most intractable difference of opinion within contemporary Anglophone philosophy. But his account is misleading in one respect. Most people who think of themselves in the quietist camp, as I do, would hesitate to say that the problems studied by our activist colleagues are *unreal*. They do not divide philosophical problems into the real and the illusory, but rather into those that retain some relevance to cultural politics and those that do not. Quietists, at least those of my sect, think that such relevance needs to be demonstrated before a problem is taken seriously. This view is a corollary of the maxim that what does not make a difference to practice should not make a difference to philosophers.

From this point of view, questions about the place of values in a world of fact are no more unreal than questions about how the Eucharistic blood and wine can embody the divine substance, or about how many sacraments Christ instituted. Neither of the latter problems are problems for *everybody*, but their parochial character does not render them illusory. For what one finds problematic is a function of what one thinks important. One's sense of importance is in large part dependent on the vocabulary one employs. So cultural politics is often a struggle between those who urge that a familiar vocabulary be eschewed and those who defend the old ways of speaking.

---

[2] Brian Leiter, ed., *The Future for Philosophy* (Oxford: Oxford University Press, 2004), 2.
[3] Ibid., 2–3.

Consider Leiter's assertion that "Neuroscientists tell us about the brain, and philosophers try to figure out how to square our best neuroscience with the ability of our minds to represent what the world is like."[4] The quietist response is to ask whether we really want to hold on to the notion of "representing what the world is like." Perhaps, they suggest, it is time to give up the notion of "the world," and of shadowy entities called "the mind" or "language" that contain representations of the world. Study of the history of culture helps us understand why these notions gained currency, just as it shows why certain theological notions became as important as they did. But such study also suggests that many of the central ideas of modern philosophy, like many topics in Christian theology, have become more trouble than they are worth.

Philip Pettit, in his contribution to *The Future for Philosophy*, gives an account of the naturalists' metaphilosophical outlook that is somewhat fuller than Leiter's. Philosophy, he says, is an attempt to reconcile "the manifest image of how things are" and the "ideas that come to us with our spontaneous everyday practices" with "fidelity to the intellectual image of how things are."[5] In our culture, Pettit says, the intellectual image is the one provided by physical science. He sums up by saying that "a naturalistic, more or less mechanical image of the universe is imposed on us by cumulative developments in physics, biology and neuroscience, and this challenges us to look for where in that world there can be room for phenomena that remain as vivid as ever in the manifest image: consciousness, freedom, responsibility, goodness, virtue and the like."[6]

Despite my veneration for Wilfrid Sellars, who originated this talk of manifest and scientific images, I would like to jettison these visual metaphors. We should not be held captive by the world-picture picture. We do not need a synoptic view of something called "the world." At most, we need a synoptic narrative of how we came to talk as we do. We should stop trying for a unified picture, and for a master vocabulary. We should confine ourselves to making sure that we are not burdened with obsolete ways of speaking, and then ensuring that those vocabularies that are still useful stay out of each other's way.

Narratives that recount how these various vocabularies came into existence help us see that terminologies we employ for some purposes need not link up in any clear way with those we employ for other purposes – that we

---

[4] Ibid., 3.
[5] Philip Pettit, "Existentialism, Quietism and Philosophy," in Leiter, *The Future for Philosophy*, 306.
[6] Ibid., 306. Pettit adds that "philosophy today is probably more challenging, and more difficult, than it has ever been." This is probably true, but the same can be said of Christian theology.

can simply let two linguistic practices coexist peaceably, side by side. This is what Hume suggested we do with the vocabulary of prediction and that of assignment of responsibility. The lesson the pragmatists drew from Hume was that philosophers should not scratch where it does not itch. When there is no longer an audience outside the discipline that displays interest in a philosophical problem, that problem should be viewed with suspicion.

Naturalists like Pettit and Leiter may respond that they are interested in philosophical truth rather than in catering to the taste of the day. This is the same rhetorical strategy that was used by seventeenth-century Aristotelians trying to fend off Hobbes and Descartes. Hobbes responded that those still sweating away in what he called "the hothouses of vain philosophy" were in the grip of an obsolete terminology, one that made the problems they discussed seem urgent. Contemporary quietists think the same about their activist opponents. They believe that the vocabulary of representationalism is as shopworn and as dubious as that of hylomorphism.

This anti-representationalist view can be found in several contributions to a recent collection of essays titled *Naturalism in Question*, edited by Mario de Caro and David Macarthur, but is most explicit in Huw Price's "Naturalism without Representationalism." Price makes a very helpful distinction between object naturalism and subject naturalism. Object naturalism is "the view that in some important sense, all there is is the world studied by science."[7] Subject naturalism, on the other hand, simply says that "we humans are natural creatures, and if the claims and ambitions of philosophy conflict with this view, then philosophy needs to give way."

Whereas object naturalists worry about the place of non-particles in a world of particles, Price says, subject naturalists view these "placement problems" as "problems about human linguistic behavior."[8] Object naturalists ask how non-particles are related to particles because, in Price's words, they take for granted that "substantial 'word–world' semantic relations are a part of the best scientific account of our use of the relevant terms."[9] Subject naturalists, on the other hand, are semantic deflationists: they see no need for such relations – and, in particular, for that of "being made true by." They think once we have explained the uses of the relevant terms, there is no further problem about the relation of those uses to the world.

---

[7] Mario de Caro and David Macarthur, eds., *Naturalism in Question*, Cambridge, MA: Harvard University Press 2004, 73.   [8] Ibid., 76.   [9] Ibid., 78.

Bjorn Ramberg, in an article called "Naturalizing Idealizations," uses "pragmatic naturalism" to designate the same approach to philosophical problems that Price labels "subject naturalism." Ramberg writes as follows:

Reduction, says the pragmatist, is a meta-tool of science; a way of systematically extending the domain of some set of tools for handling the explanatory tasks that scientists confront. Naturalization, by contrast, is a goal of philosophy: it is the elimination of metaphysical gaps between the characteristic features by which we deal with agents and thinkers, on the one hand, and the characteristic features by reference to which we empirically generalize over the causal relations between objects and events, on the other. It is only in the context of a certain metaphysics that the scientific tool becomes a philosophical one, an instrument of legislative ontology.[10]

Pragmatic naturalism, Ramberg continues, "treats the gap itself, that which transforms reduction into a philosophical project, as a symptom of dysfunction in our philosophical vocabulary." The cure for this dysfunction, in Ramberg's words, is to provide "alternatives to what begins to look like conceptual hang-ups and fixed ideas . . . [and to explain] how our practice might change if we were to describe things . . . in altered vocabularies."[11]

Frank Jackson's book *From Metaphysics to Ethics* is a paradigm of object naturalism. Jackson says that "serious metaphysics . . . continually faces the location problem." The nature of this problem is explained in the following passage:

Because the ingredients are limited, some putative features of the world are not going to appear *explicitly* in some more basic account . . . There are inevitably a host of putative features of our world which we must either eliminate or locate.[12]

Subject naturalists, by contrast, have no use for the notion of "merely putative feature of the world," unless this is taken to mean something like "topic not worth talking about." Their question is not "What features does the world *really* have?" but "What topics are worth discussing?" Subject naturalists may think that the culture as a whole would be better off if a certain language game were no longer played, but they do not argue that some of the words deployed in that practice signify unreal entities. Nor do they urge that some sentences be understood as about something quite different from what they are putatively about.

For Jackson, the method of what he calls "serious metaphysics" is conceptual analysis, for the following reason:

---

[10] Bjorn Ramberg, "Naturalizing Idealizations: Pragmatism and the Interpretive Strategy," *Contemporary Pragmatism* 1, no. 2 (2004), 43.   [11] Ibid., 47.

[12] Frank Jackson, *From Metaphysics to Ethics: A Defence of Conceptual Analysis* (Oxford: Oxford University Press, 1998), 5.

Serious metaphysics requires us to address when matters described in one vocabulary *are made true by* matters described in another vocabulary. But how could we possibly address this question in the absence of a consideration of when it is right to describe matters in the terms of the various vocabularies? . . . And to do that . . . is to do conceptual analysis.[13]

But conceptual analysis does not tell the serious metaphysician which matters make which statements about other matters true. He already knows that. As Jackson goes on to say, "Conceptual analysis is not being given a role in determining the fundamental nature of the world; it is, rather, being given a central role in determining what to say in less fundamental terms given an account of the world stated in more fundamental terms."[14]

As I have already emphasized, subject naturalists have no use for Jackson's key notion – that of "being made true by." They are content, Price says, with "a use-explanatory account of semantic terms, while saying nothing of theoretical weight about whether these terms 'refer' or 'have truth-conditions.' "[15] The subject naturalist's basic task, he continues, is "to account for the uses of various terms – among them, the semantic terms themselves – in the lives of natural creatures in a natural environment."

If you think that there is such a relation as "being made true by" then you can still hope, as Jackson does, to correct the linguistic practices of your day on theoretical grounds, rather than merely cultural–political ones. For your a priori knowledge of what makes sentences true permits you to evaluate the relation between the culture of your day and the intrinsic nature of reality itself. But subject naturalists like Price can criticize culture only by arguing that a proposed alternative culture would better serve our larger purposes.

Price confronts Jackson with the following question: "[if we can explain] why natural creatures in a natural environment come to *talk* in these plural ways – of 'truth', 'value', 'meaning', 'causation', all the rest – what puzzle remains? What debt does philosophy now owe to science?"[16] That question can be expanded along the following lines: if you know not only how words are used, but what purposes are and are not served by so using them, what more could philosophy hope to tell you?

If you want to know about the relation between language and reality, the quietist continues, consider how the early hominids might have started

---

[13] Ibid., 41–2; emphasis added.   [14] Ibid., 42–3.

[15] Price, "Naturalism without Representationalism," in Caro and Macarthur, *Naturalism in Question*, 79.   [16] Ibid., 87.

using marks and noises to coordinate their actions. Then consult the anthropologists and the intellectual historians. These are the people who can tell you how our species progressed from organizing searches for food to building cities and writing books. Given narratives such as these, what purpose is served by tacking on an account of the relation of these achievements to the behavior of physical particles?

Both Jackson and Price pride themselves on being naturalists, but different things come to their minds when they speak of "nature." When Jackson uses that word he thinks of particles. A subject naturalist like Price thinks instead of organisms coping with, and improving, their environment. The object naturalist expresses his fear of spooks by insisting that everything be tied in, somehow, with the movements of the atoms through the void. The subject naturalist expresses his fear of spooks by insisting that our stories about how evolution led from the protozoa to the Renaissance should contain no sudden discontinuities – that it be a story of gradually increasingly complexity of physiological structure facilitating increasingly complex behavior.

For the subject naturalist, the import of Price's dictum that "we are natural creatures in a natural environment" is that we should be wary of drawing lines between kinds of organisms in non-behavioral and non-physiological terms. This means that we should not use terms such as "intentionality," or "consciousness" or "representation" unless we can specify, at least roughly, what sort of behavior suffices to show the presence of the referents of these terms.

For example, if we want to say that squids have intentionality but paramecia do not, or that there is something it is like to be a bat but nothing it is like to be an earthworm, or that insects represent their environment whereas plants merely respond to it, we should be prepared to explain how we can tell – to specify what behavioral or physiological facts are relevant to this claim. If we cannot do that, we are merely inventing spooks in order to provide work for ghost-busters.

This emphasis on behavioral criteria is reminiscent of the positivists' verificationism. But it differs in that it is not the product of a general theory about the nature of meaning, one that enables us to distinguish sense from nonsense. The subject naturalist can cheerfully admit that any expression will have a sense if you give it one. It is rather that traditional philosophical distinctions complicate narratives of biological evolution to no good purpose. In the same spirit, liberal theologians argue that questions about the number of the sacraments, though perfectly intelligible, are distractions from the Christian message.

Fundamentalist Catholics, of course, insist that such questions are still very important. Object naturalists are equally insistent that it is important to ask, for example, how collocations of physical particles manage to display moral virtue. Quietist Christians think that the questions insisted on by these Catholics are relics of a relatively primitive period in the reception of Christ's message. Quietist philosophers think that the questions still being posed by their activist colleagues were, in the seventeenth century, reasonable enough. They were a predictable product of the shock produced by the New Science. By now, however, they have become irrelevant to intellectual life. Christian faith without sacramentalism and what Price calls "naturalism without representationalism" are both cultural-political initiatives.

So far I have been painting the object naturalist vs. subject naturalist opposition with a fairly broad brush. Now I shall try to show the relevance of this opposition to a couple of current philosophical controversies.

The first of these is a disagreement between Timothy Williamson and John McDowell. The anthology edited by Brian Leiter to which I have already referred includes a lively polemical essay by Williamson titled "Past the Linguistic Turn?" Williamson starts off by attacking a view that John McDowell takes over from Hegel, Wittgenstein, and Sellars: viz., "Since the world is everything that is the case . . . there is no gap between thought, as such, and the world." Williamson paraphrases this as the claim that "the conceptual has no outer boundary beyond which lies unconceptualized reality" and again as the thesis that "any object can be thought of."[17]

Williamson says that "for all that McDowell has shown, there may be necessary limitations on all possible thinkers. We do not know whether there are elusive objects. It is unclear what would motivate the claim that there are none, if not some form of idealism. We should adopt no conception of philosophy that on methodological grounds excludes elusive objects."[18]

I think that McDowell, a self-professed quietist, might respond by saying that we should indeed adopt a conception of philosophy that excludes elusive objects. We should do so for reasons of cultural politics. We should say that cultures that worry about unanswerable questions like "Are there necessary limitations on all possible thinkers?", "Could God change the truths of arithmetic?", "Am I dreaming now?" and "Is my color

[17] Timothy Williamson, "Past the Linguistic Turn?," in Leiter, *The Future for Philosophy*, 109.
[18] Ibid., 110.

spectrum the inverse of yours?" are less advanced than those that respect Peirce's pragmatic maxim. Superior cultures have no use for what Peirce called "make-believe doubt."

Williamson is wrong to suggest that only idealism could motivate McDowell's thesis. The difference between idealism and pragmatism is that between metaphysical or epistemological arguments for the claim that any object can be thought of and cultural-political arguments for it. Pragmatists think that the idea of necessary limitations on all possible thinkers is as weird as Augustine's thesis about the inevitability of sin – *non posse non peccare.* Neither can be refuted, but healthy-mindedness requires that both be dismissed out of hand.[19]

The clash of opinion between McDowell and Williamson epitomizes the opposition between two recent lines of thought within analytic philosophy. One runs from Wittgenstein through Sellars and Davidson to McDowell and Brandom. The other is associated with what Williamson calls "the revival of metaphysical theorizing, realist in spirit . . . associated with Saul Kripke, David Lewis, Kit Fine, Peter van Inwagen, David Armstrong and many others."[20] The goal of such attempts to get past the linguistic turn is, Williamson says, "to discover what fundamental kind of things there are, and what properties and relations they have, not how we represent them."[21] The contrast between these two lines of thought will become vivid to anyone who flips back and forth between the two collections of articles from which I have been quoting – Leiter's *The Future for Philosophy* and De Caro's and Macarthur's *Naturalism in Question.*

Quietists think that no kind of thing is more fundamental than any other kind of thing. The fact that, as Jackson puts it, you cannot change anything without changing the motions or positions of elementary physical particles, does nothing to show that there is a problem about how these particles leave room for non-particles. It is no more philosophically pregnant than the fact that you cannot mess with the particles without simultaneously messing with a great many other things. Such expressions as "the nature of reality" or "the world as it really is" have in the past, quietists admit, played a role in producing desirable cultural change. But so have many other ladders that we were well advised to throw away.

---

[19] Pragmatism takes its stand against all doctrines that hold, in the words of Leo Strauss, that "Even by proving that a certain view is indispensable to living well, one merely proves that the view in question is a salutary myth: one does not prove it be true": *Natural Right and History* (Chicago: Chicago University Press, 1968), 6. Strauss goes on to say that "Utility and truth are two entirely different things." Pragmatists do not think they are the same thing, but they do think that you cannot have the latter without the former.

[20] Williamson. "Past the Linguistic Turn?", 111.   [21] Ibid., 110–11.

Quietists who have no use for the notion of "the world as it is apart from our ways of representing it" will balk at Williamson's thesis that "what there is determines what there is for us to mean." But they will also balk at the idealists' claim that what we mean determines what there is. They want to get beyond realism and idealism by ceasing to contrast a represented world with our ways of representing it. This means giving up on the notion of linguistic representations of the world except insofar as it can be reconstructed within an inferentialist semantics. Such a semantics abjures what Price calls "substantial word–world relations" in favor of descriptions of the interaction of language-using organisms with other such organisms and with their environment.

The controversy about inferentialist semantics is the second of the two I want briefly to discuss. The best-known objection to Brandom's inferentialism is Fodor's. The clash between Fodor and Brandom epitomizes not only the difference between representationalist and inferentialist semantics but the larger atomist–holist conflict to which I referred earlier. Fodor thinks that philosophy can team up with cognitive science to find out how the mechanisms of mind and language work. Brandom is skeptical about the idea that there are any such mechanisms.

Brandom takes Davidsonian holism to the limit. As Davidson did in "A Nice Derangement of Epitaphs," he repudiates the idea that there is something called "a language" – something that splits up into bits called "meanings" or "linguistic representations" which can then be correlated with bits of the physical world. He tries to carry through on the Quine–Davidson hope for, as Kenneth Taylor has put it, "a theory of meaning in which meanings play no role."[22] So he abandons the notion of a sentence having a "cognitive content" that remains constant in all the assertions it is used to make. Brandom cheerfully coasts down what Fodor derisively describes as "a well-greased and well-traveled slippery slope" at the bottom of which lies the view that "no two people ever mean the same thing by what they say."[23]

Brandom does this because he wants to dismiss the idea that I get what is in my head – a cognitive content, a candidate for accurate representation

---

[22] Kenneth Taylor, *Truth and Meaning: An Introduction to the Philosophy of Language* (Oxford: Blackwell, 1998), 147. Taylor thinks of Davidson's distaste for meanings as a result of his preference for extensional languages. That preference played a role in Davidson's (early) thinking, but it plays none in Brandom's. Once one gets rid of the "making true" relation, there is no reason to think non-extensional languages fishy.

[23] Jerry Fodor, "Why Meaning (Probably) Isn't Conceptual Role," *in* Stephen Stich and Ted Warfield, eds., *Mental Representations* (Oxford: Oxford University Press, 1994), 143.

of reality – into your head by making noises that effectuate this transmission. He hopes to replace it with an account of what he calls "doxastic scorekeeping" – keeping track of our interlocutors' commitments to perform certain actions in certain conditions (including assent to or dissent from certain assertions).

Such commitments are attributed by reference to social norms. These norms authorize us to gang up on people who, having said "I promise to pay you back," or "I will join the hunt," make no move to do so. The same goes for people who, having uttered "p" and "if p then q," obstinately refuse to assent to "q." We, unlike the brutes, can play what Brandom calls the "game of giving and asking for reasons." Our ability to play this game is what made it possible for us to assume lordship over the other animals. To say that we, unlike the brutes, have minds is just another way of saying that we, but not they, play that game. *Pace* Fodor, finding out how the brain works will not help us find out how the mind works.[24] For the mind is not a representational apparatus, but rather a set of norm-governed social practices.

Brandom does not call himself a "naturalist," perhaps because he thinks the term might as well be handed over to the fans of elementary particles. But the whole point of his attempt to replace representationalist with inferentialist semantics is to tell a story about cultural evolution – the evolution of social (and, in particular, linguistic) practices – that focuses on how these practices gave our ancestors an evolutionary edge. Unless one is convinced that particles somehow enjoy an ontological status superior to that of organisms, that will seem as naturalistic as a story can get.

We are likely to look for substantive word–world relations as long as we ask Fregean questions about little atoms of linguistic significance such as "Does the assertion that the morning star is the evening star have the same cognitive content as the assertion that the thing we call the morning star is the same thing as the one we call the evening star?" If "same cognitive content" just means "will do as well for most purposes," then the answer is yes. But Fregeans, invoking Church's Translation Test, brush aside the fact that either sentence can usually be used to get the job done. The real question, they say, is not about uses but about senses, meanings, intentions. Sense, these philosophers say, determines reference in the same way that the marks on the map determine which slice of reality the map maps. Meanings cannot be the same thing as uses, for there is a difference between semantics

---

[24] I have argued to this effect in more detail in "The Brain as Hardware, Culture as Software," *Inquiry* 47, no. 3 (2004), 219–35.

and pragmatics. It is semantics that determines sameness and difference of cognitive content.

But we shall have a use for the notion of "same cognitive content" only if we try to hold belief and meaning apart, as Frege thought we should and Quine told us we should not. If we continue on along the path that Quine and Davidson cleared, we shall come to agree with Brandom that "particular linguistic phenomena can no longer be distinguished as 'pragmatic' or 'semantic.'"[25] Brandom has no more use for a distinction between these two disciplines than Davidson did for a distinction between knowing a language and knowing our way around the world generally.

I hope that my discussion of the disagreements between McDowell and Williamson and between Brandom and Fodor shows why I find Price's distinction between two forms of naturalism so useful. People like Price, Ramberg, and I would like our activist colleagues to stop talking about great big things like Experience or Language, the shadow entities that Locke, Kant, and Frege invented to replace Reality as the subject-matter of philosophy. We hope that doing so will eventually result in the evacuation of the so-called "core areas" of philosophy. Object naturalists like Jackson, Leiter, Petit, and Fodor fear that philosophy might not survive if it purged itself in this way. But subject naturalists suspect that the only thing our discipline would lose would be its insularity.

[25] Robert Brandom, *Making it Explicit* (Cambridge, MA: Harvard University Press, 1994), 592.

Wittgenstein and the linguistic turn

There are profound differences of opinion among contemporary philosophers both about whether Wittgenstein is worth reading and about what one can learn from him. They parallel disagreements about whether, and in what sense, philosophical problems are problems of language. In this chapter, I shall describe three views of Wittgenstein, corresponding to three ways of thinking about the so-called "linguistic turn in philosophy." Doing so will help me defend two claims for which I have argued in the past. First: there is no interesting sense in which philosophical problems are problems of language. Second: the linguistic turn was useful nevertheless, for it turned philosophers' attention from the topic of experience toward that of linguistic behavior. That shift helped break the hold of empiricism – and, more broadly, of representationalism.

Contemporary philosophers who call themselves "naturalists" typically see little value in Wittgenstein's work. For them, the central topic of philosophy is what Philip Pettit calls, in Sellarsian language, the clash between "the manifest image" and "the scientific image." The manifest image incorporates what Pettit calls "the ideas that come with our spontaneous, everyday practices, such as the ideas we naturally have about freedom and consciousness, causation and law, value and duty." The scientific image, he says, "challenges us to look for where in that world there can be room for phenomena that remain as vivid as ever in the manifest image: consciousness, freedom, responsibility, goodness, virtue and the like."[1]

Nothing in Wittgenstein's writings is of any help with what Pettit calls problems about the "place" of these phenomena in a world of physical particles. For these so-called "location problems" are the good old metaphysical ones – problems about how the really real is related to the merely apparently real. Those who, like myself, have been convinced by

---

[1] Philip Pettit, "Existentialism, Quietism, and the Role of Philosophy," in Brian Leiter, ed., *The Future for Philosophy* (Oxford: Oxford University Press, 2004), 308.

Wittgenstein that philosophy should dissolve such problems rather than solve them regard the naturalists as reactionaries. They are turning their backs on advances that Wittgenstein helped us make.

Naturalists typically doubt that what Gustav Bergmann dubbed "the linguistic turn" was a good idea. Bergmann said that taking that turn was a result of the discovery that "the relation between language and philosophy is closer than, as well as essentially different from, that between language and any other discipline."[2] Though many admirers of Wittgenstein still believe something like this, most naturalists do not. As Timothy Williamson has written, "there is a increasingly widespread sense that the linguistic turn is past."[3]

Williamson remarks that, from the point of view of admirers of Wittgenstein, "the revival of metaphysical theorizing, realist in spirit" will look like "a throwback to pre-Kantian metaphysics."[4] It does indeed. Williamson wants to break free of both Kantian and Wittgensteinian ways of thinking. Whereas Kant wanted philosophers to study thought rather than reality, Wittgenstein wanted them to study language. But, Williamson says, "perhaps one cannot reflect on thought or talk about reality without reflecting on reality itself . . . What there is determines what there is for us to mean."[5]

Discussion of the issues that divide naturalists like Pettit and Williamson from admirers of Wittgenstein is complicated by disagreements about the import of Wittgenstein's work. Some Wittgensteinians take seriously his suggestion that what philosophers do "is to bring words back from their metaphysical to their everyday use"[6] and his claim that "philosophy simply puts everything before us, and neither explains nor deduces anything."[7] They cite the concluding passages of the *Tractatus*, and sections 89–133 of *Philosophical Investigations*, as evidence that Wittgenstein must not be thought of as offering any theses or theories about language, or about anything else. He was, on their view, *exclusively* a therapist.

Let us call the people I have just described "Wittgensteinian therapists." Their understanding of Wittgenstein's importance differs from that of philosophers who, as I do, find support in his writings for pragmatist views of truth and knowledge. Call these people "pragmatic Wittgensteinians." They tend to brush aside just those passages that the therapists think most

[2] Gustav Bergmann, "Logical Positivism, Language, and the Reconstruction of Metaphysics," reprinted in Richard Rorty, ed., *The Linguistic Turn: Essays in Philosophical Method* (Chicago: University of Chicago Press, 1967; 2nd edn 1992), 64–5.

[3] Timothy Williamson, "Past the Linguistic Turn," in Leiter, *The Future for Philosophy*, 106.

[4] Ibid., 111.   [5] Ibid.

[6] Ludwig Wittgenstein, *Philosophical Investigations*, 2nd edn, trans. G. E. M. Anscombe (Oxford: Blackwell, 1953), section 116.   [7] Ibid., section 126.

important – his dicta about the origin of philosophical problems and the need to abjure philosophical theorizing. The pragmatic Wittgensteinians think that their hero's importance consists in having replaced a bad theory about the relation between language and non-language, such as that offered in the *Tractatus*, with a better theory, the one offered in the *Philosophical Investigations*.

Neither the naturalists' location problems nor "analytic metaphysics," pragmatic Wittgensteinians say, will interest you unless you hold two false beliefs. First: that language is a medium of knowledge only because it is tied down to non-language at certain particular points. Second: that the scientific image, by telling you what is really real, tells you what non-linguistic hitching-points are available. But *Philosophical Investigations* helped us see that this hitching-post idea can simply be dropped. On a pragmatic reading of that book, Wittgenstein is urging us to stop trying for what John McDowell calls an "external" perspective on language – a perspective enabling one to view language "sideways on."[8] If we could view it from that angle, we could spot the places where it hooks on to the world.

Wittgensteinian therapists agree with McDowell that one should not try for a sideways-on view. But they do not want to substitute an alternative view. They claim that Wittgenstein wants philosophers to engage in an activity called "elucidation," which is very different from that of propounding theses and backing them up with theories. To elucidate is not to replace one view of language by another, but to realize that any view about the relation between language and non-language is bound to be nonsense, and that philosophers who put forward such views have failed to attach a meaning to the words they use. On the therapists' reading, Wittgenstein was not telling us anything substantive, but rather conducting what he called "a battle against the bewitchment of our intelligence by means of language."[9] Therapists accept his claim that "problems arising through a misinterpretation of our forms of language have the character of depth . . . their roots are as deep in us as the forms of our language and their significance is as great as the importance of our language."[10]

The people who take this tack sometimes refer to themselves as "resolute readers" of Wittgenstein's works. Thomas Ricketts has applied this term to himself, Warren Goldfarb, Cora Diamond, James Conant, and various others. Readers of this sort accept the belief that Bergmann identified as the rationale for the linguistic turn in philosophy. They think that abandoning

---

[8] John McDowell, *Mind and World* (Cambridge, MA: Harvard University Press, 1994), 34–6, 152–3, and passim.   [9] Wittgenstein, *Philosophical Investigations*, section 109.
[10] Ibid., section 111.

that belief amounts to repudiating Wittgenstein's most important contribution to philosophy. Pragmatic Wittgensteinians, by contrast, are accurately described by Edward Minar as treating "Wittgenstein's observations on philosophy as expressions of a very particular and idiosyncratic view of its nature, a position more or less detachable from his treatments of specific philosophical problems."[11]

Pragmatic Wittgensteinians tend to be historicist in their metaphilosophical views. They think that the problems of pre-Kantian metaphysics, the problems that the naturalists have revivified, are hangovers from a particular moment in Western intellectual history. These problems originate not in a clash between common sense and science, but rather between the immaterialist notions that Christian theology had inherited from Plato and Aristotle and the mechanistic and materialistic worldpicture sketched by Galileo and Newton. That clash was between metaphysical outlooks, not between metaphysics and a premetaphysical understanding of things.

This clash produced the Cartesian notion of ideas as appearances on the stage of an inner theatre, as well as the Lockean account of words as signs of such ideas. More generally, it produced a picture of knowledge as an attempt to acquire accurate mental representations of non-mental reality. Representationalist accounts of the relation between language and non-language emerged from the attempt to divide language into assertions that represent real things and those that do not. On this historicist view, Wittgenstein's importance lies in his having helped wrench us out of our Cartesian–Lockean mind set. He helped us overcome the temptation to ask "Which pieces of our language lock on to reality, and which do not?" On this pragmatic view of his achievement, he did not show metaphysics to be nonsense. He simply showed it to be a waste of time.

I have been describing a three-cornered debate. In one corner are the naturalists, who want to get past the linguistic turn. In another are the pragmatic Wittgensteinians, who think that replacing Kantian talk about experience, thought, and consciousness with Wittgensteinian talk about the uses of linguistic expressions helps us replace worse philosophical theories with better ones. In a third are the Wittgensteinian therapists, for whom the importance of the linguistic turn lies in helping us realize that philosophers have failed to give meaning to the words they utter. The people in the first corner do not read Wittgenstein at all, and those in the

---

[11] Edward H. Minar, "Feeling at Home in Language," *Synthese* 102 (1995), 413.

other two read him very differently. I want now to describe the differences between these two readings in more detail.

The two camps disagree about the relation between early and later Wittgenstein. The therapists take the last pages of the *Tractatus* very seriously indeed. They do their best to tie them in with the metaphilosophical portions of *Philosophical Investigations*. In sharp contrast, the pragmatists tacitly dismiss the final passages of the *Tractatus* as an undigested residue of Schopenhauer. They regard sections 89–133 of the *Investigations* as an unfortunate left-over from Wittgenstein's early, positivistic period – the period in which he thought that "The totality of true propositions is the whole of natural science."[12] They have no more use for the claim that "The results of philosophy are the uncovering of one or another piece of plain nonsense"[13] than for the earlier claim that "Most of the propositions and questions to be found in philosophical works are not false but nonsensical."[14]

Pragmatic readers of Wittgenstein are not much interested in his self-image – his claim to be doing something radically different from what other philosophers do. In this respect they resemble pragmatic readers of Heidegger, who brush aside a distinction on which Heidegger insisted – that between mere philosophizing, which was what Heidegger's rivals and critics did, and a rarer and more important activity called "Thinking," in which he himself was engaged. Pragmatic Wittgensteinians do not see him as exemplary, either morally or methodologically. But they do think that he formulated an assortment of powerful and original criticisms of Cartesian–Lockean views.

On their view, Wittgenstein's contribution to philosophy consists principally of the critique of ostensive definition, the private-language argument, and the rule-following argument. So the *Tractatus* strikes them as a false start. About all they can find to salvage from that book is its account of objects, as expounded by Ishiguro and McGuinness. What Anscombe called "linguistic idealism" – the idea that the essence of an object is determined by the sorts of thing we say about it – fits in well with an anti-Lockean, non-representationalist account of knowledge. For it chimes with Davidson's thesis that most of our beliefs about an object must be true, as well as with McDowell's argument that "since the world is everything that is the case . . . there is no gap between thought, as such, and the world."[15]

---

[12] Ludwig Wittgenstein, *Tractatus Logico-Philosophicus*, trans. C. K. Ogden (London: Routledge, 1922), section 4.11.   [13] Wittgenstein, *Philosophical Investigations*, section 129.

[14] Wittgenstein, *Tractatus*, section 4.003.

[15] John McDowell, *Mind and World*, 27. Williamson quotes this passage disapprovingly in his discussion of McDowell in "Past the Linguistic Turn," 109–10.

Pragmatic Wittgensteinians think that his really important contribution was to formulate arguments that anticipate, complement, and reinforce Quine's and Davidson's criticisms of the language–fact distinction, and Sellars' and Brandom's criticism of the idea of knowledge by acquaintance. On their view, comparing and contrasting the writings of these later philosophers with the *Philosophical Investigations* helps us filter out what is merely idiosyncratic in Wittgenstein's writings. Pragmatic Wittgensteinians do not want to recapture Wittgenstein's own way of thinking, but rather to restate his best arguments in more effective ways.

Naturalists sometimes refer to philosophers who are dubious about their revival of metaphysics as "Wittgensteinian quietists."[16] But this label is more appropriate for Wittgensteinian therapists like Conant and Diamond than for pragmatic Wittgensteinians. The therapists treat "philosophy" as the name of a disease that can be cured by recognizing that one has been uttering nonsense. The pragmatists, however, are not interested in getting rid of philosophical problems as such. They are dubious about the claim that philosophical problems constitute a natural kind. They are focused on certain particular problems – those that came into prominence in the seventeenth century.

These problems no longer arise once a representationalist account of thought and language is replaced with a "social practice" account. To the pragmatists, it is a matter of indifference whether one says that the old problems are thereby dissolved or that they have now been solved. For Cartesian and Lockean ideas were, on the pragmatist view, no less clear and coherent than their replacements, just as the concepts of natural place and of phlogiston were no less coherent than those of gravity and of molecular motion. But, like their analogues in natural science, the older ideas did not pan out. They became more trouble than they were worth.

From the pragmatists' point of view, the positivists who initiated the linguistic turn in philosophy were wrong to think that there is a big difference between progress in empirical science and progress in philosophy. Consider the transition from Aristotelian hylomorphism to materialistic mechanism. Hylomorphism was neither nonsensical nor incoherent nor confused. Nor were the problems that Aristotelians discussed pseudo-problems. But those problems were forgotten once the advantages of the account offered by Galileo and Newton became evident. As with science, so with philosophy. Cartesian dualism, epistemological foundationalism, and the fact–value distinction do not embody category mistakes, nor are they the results of

---

[16] See Brian Leiter, "Introduction" to Leiter, *The Future for Philosophy*, 2–3.

conceptual confusion. They incorporated ideas that played an important part in intellectual progress. By now, however, it is time to replace them with better ideas.

Pragmatic Wittgensteinians think that the linguistic turn was an unnecessary detour. Mindful of Davidson's advice that we should cease to distinguish between knowing a language and knowing our way around in the world generally, they see no point in picking out something called "language" as the source of philosophical problems. On their view, both scientists and philosophers help us learn to get around the world better. They do not employ distinct methods. The only difference between them is that we call a new theory "scientific" if it facilitates prediction and "philosophical" if it does not.

But pragmatic Wittgensteinians agree with the therapists that there are *some* important links between early and late Wittgenstein. As José Medina puts it, "A crucial point of continuity in Wittgenstein's philosophy is the attempt to articulate a deflationary account of necessity that does away with the metaphysical view of necessity imagined as fact."[17] But they think that his later "social practice" view of necessity leaves the notion of "obtaining complete clarity" in the lurch. Once he had begun to treat the "hardness of the logical 'must'" as internalized peer pressure – pressure to use words in certain ways in certain circumstances – it would have been better for Wittgenstein to have criticized the kind of philosophy he disliked on grounds of uselessness rather than as "nonsense."

In the *Tractatus*, the idea of rigid conditions for the meaningful use of an expression – conditions that we can get a clear view of – borrowed plausibility from the identification of the totality of true propositions with those used to state facts, the ones that compose the totality of the natural sciences.[18] But once that restriction on the kind of expressions that can have a truth-value is dropped – once it is granted that moral judgments can be true in exactly the same way that empirical predictions can – it is hard to see how a sharp contrast between science and philosophy, or between philosophical discourse and other sorts of discourse, can survive.

In Wittgenstein's later work, no attempt is made to address what Popper called "the demarcation problem" – tracing the border between good science and bad metaphysics. Nor does he try to justify the linguistic turn. Rather, he simply contrasts "the everyday use" of expressions with their "metaphysical" use.[19] The former is, we are told, an unconfused

[17] José Medina, *The Unity of Wittgenstein's Philosophy* (Albany, NY: SUNY Press, 2002), 156.
[18] Cf. Wittgenstein, *Tractatus*, section 4.11.
[19] Wittgenstein, *Philosophical Investigations*, section 116.

use, the latter a confused one. Wittgenstein writes as if his readers will find it obvious that thinkers like Descartes, Locke, Hegel, and Heidegger were victims of "the bewitchment of our intelligence by means of language"[20] rather than original thinkers who, by using words in new ways, broke new paths of inquiry. He has no interest in putting himself in the shoes of the great dead philosophers, nor in treating them as responsive to the intellectual and sociopolitical exigencies of particular times and places.

In the language game of the *Tractatus*, the contrast-term for both "metaphysics" and "nonsense" was "fact-stating, reality-picturing language." Later that role is taken over by "the everyday use of words." But we are told much less about everydayness in the later books than we were told about facts in the *Tractatus*. The everyday is described purely negatively. It is simply what philosophers are out of touch with. "Philosophy," in the metaphilosophical sections of the *Investigations*, means something like "discussion of problems created by the misuse of language." But the notion of "misuse of language," like that of "nonsense," strikes pragmatic readers of Wittgenstein as an explanation of the obscure by the more obscure.

So much, for the moment, for the views of the pragmatic Wittgensteinians. I now want to offer a somewhat fuller account of the views of the therapists, the self-described "resolute readers." The most original and provocative claim that these readers make is that Wittgenstein never accepted the logical positivists' doctrine that philosophical problems arise out of misunderstandings of what they called "the logical syntax of language." He never believed that there was such a syntax. His version of the linguistic turn was as idiosyncratic as his aphoristic style. So he should not be put in the same box as Schlick, Carnap, Russell, and Ayer.

James Conant argues for this view by distinguishing between Frege's and Carnap's "substantial conception of nonsense" and Wittgenstein's own "austere" conception. Carnap explained the difference between "iggle piggle higgle" and Heidegger's "Das Nichts nichtet" as the difference between an utterance composed of signs in which no meaning can be perceived and a sentences composed of meaningful signs arranged in ways that violated syntactical rules. Conant argues, very persuasively, that Wittgenstein, when he wrote the *Tractatus*, did not believe that there were such things as "syntactical rules." So the only sort of nonsense that he could

---

[20] Ibid., section 109.

countenance was "mere nonsense," the sort exemplified by "iggle piggle higgle." Conant writes as follows:

Tractatrian elucidation aims to show that these sentences that apparently express substantially nonsensical thoughts actually express no thoughts . . . The "propositions" we come out with when we attempt to formulate these problems are to be recognized as *Unsinn*. The only "insight" that a Tractarian elucidation imparts, in the end, is one about the reader himself: that he is prone to such illusions of thought . . . The illusion that the *Tractatus* seeks to dispel, above all, is that we can run up against the limits of language.[21]

Edward Witherspoon agrees with Conant, and cites a passage in Wittgenstein's Cambridge lectures of the 1930s. There Wittgenstein explicitly criticizes Carnapian attempts to distinguish two kinds of nonsense. He explicates this passage by noting that Carnapians "want to say that there are certain rules or conditions that these sentences do not conform to, and that they are therefore nonsense." But to do this they "have had to quasi-analyze the utterance so as to show that it consists of meaningful concepts combined into a determinate quasi-logical form."[22] By contrast, he says,

when Wittgenstein is confronted with an utterance that has no clearly discernible place in a language game, he does not assume that he can parse the utterance; rather, he invites the speaker to explain how she is using her words, to connect them with other elements of the language-game in a way that displays their meaningfulness . . . When Wittgenstein criticizes an utterance as nonsensical, he aims to expose, not a defect in the words themselves, but a confusion in the speaker's relation to her words – a confusion that is manifested in the speaker's failure to specify a meaning for them.[23]

I have been persuaded by reading Conant, Witherspoon, Diamond, and other contributors to *The New Wittgenstein*, that Wittgenstein did indeed use "*Unsinn*" in a way different from either Frege or Carnap. I have also become convinced by them that Wittgenstein designed the *Tractatus* to be a self-consuming artifact. The recognition that the sentences of that book are *Unsinn* depends, as Conant puts it, "upon the reader's actually undergoing a certain experience," the attainment of which is "the sign that reader has understood the author of the work."[24] Wittgenstein, Conant continues, "does not call upon the reader to understand his sentences, but rather to understand *him*, namely the author and the kind of activity in which he

---

[21] James Conant, "Elucidation and Nonsense in Frege and Early Wittgenstein," in Alice Crary and Rupert Read, eds., *The New Wittgenstein* (London: Routledge, 2000), 197.

[22] Edward Witherspoon, "Conceptions of Nonsense in Carnap and Wittgenstein," in *The New Wittgenstein*, 345. [23] Ibid. [24] Conant, "Elucidation and Nonsense," 197.

is engaged – one of elucidation . . . When the elucidation has served its purpose, the illusion of sense is exploded from within."[25]

But though I am inclined to accept this as an accurate account of Wittgenstein's intentions, and am grateful to his resolute readers for providing it, I have no interest in undertaking the project Conant describes. My reaction to Wittgenstein's attempt to explode illusions of sense from within is the same as to Kierkegaard's attempt to escape from the aesthetic to the ethical, and then from the ethical to the consciousness of Sin: *C'est magnifique, mais ce n'est pas la guerre.* Admirers of Dewey like myself think that the point of reading philosophy books is not self-transformation but rather cultural change. It is not to find a way of altering one's inner state, but rather to find better ways of helping us overcome the past in order to create a better human future.

Despite their disagreements with Dewey, the positivists shared his conception of philosophy as a form of cultural politics. Carnap and Ayer thought that they might be able to make society more rational by formulating the rules that govern our use of language. They believed themselves to have acquired a superior grasp of those rules, thanks to their familiarity with symbolic logic. By spelling out those rules, they hoped to get undisciplined thinkers back on the rails. Their understanding of "the logical syntax of language" would enable them to draw a clear line between the cognitively meaningful and the cognitively meaningless. But once one gives up the notion that there is such a syntax, it is hard to see why one should take the linguistic turn. By turning his back on that notion, Wittgenstein may have made it impossible to defend Bergmann's claim that "the relation between language and philosophy is closer than, as well as essentially different from, that between language and any other discipline."

Nobody now thinks that the positivists' *Kulturpolitisch* initiatives bore fruit. If Carnap had been less eager to bring symbolic logic to bear, and a bit more patient, he could easily have connected "Das Nichts nichtet" with "other elements of the language-game in a way that displays its meaningfulness" (to use Witherspoon's phrasing). The language game in question is one that Heidegger deliberately and self-consciously created. It is utterly implausible to think that Heidegger might have been led, by a process of elucidation, to find himself "confused about his relation to his own words." Like Descartes, Locke, Kant, Newton, and Einstein, he gave a technical sense to familiar terms, and invented neologisms, hoping thereby to expand our linguistic repertoire in ways that would bear fruit.

---

[25] Ibid., 198.

Pragmatists like myself typically find most of the language games Heidegger invented unprofitable. We think it unlikely, for example, that there is anything useful to be said about the relation between Being and Nothing. But we also suspect that there is nothing interesting to be said about the distinction between sense and nonsense. If we adopt the social-practice view of language, there seems no way to reconstruct the relevant idea of "confusion." Anything will have a sense if you try hard enough to give it one. Nor will there be any way to identify a disease called "philosophy," one that needs to be elucidated away.

To see this point, it helps to consider the difference between the everyday use of epithets like "confused" and "nonsensical" and their technical use by Wittgensteinian therapists. When Descartes mocked the Aristotelian definition of motion ("the actualization of the potential qua potential") as unintelligible, he did not try to back up this charge with argument. The term "unintelligible" was just a rhetorical flourish. His point was simply that it would be better to treat "motion" as a primitive term than to try to synthesize mechanism with hylomorphism. When other fans of the New Science called various Scotist and Ockhamite doctrines "nonsense" they did not mean that these authors had failed to attach meaning to the words they used. Rather, they used "nonsense" to mean something like "not worth bothering about, now that Aristotle has been dethroned by Galileo and Newton." "Useless" would have been as appropriate an epithet as "confused."

It was Kant who first made charges of confusion and senselessness more than casual polemical rhetoric. When he rebuked the natural theologians for misusing the terms "cause" and "substance," he backed up his point by argument. One such argument started off by exhibiting the antinomies created by the attempt to use those terms to describe non-spatio-temporal entities. These antinomies were already familiar, and Kant's originality lay in his attempt to erect a general theory about proper and improper use of concepts. This theory was put forward as the fruit of a newfangled discipline called "transcendental philosophy." Kant thought that we needed a general theory of representation if we were to understand what had gone wrong in the history of philosophy. By erecting one, he gave philosophy a new lease on life, and ensured its survival as an academic discipline.

Kant's own theory, however, seemed to many of his critics to be more trouble than it was worth. To replace metaphysics with transcendental philosophy, they suggested, was to adopt a remedy as bad as the disease it claimed to cure. For this new kind of philosophy required one to take seriously what Strawson was to call "the mythical subject of transcendental psychology" – a mongrel discipline, neither logic nor psychology. It also required one to profess an understanding of the term "thing-in-itself" – a willingness that many who relished Kant's criticisms of both Hume and Leibniz were unable to muster.

When the initiators of the linguistic turn decided that it was time to draw a bright line between logic and psychology, they still wanted to do what Kant had failed to do: to put philosophy on the secure path of science. So they announced the discovery of a new discipline – one that would serve many of the same purposes as Kantian transcendental psychology, but would be "purely formal." This one – variously named "linguistic philosophy," "philosophy of language," and "a systematic theory of meaning" – would enable us to do what Kant had tried and failed to do. It would let us either solve or dissolve all the old philosophical problems. It could do this because it would be a theory not of representation in general, but of *linguistic* representation.

As a result of the popularity of the linguistic turn, "nonsense" became a term of philosophical art – just as "representation" had become one in the wake of Kant. Philosophers began to think of themselves as specialists in detecting nonsense. Philosophy's job would be done, they suggested, when all our concepts had been analyzed. All that we had to do was use some common sense, and some symbolic logic, and the traditional problems of philosophy would dissolve. Once we realized that the problems of philosophy were, in some sense or other, problems of language, all would be plain sailing.

But the failure of the positivists' intervention in cultural politics is now evident. The idea that philosophers should employ "linguistic methods" to expose the illusory character of philosophical problems has come to seem merely quaint. Despite the importance of Ryle's work in clearing the way for philosophers of mind such as Sellars, Dennett, and Davidson, nobody now wants to charge Descartes with having made a "category mistake." Nobody thinks he unhappily did not notice that statements about the mind are "mongrel categorical-hypotheticals." Nor does anyone nowadays see much point in Austin's maxim that "ordinary language is always the first word." Though many philosophers still accept the label "analytic," they no longer undertake to explain what a "philosophical analysis" of a concept is, nor by what rigorous standards alternative analyses are to be judged. They are content simply to argue for one or another philosophical theory, without claiming to wield special, specifically linguistic, methodological tools.

The transcendental turn and the linguistic turn were both taken by people who thought that disputes among philosophers might fruitfully be viewed from a neutral terrain, outside the controversies these philosophers conduct. The idea, in both cases, was that we should step back from the controversy and show that the clash of theories is possible only because both sets of theorists missed something that was already there, waiting to be noticed. For Kant, they did not notice the limits set by the nature of our faculties. For those who initiated the linguistic turn, they failed to grasp the conditions of linguistic significance.

This "stepping back" move is hard to reconcile with the "social practice" view of language and thought that pragmatic readers find between the lines of the *Investigations*. That is the view epitomized in the Wittgensteinian maxim "Don't look for the meaning, look for the use." It is not a "use-theory of meaning," but rather a repudiation of the idea that we need a way of determining meanings.[26] It sees the attempt to have such a theory as succumbing to the hope that language can be viewed sideways-on, making visible the hitching-posts at which language is tied to the world. Wittgenstein's maxims suggest to pragmatic readers that any utterance can be given significance by being batted around long enough in more or less predictable ways. One can distinguish more useful from less fruitful ways of speaking, and thus better scientific or philosophical theories from worse theories. But it is hard to make a place for Wittgenstein's notion of "disguised nonsense."

Alice Crary explicitly rejects pragmatic appropriations of Wittgenstein. She thinks it a mistake to read Wittgenstein as having favored "certain metaphysical theses about the nature of logic and language in the *Tractatus*" and as having rejecting them later "in favor of something like their negations."[27] The view she thinks wrong is pretty much the one I hold, but

---

[26] Davidson does not think that anybody should try to write out a T-theory for a natural language, nor that doing so would put us in a position to dissolve pseudo-problems. Brandom thinks that the content of an assertion is rarely, if ever, the same for any two users of the same linguistic expression. Neither invokes the claim that philosophical problems are problems of language. In "Wittgenstein's Philosophy in Relation to Political Thought" in *The New Wittgenstein*, at 131, Crary rightly says that if we view a "use-theory of meaning" as a view about how to *fix* meaning, then we should not attribute any such theory to Wittgenstein. Quite so, but neither should we attribute it to Davidson or Brandom.

Crary (ibid., 127) notes that I have come to repudiate the idea that philosophical views I dislike are "incoherent," but thinks that I am thereby committed to denying our "entitlement to certain epistemic ideals." Her criticism of me, and in particular of what she calls my "relativism," seems to depend upon attributing to me a view I would neither accept nor ascribe to Wittgenstein: that because use fixes meaning, and because meaning must change as use does, the boundaries between differing uses are "inviolable." Someone who accepts Brandom's inferentialist view of content, or Davidson's criticisms of the very idea of a conceptual scheme, has no use for the idea of inviolable barriers – barriers that further conversation cannot break down.

[27] Crary, "Introduction," in *The New Wittgenstein*, 4.

I would reformulate her statement of it by omitting both the word "metaphysical" and the phrase "the nature of." Pragmatists, at least those of my persuasion, would rather just say that Wittgenstein changed his mind about how best to talk about logic and language.

I suspect that Crary, Conant, and Diamond would reply that one cannot eschew metaphysics while still offering theories about the relation between language and reality. For Crary defines a metaphysical sentence as one "presented from an external point of view on language." Presumably she regards "social practice" accounts of language such as Davidson's and Brandom's as so presented. She thinks that such a point of view is one "we aspire to or think we need to assume when philosophizing – a point of view on language as if outside from which we imagine we can get a clear view of the relation between language and the world." This, she says, is "no more than the *illusion* of a point of view." When we assume such a point of view "we don't wind up saying anything coherent about how things stand."[28]

Pragmatic Wittgensteinians are willing to go along with this line of thought to the following extent: we agree that there is nothing useful to say about the relation between two large entities called "Language" and "World." We suspect that these are just the familiar, and rather disreputable, entities formerly known as "Subject" and "Object." There is, however, a lot to be said about our linguistic behavior. One example is Davidson's thesis that most of our beliefs must be true. Another is Brandom's explanation of why we have de re predication, and singular terms, in our language. A suitable selection of such holist and inferentialist doctrines is what I have been referring to, casually and for convenience of reference, as a "social practice" theory of language. This theory found much of its initial inspiration in Wittgenstein's critique of ostensive definition and of "knowledge by acquaintance."

Are Sellars, Davidson, McDowell and Brandom assuming "the illusion of a point of view"? I see no reason to think so. They do not seem to suffer from the "natural disappointment with the conditions of human knowledge" that Crary, following Stanley Cavell, says gives rise to "our tendency to become entangled in philosophical confusion."[29] Their writings do not display any sign of ever having taken epistemological skepticism very seriously.

But Wittgensteinian therapists seem to agree with Cavell that such disappointment comes as naturally to us as does, according to Freud, Oedipal resentment. On this view, philosophy is not just one area of culture among others, an area some people find of interest and many others do not, but

[28] Crary, "Wittgenstein's Philosophy," 6.   [29] Ibid., 8.

rather a trap into which anyone who begins to reflect is bound to fall. "The problems arising through a misinterpretation of our forms of language . . . are deep disquietudes."[30]

I do not think that that sort of disappointment is widespread, but I do think that the therapists are on to something. That is the fact that many, though hardly all, people who find philosophy intriguing are in search of the ineffable – something that cannot be put into words. Sometimes this is for a vision of the Good or of God. In recent times, however, partially as a cause and partially as an effect of the linguistic turn in philosophy, it has expressed itself as a a desire for contact with "the World" that is not mediated through language. I think Wittgenstein felt this desire very deeply but recognized, early and late, that it could not possibly be fulfilled. So I think that Conant is on the right track when he says that "The aim of [the *Tractatus*] is to show us that beyond 'the limits of language' lies – not ineffable truth, but rather . . . *einfach Unsinn*, simply nonsense."[31]

Wittgenstein seems to have thought that the urge to penetrate beyond the effable, the need to break through language to something better, was more than just a relatively uncommon form of obsessional neurosis – one that he himself shared with certain other unfortunates. He apparently believed it to be part of the human condition. He thought that by looking more closely at the results of succumbing to this urge we might come to understand better what it is to be a human being.

It is certainly true that the desire to get in touch with something that stays the same despite being described in many different ways keeps turning up in philosophy. Resistance to Wittgenstein's critique of ostensive definition, or to Putnam's doctrine of the relativity of reference, can easily be seen as manifestations of this desire. The need to shove language aside and get at reality "directly" reinforces the idea that demonstratives mark the location of hitching-posts, the places where language locks on to the world: "*This* is what we mean by red!"

The same desire, I think, underlies Kripke's attempt to use the expression "This very thing" as a way of pinning down an object independent of its description. It motivates Timothy Williamson's insistence that ontology is prior to philosophy of language because, *pace* Sellars, "In defining words – for example, natural kind terms – we must point at real specimens."[32] It produces many other such attempts to find what Derrida called "a serene presence beyond the reach of play."

---

[30] Wittgenstein, *Philosophical Investigations*, section 111.
[31] Conant, "Elucidation and Nonsense," 197.   [32] Williamson, "Past the Linguistic Turn," 111.

But it is not obvious that this desire, the one that sometimes manifests itself as the need to "emit an inarticulate sound"[33] has deep roots. A desire may be shared by Parmenides, Meister Eckhart, Russell, Heidegger, and Kripke without being intrinsic to the human condition. Are we really in a position to say that this desire is a manifestation of what Conant calls "our most profound confusions of soul"?[34] Wittgenstein was certainly convinced that it was. But this conviction may tell us more about Wittgenstein than about philosophy. The more one reflects on the relation between Wittgenstein's technical use of "philosophy" and its everyday use, the more he appears to have redefined "philosophy" to mean "all those bad things I feel tempted to do."

Such persuasive redefinitions of "philosophy" are characteristic of the attempt to step back from philosophy as a continuing conversation and to see that conversation against a stable, ahistorical background. Knowledge of that background, it is thought, will permit one to criticize the conversation itself, rather than joining in it. The Kantian transcendental turn and the later linguistic turn were, as I have already said, examples of such inevitably unsuccessful attempts to step out of the conversation. Kant could not answer the question of how he had managed to acquire so much non-empirical knowledge about the limits of thought. The philosophers who agreed with Bergmann that philosophical problems are problems of language were unable to cope with the fact that their accounts of "the logic of language" were just practical suggestions about how it might be best for us to talk.

Once we give up on the project of "stepping back," we will think of the strange ways in which philosophers talk not as needing to be elucidated out of existence, but as suggestions for talking differently, on all fours with suggestions made by scientists and poets. A few philosophers, we may admit, are "like savages, primitive people, who hear the expressions of civilized men, and then draw the queerest conclusions from it."[35] But most of them are not. They are, rather, contributors to the progress of civilization. Knowledgeable about the dead ends down which we have gone in the past, they are anxious that future generations should fare better. If we see philosophy in this historicist way, we shall have to give up on the idea that there is a special relation between something called "language" and something else called "philosophy."

[33] Wittgenstein, *Philosophical Investigations*, section 216.
[34] Conant, "Elucidation and Nonsense," 196.
[35] Wittgenstein, *Philosophical Investigations*, section 194.

12

Holism and historicism

Philosophers of mind and language in the analytic tradition divide into atomists and holists. The ambition of the atomists is to explain, as they often put it, how the mind works and how language works. The holists doubt that this is a fruitful project, because they think it a mistake to treat mind and language as entities that have either elementary parts, or a structure, or inner workings. They do not believe that there are things called "beliefs" or "meanings" into which minds and languages can be broken up. Atomists, holists believe, fail to realize that rationality – the thing that makes us special – is a social phenomenon, not one that a human organism can exhibit all by itself.

This quarrel has metaphilosophical implications. Atomists prefer to think of philosophy as a quasi-scientific, problem-solving discipline. They see themselves as collaborating with cognitive scientists in order to find out facts about the capabilities of the human organism – facts that can be studied without reference to history. But if, like the holists, you think of rationality in social-practice terms, you will try instead to explain how certain organisms managed to become rational by telling stories about how various different practices came into being. You will be more interested in historical change than in neurological arrangements.

Atomists and holists agree that what makes human beings special is their possession of mind and language. They also agree that the big problem is to explain the existence of mind and language without appealing to the sort of non-physical entities postulated by Plato, Augustine, and Descartes. Both are physicalists, believing that, as Frank Jackson has put it, "if you duplicate our world in all physical respects and stop right there, you duplicate it in *all* respects."[1]

But there the similarities end. Atomists think that by breaking mind and language down into parts we can get psychology in touch with neurology

---

[1] Frank Jackson, *From Metaphysics to Ethics* (Oxford: Oxford University Press, 1998), 12.

in roughly the same way that chemistry has been brought together with physics and biology with chemistry. They find it useful and important to say that the mind is, in some important sense, the brain. So they spend much of their time explaining how beliefs and meanings can reside within the collection of physical particles which is the human central nervous system.

The holists find this identification of mind and brain thoroughly misleading. As they see it, the atomists are simply taking for granted that what worked for matter – namely, the explanation of macrostructural behavior by reference to transactions between microstructural components – will work for mind. The holists agree that there is much to be discovered about how the brain works, but they doubt that a perfected neurophysiology would tell us anything interesting about mind or language. For, they insist, the mind is no more the brain than the computer is the hardware.

A perfect understanding of its electrical circuits, holists points out, does very little to help you understand how your computer manages to do all the wonderful things it does. To understand that you have to know a lot about software. For the computer will run a fabulous variety of different programs while remaining indifferent to which ones it is running; the same program can be run on many different sorts of hardware. According to the holists, mind and brain, culture and biology, swing as free from one another as do software and hardware. They can and should be studied independently.

Understanding mind and language, the holists say, is a matter of understanding the evolution of the social practices in which we presently engage. We could not, they cheerfully admit, have engaged in those practices unless we had the requisite neurological equipment. Cultural evolution could not begin until biological evolution had reached a certain point. But they are dubious when Steven Pinker says that "The mind is a system of organs of computation, designed by natural selection to solve the kinds of problems our ancestors faced in their foraging way of life."[2]

The holists point out that explanations of human behavior which tie in with neurology or with evolutionary biology will tell us only about what we share with the chimpanzees. It will not tell us about what we, but not the chimpanzees, share with the creatures who painted pictures on the walls of caverns, nor with those that built the ships that sailed to Troy. We can

[2] Steven Pinker, *How the Mind Works* (New York: Norton, 1997), 21. For further discussion of Pinker's views, see my "Philosophy-envy," *Daedelus* 133, no. 44 (Fall 2004), 18–24. I discuss the relation between philosophy and cognitive science at greater length in "The Brain as Hardware, Culture as Software," *Inquiry* 47 (2004), 219–33.

learn about the processes that transformed those ancestors into ourselves only by constructing a narrative, telling a story about how they became us.

Holist philosophers of mind and language think that the best way to show that we need not postulate immaterial entities to explain our uniqueness is to tell an imaginative story about how grunts mutated into assertions. This is the story of how, to use Robert Brandom's terminology, sapience replaced mere sentience. Brandom argues that to count as an assertion, and thus as a sign of sapience, a series of noises must be explicitly criticizable by reference to social norms. Such a norm is already in place when a hominid first realized that, having grunted "P," she might well be beaten with sticks if she did not grunt "Q" on appropriate occasions. But the norm only became explicit, and what Brandom calls "the game of giving and asking for reasons" only began a few hundreds of thousands of years later. At that point, descendants of the original grunter realize that if they have asserted both *P* and *If P then Q,* they will deservedly be denounced as "irrational" if they cannot produce good reasons for refusing to assert *Q.*

Whereas the holists take the social practice of criticizing assertions to be indispensable for both mentality and language, the atomists think that we had minds before we had language, and indeed that non-human animals have minds. This is because they think that the crucial notion in this area of philosophy is *representation* rather than, as Brandom does, *inference.* Atomism in philosophy of mind and language is closely tied to the idea that cognitive science will help us see the mind as the central nervous system by linking up perceptual representations – physiological states that can be put in some more or less isomorphic relation to the environment – with linguistic representations.

The hope that cognitive science will help us understand why we are so special is a legacy from Locke. It derives from his suggestion that the mind should be viewed as a storehouse of simple and complex ideas. This suggestion led to Hume's deliberately provocative reference to "the reason of animals," nineteenth-century associationist psychology, Ayer's linguistified version of Hume, and McDowell's linguistified version of Kant. Holists think that it was a pity that Locke put us on this path, and they blame Descartes for misleading him. For Descartes provided Locke with the image of the mind as an inner theater – a room equipped with a screen on which immaterial representations are displayed. An immaterial viewer of this screen then decides what the extra-mental world is like on the basis of the clarity or the coherence of those representations.

Holists also blame Descartes for the idea that the mind is a thing that has workings that might be better understood. To think of it this way – as what Gilbert Ryle mockingly called a non-material mechanism – is, they argue, a fundamental mistake. For the mind should be thought of not as a mysterious entity but as a cluster of capacities brought into existence by making social norms explicit. Holists think that cognitive science may help us understand *sentience* better, for the notion of "mechanisms of perception" does have a use. As long as you stick to sentience, and do not go on to sapience, it makes sense to connect physiological states with dispositional responses. But, holists insist, to have very complex dispositional responses is not yet to have mentality, as long as these responses are not subject to criticism by explicit reference to norms.

As holists see the matter, there is nothing intermediate between the neurons and the social practices for cognitive science to study. To study what makes human beings special, and so very different from the chimpanzees, is to study those practices – to study culture. We neither have nor need a bridge between the neurons and the practices, any more than we need one between hardware and software. Software is just a way of putting hardware to use, and culture is just a way of putting our physiological equipment to use. To understand how hardware works is one thing, but to understand the uses to which it is put is something quite different. Understanding electrical circuits, in the neurons or in the chips, does nothing to help us understand how the sophisticated software of the 1990s evolved out of the primitive software of the 1950s, nor how assertions replaced grunts.

The atomists think, to quote Steven Pinker again, that "the computational theory of mind . . . is one of the great ideas in intellectual history, for it solves one of the puzzles that make up the mind–body problem." This is the puzzle first posed by Descartes: the problem of how beliefs, which do not seem to be physical objects, can cause physical events. Pinker says that the computational theory resolves the paradox by saying that beliefs are

information, incarnated as configurations of symbols. The symbols are physical states of bits of matter, like chips in a computer or neurons in the brain. They symbolize things in the world because they are triggered by those things via our sense organs . . . Eventually the bits of matter constituting a symbol bump into bits of matter connected to the muscles and behavior happens . . . The computational theory of mind thus allows us to keep beliefs and desires in our explanations of behavior while planting them squarely in the physical universe. It allows meaning to cause and be caused.[3]

For the holists, however, there never was a mind–body problem to be solved, because there never were little mental entities called "beliefs," or

---

[3] Pinker, *How the Mind Works*, 25.

little linguistic entities called "meanings" that needed to be placed within the physical universe. Not all causal explanation, the holists say, proceeds by picking out little things that bump into other little things.

Atomism went largely unchallenged among analytic philosophers during the first half of the twentieth century. But the holist reaction began about fifty years ago, with the publication of Ryle's *The Concept of Mind*, Wittgenstein's *Philosophical Investigations*, Sellars' "Empiricism and the Concept of Mind," and Quine's "Two Dogmas of Empiricism." Wittgenstein cast doubt on the very idea of a systematic theory of meaning. Quine mocked the idea that there were entities called "meanings" associated with linguistic expressions. Ryle, like Wittgenstein, was dubious about empirical psychology. He thought that projects of replacing little spooky explainers with little non-spooky explainers was a residue of Descartes' bad picture of the mind as a para-mechanical system. Sellars followed up on Wittgenstein by arguing that what makes human beings special is the ability to argue with one another, not the ability to have inner mental states that are somehow isomorphic to states of the environment.

The holists of the present day include such philosophers of language as Donald Davidson, who follows up on Quine, and Brandom, who follows up on Sellars. The holist ranks are swelled by philosophers of mind who are following up on Ryle and Wittgenstein – notably Vincent Descombes, Jennifer Hornsby, Helen Steward, Arthur Collins, and Lynn Baker. These holists are locked in battle with atomists such as Chomsky, Pinker, Fodor, and all the other philosophers and cognitive scientists who hope to develop what Fodor calls "a semantic theory for mental representations." Holists think that there is neither a need for such a theory nor any chance of getting it.

I hope that my sketch of the atomist–holist quarrel helps to explain why many atomists suspect that holism puts the very idea of analytic philosophy in danger As the battle between the holists and the analysts has worn on, it has come to look more and more like a disagreement about what sort of thing philosophers should see themselves as doing – about the self-image of the discipline.

If philosophy is to be analytic, there must be some little things to analyze bigger things into. Philosophical analysis of the sort Russell envisaged requires that there be such things as concepts or meanings that can be isolated and treated as elements of beliefs. But if, as Wittgenstein suggested, a concept is just the use of a word, and if the proper use of the words that interest philosophers is always going to be a matter of controversy, it is not clear that "analysis" is an apposite term for what philosophers do. For a philosopher's claim to have discovered the contours of a concept can never be more than a suggestion about how a word should be used. Philosophers' diagnoses of "conceptual confusion," as well as their claims to have achieved "conceptual clarity" look, from a Wittgensteinian point of view, like disingenuous ways of going about the transformation of culture, rather than ways of making clearer what has previously been going on.

The idea that Russell and his followers put our discipline on the secure path of a science is very dear to many analytic philosophers. One of the reasons they resist holism is the fear that if they walk away from the natural scientists in the direction of the historians they will open the gates to obscurantism. Many analytic philosophers dislike the idea that philosophy is one of the humanities, and insist that it is one of the sciences.

Holists, however, see no more promise in inquiry into how mind and language work than inquiry into how conversation works. So they think that the best we can do in the way of understanding how mind and language work is to tell stories, of the sort told by Sellars and Brandom, about how metalinguistic and mentalistic vocabularies came into existence in the course of time, as well as stories about how cultural took over from biological evolution. The latter stories recount how we got out of the woods and into the painted caverns, out of the caverns and into the villages, and then out of the villages into the law courts and the temples. The kind of understanding that narratives of this sort give us is not the sort that we get from seeing many disparate things as manifestations of the same underlying thing, but rather the sort that comes from expanding our imagination by comparing earlier with later ways of being human.

Obviously, I am in the holist camp. I think that philosophers should give up on the question "What is the place of mental representations, or meanings, or values, in a world of physical particles?" They should describe talk about particles, talk about beliefs, and talk about what ought to be done, as cultural activities that fulfill distinct purposes. These activities do not need to be fitted together in a systematic way, any more than basketball and cricket need to be fitted together with bridge and chess. If we have a plausible narrative of how we became what we are, and why we use the words we do as we do, we have all we need in the way of self-understanding.

The analogy with fitting together pieces of a puzzle is entirely appropriate for many areas of inquiry – for example, paleontology, particle physics, and epigraphy. These are all areas of culture in which there is enough consensus to give a use to the notion of "getting it right." The idea that philosophy can become such an area by being put on the secure path of a science remains plausible only as long as concepts and meanings are seen as isolable from social practices and from history. For only if such isolation were possible would we be able to identify atoms of thought or of language whose relations with one another would remain constant no matter what use is made of them, in the way that the relations between bits of hardware remain constant no matter what program is being run. Suspicion of attempts at such isolation becomes explicit in Wittgenstein's *Philosophical Investigations,* which is why Russell's review of that book was so furious. Russell was appalled by the suggestion that we stop asking about meaning and start asking about use. He was right to suspect that if Wittengestein were taken seriously, the movement he initiated would be seen as having put us on a false scent.

Once one gives up on atomism, one will begin to wonder, as Wittgenstein did, why logic was once thought to be something sublime. One may then start thinking of logic as Brandom does – as a device for making our social norms explicit. This will lead to taking changes in social norms seriously, and to abandoning the notion that mind or language are things that can be gotten right once and for all.

Brandom is one of the few analytic philosophers to take Hegel seriously. Hegelians are inclined to substitute questions about what makes *us*, in our time and place, special for questions about what makes human beings in general special. They replace questions about what we share with every human everywhere with questions about how we differ from our ancestors and how our descendants might differ from us. They think of philosophy not as a matter of fitting together pieces of a puzzle but of reinterpreting and recontextualizing the past.

This difference of opinion about what it is important to think about explains why what I have been calling "historicist philosophy" is often called "hermeneutic philosophy." The term "hermeneutic" signals a shift of interest from what can be gotten right once and for all to what can only be reinterpreted and recontextualized over and over again. That is why Brandom takes the common law, rather than the discovery of physical microstructure, as a paradigm of rational inquiry. Brandom argues that Hegel taught us how to think of a concept on the model of a person – as the kind of thing that is understood only when one understands its history. The best answer to a question about who a person really is is a story about her past that helps explain her recent conduct. The most useful response to questions about a concept is to tell a story about the ways in which the uses of a certain cluster of words have changed in the past, as a prelude to a description of the different ways in which these words are being used now. The clarity that is achieved when these different ways are distinguished from one another, and when each is rendered intelligible by being placed within a narrative of past usage, is analogous to the increased sympathy we bring to the situation of a person whose life-history we have learned.

13

Kant vs. Dewey
The current situation of moral philosophy

In recent decades, Anglophone philosophy professors have had a harder and harder time explaining to their fellow-academics, and to society at large, what they do to earn their keep. The more specialized and professionalized the study of philosophy becomes, the less respect it is paid by the rest of the academy or by the public. By now it runs some risk of being ignored altogether, regarded in the same way that classical philology is, as a quaint, albeit rather charming, survival.

This problem is less acute, however, in the case of moral philosophy, which is the most visible and generally intelligible of the various philosophical specialties. But even moral philosophers are hard pressed to explain what they think they are doing. They need to claim an ability to see more deeply into matters of right and wrong than most people. But it is not clear what it is about their training that permits them to do so. People who have written their Ph.D. dissertations in this area of philosophy can hardly claim to have had more experience with difficult moral choices than most. But what exactly *can* they claim?

A familiar sort of answer to this line of questioning was given by Peter Singer thirty-odd years ago in a much-discussed article in the *New York Times Magazine*. The article was called "Philosophers Are Back on the Job."[1] Singer thought of himself as bringing glad tidings. Philosophers, he explained, had once held that moral judgments were unarguable expressions of emotion, but now they had come back to their senses. They had joined the rest of the population in believing that there were good and bad arguments in favor of alternative moral choices.

Now that they had come to appreciate this fact, Singer continued, the public would be well advised to listen to moral philosophers' views on such vexed topics as abortion. For, he explained, "No conclusions about what we ought to do can validly be drawn from a description of what most

---

[1] Peter Singer, "Philosophers Are Back on the Job," *The New York Times Magazine*, July 7, 1974, 6–7, 17–20.

people in our society think we ought to do."[2] On the contrary, "if we have a soundly based moral theory, we ought to be prepared to accept its implications even if they force us to change our moral views on major issues." Fortunately, he continued, philosophers are capable of providing such theories and thus correcting society's moral intuitions. As he put it, "the philosopher's training makes him more than ordinarily competent in assessing arguments and detecting fallacies. He has studied the nature of moral concepts, and the logic of moral argument."[3] Singer concluded his article by saying that "the entry of philosophers into areas of ethical concern from which they have hitherto excluded themselves is the most stimulating and potentially fruitful of all the recent developments in philosophy."[4]

When I first read this article, I squirmed in embarrassment. Singer's view of the social role of philosophy professors struck me as calculated to make the public even more suspicious of us philosophers than it already was. For, on his account, moral philosophers have "soundly based theories" that are grounded on something quite different from the moral intuitions of the public. They have a different, and better, source of moral knowledge than those intuitions can provide. This source, which philosophers traditionally refer to as "reason," has an authority that takes precedence over any alternative source.

On Singer's account, moral philosophers are somehow more in touch with this source, and therefore more rational, than the vulgar. It is not clear whether this is the cause or the effect of their superior grasp of what Singer calls "the nature of moral concepts of the logic of moral argument." However that may be, I think the notion of a moral theory based on something sounder than a set of moral intuitions as dubious as the idea that moral concepts have a special nature that the experts understand better than the vulgar, and as the idea that moral argument has a special logic that philosophical training enables one to appreciate.

To grasp a concept is just to know how to use a word. You grasp the concept of "isotope" if you know how to talk about physical chemistry, and the concept of "mannerism" when you know how to talk about the history of European painting. But concepts like "right," "ought," and "responsible" are not technical concepts, and it is not clear what special training could enable you to grasp the uses of these words better than do the laity.

When it comes to "the logic of moral arguments," I am again baffled. I cannot think of any sense of the word "logic" in which arguments about

---

[2] Ibid., 19.   [3] Ibid., 20.   [4] Ibid.

the right thing to do have a different *logic* than arguments about what profession to go into or what house to buy or whom to vote for. I cannot imagine how Singer would defend the claim that judges and social workers, for example, are less familiar with this "logic" than are trained moral philosophers, or the claim that philosophical training would help such people do their jobs better.

I do not mean to be philistine about this. I quite agree that widely read people are often better at making moral choices than people with little learning and, consequently, little imagination. Moral philosophes are, typically though not invariably, widely read and imaginative people. But I do not think that Singer, and others who agree with his evaluation of the social value of moral philosophy, give us much reason to believe that training in philosophy rather than in, for example, anthropology or the history of European literature or the criminal law will be especially helpful in giving one a superior ability to make moral decisions. I admire many of my colleagues who specialize in moral philosophy, and I read many of their books with pleasure and profit. But I should never dream of making the sorts of claims for them that Singer did.

I would like to suggest an alternative answer to the question of what most professors of moral philosophy have that others do not. They do not have more rigor or clarity or insight than the laity, but they do have a much greater willingness to take seriously the views of Immanuel Kant. More than any other author in the history of philosophy, Kant gave currency and respectability to notions like "the nature of moral concepts" and "the logic of moral argument." For he claimed that morality was like nothing else in the world – that it was utterly distinctive. He argued that there is a vast and unbridgeable difference between two realms – the realm of prudence and that of morality. If one agrees with him about this, as many moral philosophers still do, then one will be predisposed to think that one might make a professional specialty out of the study of moral concepts. But if one has not read Kant, or if one's response to reading *The Fundamental Principles of the Metaphysics of Morals* is either revulsion or a fit of the giggles, the idea that morality can be an object of professional study may well seem farfetched.

Again, if one takes Kant seriously, then Singer's idea that there is a separate source for moral principles, one that provides the principles that ground a "soundly based moral theory," will sound plausible. If you have not read Kant, or have failed to find his views attractive, you may think, as I do, that all a moral principle can possibly do is to abbreviate a range of moral intuitions. Principles are handy for summing up a range of moral reactions, but they do not have independent force that can correct such reactions. They draw all their force from our intuitions concerning the consequences of acting on them.

As I read the history of philosophy, Kant is a transitional figure – somebody who helped us get away from the idea that morality is a matter of divine command, but who unfortunately retained the idea that morality is a matter of unconditional obligations. I would accept Elizabeth Anscombe's suggestion that if you do not believe in God, you would do well to drop notions like "law" and "obligation" from the vocabulary you use when deciding what to do.

Like other great thinkers of the Enlightenment, Kant wanted to get rid of the idea that the priests were moral experts, and to establish the democratic doctrine that every human being, or at least every male human, had the inner resources necessary to make sound moral decisions. But he thought that these resources consisted in the possession of an unconditional principle – the categorical imperative – that would enable us to decide how to resolve moral dilemmas. He saw this imperative as the product of a special faculty that he called "pure practical reason," a faculty whose deliverances were entirely unaffected by historical experience. We can appeal from society's moral intuitions to that faculty, and it will tell us which intuitions to keep and which to throw out.

Nietzsche said that a bad smell of blood and the lash hangs over Kant's categorical imperative. My favorite contemporary moral philosopher, Annette Baier, detects the same stench. As Baier sees the matter, the Kantian notion of unconditional obligation is borrowed from an authoritarian, patriarchal, religious tradition that should have been abandoned rather than reconstructed. Had we followed Hume's advice, we should have stopped talking about unconditional obligations when we stopped being afraid of postmortem tortures. When we ceased to agree with Dostoevsky that if God did not exist, everything would be permitted, we should have put aside the morality–prudence distinction. We should not have substituted "Reason" for "God" as the name of a law-giver.

We are often told by contemporary moral philosophers that Kant made a breathtaking discovery, and gave us a vitally important new idea, that of moral autonomy. But I suspect that when Kant is given credit for this discovery, we are using the term ambiguously. Everybody thinks autonomy in the sense of freedom from outside impositions is a fine thing. Nobody likes either human or divine tyrants. But the specifically Kantian sense of autonomy – having one's moral decisions made by reason rather than by anything capable of being influenced by experience – is quite a different matter. Relatively few people agree with devotees of Kant such as Christine Korsgaard – perhaps the most eminent, and certainly the most uncompromising, of contemporary Kantian moral philosophers. She thinks that Kant was right to hold that there is a special kind of motivation called "moral" and that "moral motivation, if it exists, can only be autonomous."[5] Autonomy in the sense of obedience to reason's unconditional command is a very special, very technical, concept – one that has to be learned in the way that any other technical concept is learned, by working one's way into a specifically Kantian language game.

This language game is one that you have to know how to play in order to get a Ph.D. in moral philosophy. But a lot of people who spend their lives making hard moral decisions get along nicely in blithe ignorance of its existence. A great deal of contemporary Anglophone moral philosophy takes for granted a discourse in which the idea of "specifically moral motivation" goes unquestioned, as does the idea that "morality" is the name of a still rather mysterious entity that requires intensive study. Reading Kant is a good way to get initiated into this discourse.

Reading my own philosophical hero, John Dewey, is a good way to find one's way out of this discourse. Dewey hoped that there would be fewer and fewer people who found Kant's way of talking about moral choice attractive. Dewey thought that it was a very bad idea to separate morality from prudence, and a particularly bad idea to think that moral imperatives have a different source than prudential advice. He viewed Kant as a figure whose view of human beings could never be reconciled with Darwin's naturalistic account of our origins. On a post-Darwinian view, Dewey argued, there can be no sharp break between empirical and non-empirical knowledge, any more than between empirical and non-empirical practical considerations, or between fact and value. All inquiry – in ethics as well as physics, in politics as well as logic – is a matter of reweaving our webs of beliefs and desires in such a way as to give ourselves more happiness and richer and freer lives. All our judgments are experimental and fallible. Unconditionality and absolutes are not things we should strive for.

As Dewey saw these matters, the Kantian split between the empirical and the non-empirical was a relic of the Platonic distinction between the material and the immaterial, and thus of the theologico-metaphysical distinction between the human and the divine. Dewey thought this "brood

---

[5] Christine Korsgaard, *Creating the Kingdom of Ends* (Cambridge: Cambridge University Press, 1999), 23.

and nest of dualisms," as he called it, should be swept aside, taking Plato and Kant with it.

I think of contemporary moral philosophy as trapped between Kant and Dewey because most philosophers these days are naturalists who would like their views to be readily reconcilable with a Darwinian view of how we got here. But Darwinians cannot be at ease with the Kantian idea of a distinctively moral motivation, or of a faculty called "reason" that issues commands. For them, rationality can only be the search for intersubjective agreement about how to carry out cooperative projects. That view of rationality is hard to reconcile with the Kantian distinction between morality and prudence.

Learning how to play the language game in which the Kantian concept of autonomy has its original home requires taking Kant's baroque faculty psychology seriously. For to wield this concept one must first break up the person so as to distinguish the law-giving from the law-receiving psychical elements. Dewey devoted a lot of energy to helping us get rid of this distinction, and he was largely successful. The idea of a law-giving faculty called "reason," it seems to me, lingers on only among two sorts of people. The first are masochists who want to hold on to a sense of sin while still enjoying the comforts of a clean, well-lighted, fully mechanized, Newtonian universe. The second are professors of moral philosophy whose job descriptions presuppose a clear distinction between morality and prudence, and so are suspicious of Deweyan attempts to break that distinction down.

Dewey was, I think, on the right track when he wrote:

Kant's separation of reverence [for the commands of reason], as the one moral sentiment[,] from all others as pathological, is wholly arbitrary . . . And it may even be questioned whether this feeling, as Kant treats it, is even the highest or ultimate form of moral sentiment – whether it is not transitional to love.[6]

In his thirties, when he was still a follower of T. H. Green, Dewey saw Hegel as having moved beyond Kant in the same way that the New Testament had moved beyond the Old – by replacing the law and the prophets with love. Both Hegel and Christ, as Dewey read them, had managed to move beyond the obsessive desire for ritual purity (or, as Kant called it, the need to cleanse morality of all traces of the merely empirical). Even after Dewey had ceased to think of himself as a Hegelian, he never faltered in his attempt to tear down the dualisms that moral philosophy had inherited from Kant.

[6] John Dewey, *Outline of a Critical Theory of Ethics*, in *The Early Works of John Dewey*, vol. III (Carbondale: Southern Illinois University Press, 1971), 295.

My other favorite contemporary moral philosopher, J. B. Schneewind, manages to respect and admire Kant in a way that Baier and I do not. But he has tried to distance himself from the worst parts of Kant in various essays. One of these is an early article, published in 1968, called "Moral Knowledge and Moral Principles." There he urges that we drop the idea that moral philosophers have a duty to provide us with moral principles that are completely context-free, in the sense of "capable of being applied to any kind of situation."[7] He supports this point by saying:

From the fact that a given principle is supreme in resolving conflicts it does not follow that it must be supreme in every context. To suppose that it does follow would be like supposing that every decision and rule agreed upon by a happily married couple depends upon the authority of the divorce court, since that court has the final word in settling all their affairs if they cannot settle them by other means . . . Any principle established with the help of argument might simply be as it were a moral ambulance, not for everyday use, having the right of precedence only in emergencies and not in the ordinary run of events.[8]

In this essay, Schneewind did not explicitly endorse this "only in emergencies" view of moral principles but much that he has said in later years seems to accord with it. Thus in an essay criticizing Korsgaard's emphasis on the unconditionality of moral principles Schneewind remarks:

In deliberations embedded in a complex context of shared assumptions and agreements there may be no practical need to continue to seek for reasons until we find one that meets Korsgaard's requirement [the requirement that justification be conclusive]. Justificational skepticism does not naturally arise in these contexts . . . Philosophical skepticisms would lead us to think that we can never rightly rely on even possibly doubtful premises. But Korsgaard would have to justify this standard in order to use it to start us on the regress argument that leads her to the principle no free agent could question.[9]

Schneewind goes on to say that in emergencies – situations in which we have reasons for criticizing some of our hitherto unquestioned moral commonplaces, or are facing radically new problems, or are dealing with or affecting people whose morality and culture are unfamiliar to us – the Kantian formulations (of the categorical imperative) are just what we need.[10] It may indeed be useful, in those cases, to ask ourselves whether we are using other human beings merely as means. But he notes that the

---

[7] J. B. Schneewind, "Moral Knowledge and Moral Principles," in *Revisions: Changing Perspectives in Moral Philosophy*, ed. Stanley Hauerwas and Alasdair MacIntyre (Notre Dame, IN: Notre Dame University Press, 1983), 116.   [8] Ibid., 117.
[9] J. B. Schneewind, "Korsgaard and the Unconditional in Morality," *Ethics* 109 (1998), 46.
[10] Ibid.

utilitarian principle may be helpful too. It may be useful, in such cases, to ask ourselves which decision will increase human happiness – will produce more pleasure and less pain. Schneewind says that

both sorts of principle possess the unlimited generality that makes them suitable for helping us reach reasoned agreement in the special kinds of deliberative situation where our "thicker" or more specific reasons no longer do the job.[11]

Although Schneewind says that he thinks Kant's ambulance service better than Mill's, he does not seem to care much about the Kant–Mill difference. Like Annette Baier, Schneewind has evinced exasperation with the fascination that this difference exerts on contemporary moral philosophers – the obsession with the opposition between consequentialism and non-consequentialism that still dominates Ethics 101. When reading later chapters of Schneewind's recent history of moral philosophy, *The Invention of Autonomy*,[12] one gets the sense that Schneewind's favorite eighteenth-century moral philosopher is not Kant but rather Diderot, of whom he writes: "Seek happiness with justice in this life; if this is a moral principle, it is the one Diderot would support."[13]

My own view is that nobody should put in much time dithering about which ambulance service to call in emergencies. The principle Schneewind puts in Diderot's mouth is all that we will ever get, and all we will ever need, in the way of a reconciliation of Mill with Kant. I agree with Baier when she says that we should stop telling students in freshman ethics classes that principles are terribly important, and that they are being intellectually irresponsible if they do not sign up with one ambulance service or the other.

So I read Schneewind as saying that the choice of which service to contract with is much less important than the realization that moral principles can do no more than summarize a lot of our previous deliberations – remind us of some of our previous intuitions and practices. Such thin and abstract reminders may help when thicker and more concrete considerations leave us still at odds with our neighbors. They do not provide algorithms, but they offer the only sort of guidance that abstraction has to offer.

Schneewind ended his 1968 article by saying that we should not mistake the decision that a certain moral principle sums up a lot of relevant experience "for a discovery that certain principles are basic because of their own inherent nature."[14] As a good Deweyan, Schneewind is not about to take

---

[11] Ibid., 47.
[12] J. B. Schneewind, *The Invention of Autonomy: A History of Modern Moral Philosophy* (Cambridge: Cambridge University Press, 1998).   [13] Ibid., 468.
[14] Schneewind, "Moral Knowledge and Moral Principles," 126.

the Kantian notion of "inherent nature" seriously. He cites Dewey as holding that "what is scientific about morality is neither some basic principle or principles on which it rests . . . but the general structure of its contents and its methods."[15] One might restate the point by saying that on a Deweyan, as opposed to a Kantian, view, what makes physics, ethics, and logic rational is not that they are axiomatizable but that each is what Wilfrid Sellars called "a self-correcting enterprise which can put *any* claim in jeopardy but not *all* at once."[16]

To say that moral principles have no inherent nature is to imply that they have no distinctive source. They emerge from our encounters with our surroundings in the same way that hypotheses about planetary motion, codes of etiquette, epic poems, and all our other patterns of linguistic behavior emerge. Like these other emergents, they are good insofar as they lead to good consequences, not because they stand in some special relation either to the universe or to the human mind. For Deweyans questions about sources and principles, about *das Ursprungliches* and *ta archaia*, are always a sign that the philosophers are up to their old Platonic tricks. They are trying to shortcut the ongoing calculation of consequences by appealing to something stable and permanent, something whose authority is not subject to empirical test.

Whenever Kantian reactionaries like Husserl and Russell gain the upper hand over progressive Hegelian historicists like Green and Dewey, philosophy professors once again start drawing non-empirical lines between science and the rest of culture, and also between morality and prudence. The former undertaking played a considerable role in creating what we now call "analytic philosophy." But it is now viewed skeptically by such post-Kuhnian, Hegelianized philosophers of science as Ian Hacking, Arthur Fine, and Bruno Latour. These writers insist that there are only sociological distinctions between science and non-science, distinctions revolving around such notions as expert cultures, initiation into disciplinary matrices, and the like. There are no metaphysical or methodological differences. There is nothing for philosophy of science, as opposed to the history and sociology of science, to be about.

I think this post-Kuhnian stance would have been welcomed by Dewey, for whom the term "scientific method" signified little more than Peirce's injunction to remain experimental and open-minded in one's outlook – to make sure that one was not blocking the road of inquiry. If

---

[15] Ibid., 120.
[16] Wilfrid Sellars, *Science, Perception and Reality* (London: Routledge and Kegan Paul, 1963), 170.

Arthur Fine's claim that "science is not special" comes to be generally accepted, there may no longer be an overarching discipline called "philosophy of science," although there may quite well be fruitful areas of inquiry called "philosophy of quantum mechanics" or "philosophy of evolutionary biology."[17]

Something analogous might happen if we were to psychologize the morality–prudence distinction in the way that the Kuhnians have sociologized the science–common sense distinction. We could do this by saying that what distinguishes morality from prudence is not a matter of sources but simply the psychological difference between matters that touch upon what Korsgaard calls our "practical identity" – our sense of what we would rather die than do – and those that do not. The relevant difference is not one of kind, but of degree of felt importance, just as the difference between science and non-science is a difference in degree of specialization and professionalization.

Since our sense of who we are, and of what is worth dying for, is obviously up for historical and cultural grabs, to follow out this line of thought would once again lead us away from Kant to Hegel, and eventually to Dewey's synthesis of Hegel with Darwin. In a Deweyan philosophical climate, disciplines such as the "philosophy of American constitutional law" or the "philosophy of diminished responsibility" or the "philosophy of sexual relationships" might flourish, but nobody would see much point in an overarching discipline called "moral philosophy," any more than they would see a point in one called "philosophy of science." Just as there would be nothing called "scientificity" to be studied, there would be nothing called "morality." The obsolescence of Kantian discourse would make the idea of study of the "nature of moral concepts" sound silly, and might thus lead to a remapping of the philosophical terrain. There is a reason, however, why we resist the suggestion that the morality–prudence distinction is simply a matter of individual psychology – why we think that morality is both special and mysterious, and that philosophers ought to have something to say about its intrinsic nature. We think it special because we think that "Why should I be moral?" is a good question in a way that "Why should I be scientific?" is not. This is because we interpret "moral" as meaning "having roughly the practical identity that we in fact have." We think that there ought to be people who can show us why our side is right – why we decent, tolerant, good-hearted liberals are something more than an

---

[17] See Arthur Fine, "The View from Nowhere in Particular," *Proceedings and Addresses of the American Philosophical Association* 72 (1998); I discuss Fine's view in "A pragmatist view of contemporary analytic philosophy," above, 133–146.

epiphenomenon of recent socioeconomic history. Moral philosophers seem good candidates for this role. Kantians of the strict observance such as Korsgaard explicitly accept it.

Here, at the beginning of the twenty-first century, we can do without philosophy of science because we have no need for reassurance about science. We can drop the idea that scientificity is an important natural kind, because science is not in danger. Philosophy of science – in its traditional form of an argument that the scientific method, and only the scientific method, could tell us how things really and truly were – seemed important back in the days when Pius IX was anathematizing modern civilization. But as the tension between religion and science gradually ceased to occupy the attention of the intellectuals, philosophy of science came to look like one more teapot in which to stir up academic tempests. Nowadays philosophy of science attracts public attention only when, for example, fundamentalist preachers decide to take another crack at Darwin, or when sociobiologists try to take over the magisterium once enjoyed by theologians.

In contrast, moral philosophy may still look indispensable. This is because there is a permanent tension between the morality of the Enlightenment and the primitive, barbaric, exclusionary moralities of cultures and populations that have not enjoyed the security and wealth we have. Those cultures have missed out on the emergence of tolerance, pluralism, miscegenation, democratic government and people like us. So non-academics are inclined to feel that this may be one area in which philosophy professors actually earn their keep – a confidence not felt about analytic philosophers who specialize in what they call "the core areas of philosophy," metaphysics and epistemology.

This favorable predisposition may not survive Ethics 101, but students who enter that course afraid of what they call "relativism" continue to provide an appreciative audience for books that will tell them, as Kant does, that morality has a special source – a special relation to something neither contingent nor historically locatable. The best recent book of this sort – Korsgaard's *The Sources of Normativity* – attempts both to reconstruct the morality–prudence wall that Dewey tried to tear down and to *prove* that our side is right – that the European Enlightenment was not just an historical contingency, but rather a rational necessity. Replying to Schneewind and other critics of her insistence on unconditionality, Korsgaard says:

> To all of the fans of the embedded, the pragmatic, the contextual, and so on, who are always insisting that justifications must come to an end somewhere, Kant would answer that justifications can come to an end only with a law you yourself will, one you'd be prepared to will for everyone, because justifications must come

to an end with you – with the dictate of your own mind. And in this, I stand with Kant.[18]

For Korsgaard, one's mind has a structure that transcendental philosophy can reveal. By revealing that structure, philosophy can provide a transcendental argument for the truth of Enlightenment morality[19] – an argument that will convince even Nazis and mafiosi if they just think hard and long enough. To be reflective, for Korsgaard, is to let one's mind work freely to explore the implications of its own existence, rather than being distracted by passion and prejudice.

Dewey agreed with the later Wittgenstein that we should avoid confusing questions about sources – which should always be treated as requests for causal explanation – with questions about justification. This is the confusion that Dewey and his follower Wilfrid Sellars diagnosed in empiricist epistemology. But the confusion is, of course, common to the empiricists, the Platonists and the Kantians. It consists in the attempt to split the soul or the mind up into faculties named "reason," "the senses," "the emotions," "the will" and the like and then to legitimize a controversial claim by saying that it has the support of the only relevant faculty. Empiricists argue that since the senses are our only windows on the world, only they can tell us what the world is like. The Platonists and the Kantians say that since unleashed desire is the source of moral evil, only something utterly distinct from desire can be the source of moral righteousness.

Korsgaard revels, as happily and unself-consciously as Kant himself, in faculty psychology. She says, for example, that "the relation of the thinking self to the acting self is one of legitimate authority,"[20] and would presumably say that any authority claimed by the passionate self would be illegitimate. Again, she says that "our identity as moral beings – as people who value themselves as human beings – stands behind our more particular practical identities."[21] It stands, so to speak, in the shadows behind my identity as parent, lover, businessman, patriot, mafioso, professor or Nazi, waiting to be revealed by reflection. How powerfully it makes itself felt depends, in Korsgaard's phrase, upon "how much of the light of reflection is on."[22]

Visual metaphors of this sort are as central to Korsgaard's thinking as to Plato's, but such metaphors are anathema to those who follow Dewey in thinking of the self as a self-reweaving and self-correcting network of beliefs

---

[18] Christine Korsgaard, "Motivation, Metaphysics, and the Value of the Self: A Reply to Ginsborg, Guyer and Schneewind," *Ethics* 109 (1998), 66.
[19] Cf. Christine Korsgaard, *The Sources of Normativity* (Cambridge: Cambridge University Press, 1996), 123.   [20] Ibid., 165.   [21] Ibid., 121.   [22] Ibid., 257.

and desires – a homeostatic mechanism. To see all inquiry (in physics and logic as well as in ethics) as such a search for homeostasis, for temporary reflective equilibrium, is to set aside the search for legitimizing faculties and, more generally, the search for sources. "Reason" is no more a source for concepts or judgments than is "sense experience" or "physical reality." The whole idea of legitimizing a concept or a judgment by finding out where it came from is a bad one.

Readers of Wittgenstein who are accustomed to treat "our concept of X" as synonymous with "our use of the word X" will be suspicious of Korsgaard's demand that philosophers tell us the source of moral concepts. For them, the question "What is the source of our uses of the normative terms we employ in our moral deliberations?" can only be interpreted as a request for historical background. Histories of moral reflection like Schneewind's, Charles Taylor's, and Alasdair MacIntyre's, rather than books like Korsgaard's own, will be thought of as providing appropriate answers to it.

Wittgensteinians will be especially suspicious when Korsgaard goes on to ask: "Where do we get these ideas that outstrip the world we experience and seem to call into question, to render judgment on it, to say that it does not measure up, that it is not what it ought to be?" Korsgaard says that it is clear that we do not get these ideas from experience. But the notion of getting ideas from experience requires us to dredge up all the dogmas of empiricism, as well as an obsolete Lockean building-block picture of language learning. The same goes for the assumption that there is a nice, neat distinction between descriptive ideas and normative ideas, the former coming from experience and the latter from a less obvious source.

Wittgensteinians think that we get ideas that outstrip the actual from the same place we get ideas that delimit the actual – from the people who taught us how to use the words that are used to formulate those ideas. From this perspective, the question "What are the sources of normativity?" has no more appeal than "What are the sources of facticity?" For a norm is just a certain kind of fact – a fact about what people do – seen from the inside.

Suppose that, as a matter of contingent fact, a community to which I am proud to belong despises people who do A. Members of this community often say they would rather be dead than do A. My identification with that community leads me to say "We [or "People of our sort" or "People I respect"] don't do A." When I say that, using the first person, I am reporting a norm. When I stand back from my community, in my capacity as anthropologist or intellectual historian and say "They would rather die than do A," I am reporting a fact. The source of the norm is, so to speak, my internalization of the fact. Or, if you like, the source of the fact is the externalization of the norm.

This was Sellars' account of the relation between fact and value, and of the moral point of view. For Sellars, as for Dewey, the former relation was sufficiently clarified by pointing out the relation between "Young men in Papua feel obliged to hunt heads" and "All of us young men here in Papua would be ashamed of ourselves if we did not hunt heads." It is the token-reflexive pronoun that makes the big difference, and the only difference.[23]

Korsgaard herself seems to come close to this view when she says that the answer to her question about the sources of normativity "must appeal, in a deep way, to the sense of who we are, to our sense of our identity."[24] She goes on to say that one condition on "a successful answer to the normative question" is that "it must show that sometimes doing the wrong thing is as bad or worse than death." She adds that "the only thing that could be as bad or worse than death is something that for us amounts to death – not being ourselves any more."

Dewey could agree completely with this point, but he would think that once it has been made, we know all that we shall ever know about the sources of normativity. So Deweyans will regret that Korsgaard thinks that there is more to be discovered, and that only such a discovery will enable philosophers to meet the challenge of an agent facing a difficult moral demand who asks "Why must I do it?" Korsgaard tells us that "an agent who doubts whether he must really do what morality says also doubts whether it is so bad to be morally bad."

But one will take the question "Why should I be moral?" seriously only if one thinks that the answer "Because you might not be able to live with yourself if you thought yourself immoral" is not good enough. But why should it not suffice? Only, it seems to me, because the person who doubts that she should be moral is already in the process of cobbling together a new identity for herself – one that does not commit her to doing the thing that her old identity took to be obligatory.

Huck Finn, for example, fears that he may not be able to live with himself if he does not help return Jim to slavery. But he winds up giving it a try. He would not be so willing, presumably, if he were completely unable to imagine a new practical identity – the identity of one who takes loyalty to friends as releasing one from legal and conventional obligations. That, presumably, is the identity Huck will claim when explaining to St. Peter

[23] See Wilfrid Sellars, *Science and Metaphysics* (London: Routledge and Kegan Paul, 1963), ch. 7.
[24] Korsgaard, *The Sources of Normativity*, 17.

why he should not be sent to hell as a thief. Analogously, a Catholic doctor who thinks she would rather die than kill a fetus may find herself hastily weaving a new practical identity for herself when she turns out to be a desperate rape victim's only hope.

Socrates was able to make the thesis that nobody knowingly does evil sound plausible only because most of us share Huck's, or my imagined doctor's, ability to whip up a new practical identity to suit the occasion. Most of us have had experience with doing just that. We find Socrates himself explaining, in the *Apology*, that he has spent his life fashioning a new identity for himself, and that now he would rather die than be what his judges call "moral" – that is, revert to being the person whom he and they were brought up to be. This new identity may well have looked to Socrates' audience like a rationalization of neurotic perversity, just as Huck's new-found identity would have looked like a rationalization of moral weakness to the local sheriff.

Korsgaard thinks that there is an ahistorical criterion for distinguishing a rationalization of weakness from a heartening example of moral progress. Deweyans think that there is only the criterion of how well or badly we ourselves can fit Huck's or Socrates' new practical identities together with our own. There is only, if you like, the judgment of history – that particular history that leads up to us, with the practical identities we currently have. To paraphrase the old saw about treason, Huck's and Socrates' identities prospered, and none now dare call them rationalizations of weakness or perversity. By contrast, consider young Hans, a German soldier who was assigned to murder Jewish children found hiding in the hedgerows of Poland. He hastily constructed a new practical identity for himself – that of the good, obedient servant of the Fuehrer. Thanks to the might of the Allied armies, this identity did *not* prosper.

On the Deweyan view I am sketching, the pragmatic cash value of the question "Why should I be moral?" is "Should I retain the practical identite I presently have, or rather develop and cherish the new identity I shall have to assume if I do what my present practical identity forbids?" On this way of thinking of the matter, the question "Why should I be moral?" is a question that arises only when two or more alternative practical identities are under consideration. That is why the question almost never arises in traditional societies of the sort in which the jurymen who tried Socrates were raised. These jurors could make little sense of the question, and therefore little sense of Socrates' life.

But the question arises in modern pluralistic societies all the time – not to mention societies in which cruel tyrants suddenly take control. In those societies, however, it is not usually thought of as a question for philosophers to answer by giving a satisfactory theory of the sources of normativity. Rather, it is a question about which of the many available suppliers of alternative practical identities I should buy from.

On my construal, then, the question "Why should I be moral?" is typically a preliminary to asking "What morality should I have?" The latter question is itself a way of asking "Should I continue to think certain actions to be as bad as or worse than death?" This is, of course, quite different from Korsgaard's Kantian construal. She thinks it is a question to be answered by looking not at the relative attractions of various communities and identities, but at something that exists independently of the historical contingencies that create communities and identities.

To see better how this question looks from the Deweyan point of view I am recommending, consider an analogy between "Why should I be moral?" and "Why should I think this podium and these chairs to be real?" This Cartesian question, Wittgensteinians like Bouwsma have suggested, should be taken seriously only if an alternative account of the appearances is suggested: for example, that these items of furniture are actually papier-mâché imitations of the real thing, or that they are illusions produced by needles stuck in my brain. Some such concrete and detailed account of my temptation to believe in their reality has to be offered before I shall bother to consider the claim that they are unreal. Once such an account is provided, then an alternative candidate for local reality – perhaps stage-setters or mad doctors – may become plausible. But to peruse the merits of these alternative candidates is not to do philosophy. No exploration of what "real" means or of the nature of reality is likely to help.

Analogously, I am suggesting that the question "Why should I be moral?" should be taken seriously only if an alternative morality is beginning to sound plausible. But to peruse the merits of these alternative candidates is not a task for the sort of philosopher who purports to tell us more about the meanings of the terms "real" and "moral" – the sort who investigates the "natures" of these concepts.

Korsgaard defines "a theory of moral concepts" as an answer to three questions: what moral concepts mean or contain, what they apply to, and where they come from.[25] On the view I am suggesting, only the second of these questions is a good one. The question of what moral concepts mean is as bad as the questions of what such concepts as "real podium," "cardboard imitation podium" and "needle inserted in the podium-perceiving

---

[25] Ibid., 11.

area of my brain" mean. Until somebody exhibits concrete puzzlement about when to use which term, the concepts do not need clarification.

A romantic and troubled adolescent who wonders whether to try to build her moral identity around the figures of Alyosha and Father Zossima, or rather around the figures of Ivan and Zarathustra, may be helped by literary critics and intellectual historians to see more clearly what these figures were committed to and how they thought of themselves. Hans, when sent to the *Einsatzkommando*, may be helped by a kindly anti-Nazi sergeant, or an equally kindly pro-Nazi chaplain, in the same way. This help can, if you like, be thought of as conceptual clarification. But it is hard to see how Kantian philosophers are going to get into the act. For their explanations of what "moral" means seem irrelevant to these adolescents' problems. Analogously, explanations of what "real" or "true" means, or accounts of the source of these normative notions, would seem irrelevant to someone who has begun to wonder whether she may not be the victim of a mad, needle-wielding brain surgeon.

Someone as impatient with Korsgaard's Kantian questions as I am finds ancient moral philosophy – focusing as it did on choosing heroes, debating which figures a youth should try to model himself upon – of more interest than the kind of thing you usually get in Ethics 101. For such debates concern alternative moral identities – and thus provide moral issues to get one's teeth into – in a way that debates about the alternative merits of the categorical imperative and the utilitarian principle do not. Discussion of the relative merits of Alyosha and Ivan seems continuous with debate concerning those of Odysseus and Achilles, or of Socrates and Pericles. Discussions of deontology versus consequentialism, or of whether our sense of moral obligation originates in reason or in sentiment, seem pedantic distractions from discussions of historical or literary personages.

In making this point, I am echoing some things that Schneewind has said. In a paper called "What Has Moral Philosophy Done for Us . . . Lately?"[26] he takes up some of my own doubts about moral philosophy and says that one thing that can be said for this area of culture is that "the creations of the philosopher's conceptual imagination have been as vivid and efficacious as the characters made up by the novelist or the tragedian." He cites the Epicurean and the Stoic as examples, and then goes on to say that

---

[26] J. B. Schneewind, "What Has Moral Philosophy Done for Us . . . Lately?" Lecture given at the University of Michigan Institute for the Humanities, February 2000; available on video at http://ethics.sandiego.edu/video/Schneewind. Published in German as "Vom Nutzen der Moralphilosophie – Rorty zum Trotz," trans. Harald Koehl, in *Deutsche Zeitschrift für Philosophie* 48 (2000), 855–66.

"Philosophical portraits of the good life pick up on the pre-theoretical attitudes that we are predisposed to have about how we want to live. By
showing them how to think them through, they can help us as much as fic-
tions can to self-understanding and self-critique."

I agree with the remarks I have just quoted from Schneewind, although
I should be inclined to add "yes, but no more than works of history and of
fiction can, and perhaps not as efficiently." But when Schneewind goes on
to say that when we try to articulate resemblances between ourselves and
Socrates or Mr. Casaubon we "may need to move beyond the case to something like a statement of principle," I become more dubious. Some of us,
those with a taste for principles, may need to do this. But for reasons
Schneewind himself adumbrated in the 1968 essay I quoted earlier, I am
not sure that such needs should be encouraged.

As I see it, we almost never do what Singer thinks we ought to do: reject
the moral views of the community in which we have been raised because
we have found what Singer calls "a soundly based moral theory" – at least
if such a theory consists in a series of inferences from some broad general
principle that strikes us as intuitively plausible. Rather, when we find such
a principle plausible, and realize that accepting it would lead us to change
our ways, we attempt to obtain what John Rawls calls "reflective equilibrium." That is, we go back and forth between the proposed principle and
our old intuitions, trying to fabricate a new practical identity that will do
some justice to both. This involves imagining what our community would
be like if it changed its ways, and what we would be like as a member of
this reformed community. It is a detailed comparison of imagined selves,
situations and communities that does the trick, not argument from principles. Formulation of general principles is sometimes useful, but only as a
tool for summarizing the results of imagining such alternatives.

Singer and many other contemporary moral philosophers seem to
imagine that somebody could decide to overcome her reluctance to
perform abortions, or decide to help change the laws so that abortion
becomes a capital crime, simply by being struck by the plausibility of some
grand general principle that dictates one or the other decision. But this is
not the way moral progress or moral regress occurs. It is not how people
change their practical identities – their sense of what they would rather die
than do.

The advantage that well-read, reflective, leisured people have when it
comes to deciding about the right thing to do is that they are more imaginative, not that they are more rational. Their advantage lies in being aware
of many possible practical identities, and not just one or two. Such people

are able to put themselves in the shoes of many different sorts of people – Huck before he decided whether to turn Jim in and Huck afterward, Socrates and Socrates' accusers, Christ and Pilate, Kant and Dewey, Homeric heroes and Christian ascetics. Moral philosophers have provided us with some moral identities to consider, historians and biographers with others, novelists with still others.

Just as there are many imaginable individual practical identities, so there are many communal practical identities. Reflective and well-read people read history, anthropology, and historical novels in order to get a sense of what it would be like to have been a loyal and unquestioning member of a community we regard as primitive. They read science fiction novels in order to get a sense of what it might be like to have grown up in communities more advanced than our own. They read moral philosophers not to find knock-down arguments, or to become more rational or more clear or more rigorous, but to find handy ways of summarizing the various reactions they have had to these various imaginings.

Let me conclude by returning to the question with which I began: the question to which I think Singer and others give bad answers. As I see it, specialists in moral philosophy should not think of themselves as people who have better arguments or clearer thoughts than most, but simply as people who have spent a lot of time talking over some of the issues that trouble people faced with hard decisions about what to do. Moral philosophers have made themselves very useful in hospitals discussing issues created by recent advances in medical technology, as well as in many other arenas in which public policy is debated. Singer himself has done admirable work of this sort. These philosophers are perfectly respectable members of the academy and of society. They no more need to be embarrassed by demands for justification of their place at the public trough than do anthropologists, historians, theologians or poets. It is only when they get up on their high Kantian horses that we should view them with suspicion.

Index of names

CPSIA information can be obtained
at www.ICGtesting.com
Printed in the USA
LVHW040852280619
622642LV00001B/60